Fifteen Thousand Miles by Stage

Cordially Yours
Carrie Adell Strahorn

Fifteen Thousand Miles by Stage

Volume 1: 1877–1880

A Woman's Unique Experience during Thirty Years of Path
Finding and Pioneering from the Missouri to the
Pacific and from Alaska to Mexico

By

Carrie Adell Strahorn

Introduction by Judith Austin

*With 177 Illustrations from Drawings by Charles M. Russell
and others, and from Photographs*

University of Nebraska Press
Lincoln and London

First Bison Book printing: 1988
Most recent printing indicated by the first digit below:
1   2   3   4   5   6   7   8   9   10

Library of Congress Cataloging-in-Publication Data
Strahorn, Carrie Adell, 1854–1925.
    Fifteen thousand miles by stage: a woman's unique experience during thirty years of path finding and pioneering from the Missouri to the Pacifiic and from Alaska to Mexico / by Carrie Adell Strahorn.
    p.   cm.
    "A Bison Book."
    Reprint. Originally published: New York: Knickerbocker Press, 1911.
    Contents: v. 1. 1877–1880—v. 2. 1880–1898.
    ISBN 0-8032-4159-3 (vol. 1).   ISBN 0-8032-9154-X (pbk.: vol. 1).
    ISBN 0-8032-4160-7 (vol. 2).   ISBN 0-8032-9155-8 (pbk.: vol. 2).
    1. Strahorn, Carrie Adell, 1854–1925—Journeys—West (U.S.) 2. West (U.S.)—Description and travel—1880–1950. 3. West (U.S.)—Description and travel—1860–1880. 4. Coaching—West (U.S.)—History—19th century. 5. Pioneers—West (U.S.)—Biography. 6. Women pioneers—West (U.S.)—Biography.   I. Title.   II. Title: 15000 miles by stage.
F595.S89 1988   CIP 87–30064
971.8'042—dc19

Volume 1 of the Bison Book edition reprints Chapters I through XXIX of the 1911 edition published by G. P. Putnam's Sons in one volume. Four color plates by Charles Russell that appeared on unnumbered pages in the original edition have been dropped.

INTRODUCTION BY JUDITH AUSTIN

In all my girlhood the one thing that I wanted to avoid in my life was to be a pioneer. So often had I listened to tales of my elders of " '49 and spring '50" etc., that it had made me say many times that I would never be a pioneer and be called the oldest settler in a town or country, or one of the early ones in any State history. Yet there I was at the very threshold of a new land where I was to be the first woman in many then unexploited regions, and the title of "old settler" was to be indelibly and forever attached to me and mine.[1]

Carrie Adell Strahorn stood at that threshold of the American West when she married Robert Strahorn in 1877—not the threshold of a comfortable, predictable life. Strahorn had just been hired by the Union Pacific Railroad to explore and publicize the West, and he had persuaded the UP officials to allow her to accompany him. For the next thirty years she and her "Pard" would live mainly on horseback and in stagecoaches. It was a good thing for the country that she did not stay behind, for she proved his equal as a trailblazer and community builder. And it was a good thing for readers when, in 1911, she published this account of her roving life with Pard. *Fifteen Thousand Miles by Stage,* full of her wit and sense of adventure, is as fresh now as it was then.

Although she came from hardy stock, Carrie Adell Green was used to a comfortable life. She was born in Marengo, Illinois, on New Year's Day of 1854 to a family of "old settlers" in the Midwest. Her father, John W. Green, was a surgeon, said to have been the first west of Chicago to use anaesthetic. He served in the Civil War, rising to the rank of general in the Army of Tennessee under Grant. Louise Green accompanied her husband through at least one part of his war duty, the Red River campaign in Louisiana and Mississippi. the Greens had three daughters, one of whom also became a physician. Adell, the middle child, was encouraged to obtain as much education as she wished. After completing public school in Marengo, she received a degree from the University of Michigan and studied vocal music in this country and abroad.[2]

Robert Strahorn's background was more humble. He was born in Pennsylvania in 1852 to farmers who moved to Illinois four years later. His formal education ended when he was ten, but four years later he was working as a printer and soon thereafter as a budding reporter in western Missouri. Tuberculosis (and restlessness after years of watching pioneers head west) prompted a move to Denver via Cheyenne in 1870. A Denver romance ended sadly with the death of the young lady, a native of Marengo. At the end of her life she returned to Marengo, where she was nursed by Strahorn and by her close friend, Adell Green.[3]

After he returned to Denver, Strahorn set out to cover the Indian wars—chiefly as a reporter assigned to General George Crook's command. He wrote dispatches for the *Chicago Tribune, Rocky Mountain News, Omaha Republican,* and occasionally for the *New York Times* as well. His view of the causes of Indian unrest—it was "mainly due to our disregard of their rights"—was less dogmatic than might be expected.[4] But that realization did not deter him from some lively front-line reporting as he accompanied Crook's command through a series of campaigns. The experience—in which Strahorn proved himself a good shot and good also at coping with physical hardship—resulted in a lasting friendship with Crook.

The time Strahorn spent in Wyoming and Dakota territories (and presumably his awareness that the "Indian problem" had essentially been solved in that area) led him to write a book extolling their attractions in *A Hand-Book of Wyoming and Guide to the Black Hills and Big Horn Regions for Citizen, Emigrant and Tourist.*[5] He completed the book in ninety days and, en route to his wedding, gave a copy to Thomas Kimball, general passenger agent of the Union Pacific Railroad in Omaha. Strahorn had no way of knowing that Kimball was about to go off fishing with Jay Gould, president of the UP, and would show Gould the book. The result was the offer of a job with the railroad as head of a "literary bureau," preparing more such guidebooks that would serve as sources of information to prospective settlers in areas where the Union Pacific wished to extend its trackage—a band some thousand miles wide on either side of the main track from Omaha to Ogden, and west from the railhead as well.

Certainly such a position was more appealing than returning to Cheyenne and entering territorial politics, as he had planned to do. But there was a catch: the railroad expected that Strahorn would travel widely—and in country where there were no rail lines and frequently few if any amenities at all. It was not, in the view of UP officials, a suitable life for a young lady. Neither, in the Strahorns' view, was staying behind in Cheyenne acceptable, and he issued an ultimatum: either she went along or he did not take the job. J. T. Clark, general superintendent of the railroad, finally gave in and provided passes for both of them.[6] Adell would eventually become an "old settler" in spite of herself, and although the hardships of the fifteen thousand (at least) miles of stagecoach and horseback travel were less than those of the forty-niners, she had adventures and odd encounters enough to match those of any gold seeker or earlier pioneer.

The first volume of *Fifteen Thousand Miles by Stage* takes the Strahorns, tireless scouts, down nearly every primitive road in Colorado, Utah, Wyoming, Idaho, New Mexico, Montana, Washington, and Oregon in the late 1870s. They experience every kind of discomfort, mishap, and peril, and survive to laugh about it. The food at the remote stations is often inedible, so they learn to carry raisins. Pioneering means sleeping, fourteen to a room, under a leaky roof on a rainy night. More often they sleep on ground claimed by rattlesnakes. Their fellow passengers add to the adventure: singers of bawdy songs without end, garrulous old men who tell their life stories, children with whooping cough, complainers and snorers, and every kind of misfit. Sometimes as many as seventeen people crowd into (and on top of) a Concord coach. Bodies shift and elbows jab as it bumps down a corduroy road, swings out over mountain ledges, occasionally spills, and (once in the Strahorns' experience) lurches after runaway horses. But for those waiting for news and mail, the appearance of the stagecoach is the big event of the day.

No one knew better than Adell Strahorn that life is scarcely bearable without a sense of humor. She loves to tell stories, and the reader can expect some funny (and some sad) ones about assorted eccentrics and about the likes of Bill Nye, Horace Greeley, and General George A. Crook. The general, it seems, fell in love with a southern belle and — the melodramatic outcome is on pages 181–82.

In this first part, the Strahorns are still young and hardy and able to adjust to rapidly changing conditions on the frontier, some of them scary. For instance, Adell describes a tense night ride in 1878 through the area where the Bannock Indian war was being fought. On a mountainous stretch of road near Lake City, Colorado, she sits up front with a woman-hating driver who comes close to pitching her off the coach. Things happen to her and Pard; they cause things to happen. They lose their horses on treks into the wilderness to look at scenery. They climb Gray's Peak in Colorado and barely get down alive when an electrical storm boils up. Because of Pard's position, the Union Pacific granted them privileges, so they ride on a cowcatcher (does anyone remember what a cowcatcher is?) over mountain passes, through tunnels, and across the Dale Creek Bridge between Cheyenne and Ogden. They descend, on a narrow ladder, 155 feet into a mine near Bonanza, Idaho. They ride on unballasted track past Soda Springs and Blackfoot, Idaho. Nearly always they have a good time—at least in the telling afterward!

In remote places of the West, Adell Strahorn is treated royally by men starved for the sight of a woman. At the same time she has to stand up to those who would protect her from experience because she is a woman. When, in the fall of 1880, the superintendent of Yellowstone National Park discourages her from going with the men to see the Great Falls of the Yellowstone, she waits until they are out of sight and rides out alone. She is the first white woman to tour the park. In fact, she and Pard establish a number of firsts during their travels. Most memorably, on December 1877 they ride the first train on the new Colorado Central Railroad between Cheyenne and Denver, occupying the car that had carried Abraham Lincoln's body from Washington to Springfield.

Indeed, the entire book represents a kind of first, for all the places come to life in a highly individual light, as if they were being described for the first time by an intelligent being. Never mind that Robert Strahorn was a propagandist whose "worst misgivings arose from thoughts of the hardships to be encountered by the thousands who would now, largely through our early flood of alluring literature, follow in our footsteps."[7] Never mind that Adell herself said (p. xv) that she sometimes gave more of a rosy glow to their experience on the frontier than she might have. An occasional critic might take them to task for not reporting bad conditions,[8] which they certainly knew from experience; but their sense of mission, youthful enthusiasm, and genuine love of the West underlay their work. However, Adell in this book provides no Chamber of Commerce travelogue. In a succession of medallion-like images she captures what was for her the essence of towns and cities in the late 1870s— Omaha, Cheyenne, Salt Lake City, Butte, Leadville, Santa Fe, Spokane, and Walla Walla. Any romantic illusions about most of them are disspelled by her penetrating observations and wry sense of humor.

Magnificent as she is, Adell Strahorn has her share of prejudices and does not attempt to hide them. She is harsh on Mormons, especially over polygamy—and she certainly shared contemporary attitudes about Indians and Mexicans. Oddly, she is far more sympathetic toward Alaskan natives (to be encountered in Volume 2) and is particularly critical of their treatment by whites, who destroyed their culture and took their land. She is wonderfully critical of eastern ignorance of the West and of the peculiar behavior of some easterners when they came west (including the outlandish clothing they saw as most suitable in the "Wild West"). She does not spare her opinions of communities, as seen in her criticism of some denizens of Butte (p. 94).

Toward the end of Volume 1, Adell Strahorn summarizes those hectic years in which the Strahorns explored new routes and paved the way for new communities:

> With time to catch my breath at Walla Walla, I began to figure out what we had been doing. The year 1880 was nearing a close, and with it numbered three thousand miles more of stage travel for us, or six thousand miles in all since we started out on such adventurous experiences only three years before. We had run about the whole gamut of exploration—the great stock ranges, the profoundest forests, the broad grain lands, and the varied attractions for the pleasure or health seeker, with everything else that could have any possible bearing on future transportation interests. Those things were gone into with a ''fine tooth comb,'' as Pard sometimes put it. Mines of the base or precious metals were everywhere, and down in the heart of mother-earth we had explored hundreds of them. By winze and ropes and tunnels we had followed the gold, copper, and lead hidden in rocky rifts or sandy bed, or yet again from its black soft blanket of porphyry, out into the sunlight and through arastra, crusher, amalgamator, or smelter to the bright coins of commerce.The advantage of future rail routes, or even of more stage lines, was nowhere overlooked. (p. 307)

Once the Strahorns' travels have taken them all the way to the West Coast—by almost every mode of transportation then known—Adell Strahorn's life changes somewhat. In Volume 2, she is still the honored guest of all and sundry who are anxious to see the Union Pacific head their way, but now she is also a hostess to settlers streaming into places she and Pard helped to found. During these years she is, in effect, a hostess to the West. Volume 2 shows the Strahorns turning their earlier travels to consequence for a new wave of pioneers. She and Pard settle in places long enough to call them home, but they are still on the move. Carrie Adell Strahorn matures and grows as a human being in a way unique to those who are part of a great ongoing adventure.

NOTES

1. This passage, which appears on p. 14 of this volume, is quoted, with minor variations, in Robert E. Strahorn, "Ninety Years of Boyhood" (unpub. MS; carbon copy in Terteling Library, College of Idaho, Caldwell, Idaho), pp. 240–41. Strahorn's autobiography tells many of the same stories as *Fifteen Thousand Miles by Stage*, often in nearly identical language.

2. *History of the City of Spokane and Spokane Country [sic], Washington, From Its Earliest Settlement to the Present Time* (Spokane: The S. J. Clarke Publishing Company, 1912), pp. 7–8.

3. Robert Strahorn, "Ninety Years," p. 64.

4. Ibid., p. 103.

5. Cheyenne, Wyoming, 1877. No publisher is listed.

6. Robert Strahorn, "Ninety Years," pp. 240, 242, 246–47.

7. Ibid., p. 259.

8. See Oliver Knight, "Robert Strahorn, Propagandist for the West," *Pacific Northwest Quarterly* 59 (January 1968): 43–44.

PREFACE

THE West of thirty-four years ago is now only a tradition. The picturesque wilderness with its marauding bands of Indians, with its lawless white men, with its quaint stage-coaches, and with its vast tenantless reaches of mountains and plains was a reality, with all the vast resources of the great domain yet to be developed.

The bird's-eye view of to-day looks down upon thousands of miles of railways, flourishing towns, substantial cities, and millions of acres of land green with cultivation where only yesterday were the dreary solitudes of sandy waste.

In the pages of this volume, I have endeavored to give a picture of the Old West, to tell of the efforts which a Westward marching population made to establish homes on the border line of civilization and beyond, enduring hardships and privations with the courage of heroes. I have tried to restore the picturesque condition of what was the great homeless frontier of our Western country, and to trace its development.

The narrative covers nearly every highway of the country between the Missouri River and the Pacific Ocean and from the British lands to Mexico. The old Concord stage-coach with its swinging thoroughbrace and the covered "dead X" wagon were the Pullman cars for the overland traveller, and highway meals were served from the wagon box or at a wayside cabin that was frequently more than half a stable.

The circumstances that led to such a life date back to the year 1877, when my husband, Robert E. Strahorn, wrote and published a book on the resources, climatic conditions, and scenic attractions of what was then Wyoming Territory. The book fell into the hands of Jay Gould, who was then the wizard of the railroad world and the live wire of the Union Pacific Company, with its rails running from Omaha to Ogden and Salt Lake City. The fancy seized Mr. Gould to have Mr. Strahorn create a literary bureau and advertising department for the Union Pacific Railway Company, and to write a similar book on all Western States and Territories. It was a new departure for a railroad company, but as the scheme was discussed its scope broadened until it seemed to be without limit. The Company wanted to know the possibilities for extensions, the tonnage that might accrue, the tillable acres, the scenic attractions, and all the alluring inducements that could be offered to prospective home-seekers.

The offer came within a week after our marriage. To accept it meant the abandonment of plans already well matured, and the alternative of leaving me alone among strangers in the Far West, or subjecting me to a life of hardship in frontier travel that was looked upon as well nigh unendurable, either one of which seemed equally impossible for him to force upon me.

It was a career so suited to his capabilities and his liking that I determined not to be a stumbling block at the very threshold of our new life, and he was finally persuaded to accept the position, it being agreed that for a time at least I would accompany him. That stipulation the railroad officials emphatically refused. They said no woman could endure the hardships that conditions of travel then required on routes far away from the railroad, and added that he would be constantly hampered and delayed in his work. Mr. Strahorn was firm in his insistence, and they were obdurate and arbitrary; they argued and reasoned, then demurred, relented, and finally consented.

It meant going the length of nearly every stage road across our great frontier many times over; into remote districts, into lonely valleys and far-reaching mountains. It meant going into hundreds of mines, computing millions of feet of timber, the number of cattle and sheep and their increase. It involved the study of the prairies and hillsides with reference to their adaptability for raising cereals and fruits; the examination of watercourses and drainage, the determination of the climatic and scenic conditions, and, in short, every factor that would make attractive and instructive reading for the home-seeker.

Fifteen thousand miles by stage was but an incident of those strenuous years as the work progressed. When books, pamphlets, and newspapers started a fast and furious immigration, and railroads began their extensions, then came the locating of towns, colonizing the people into settlements, building bridges and irrigating-canals, schools, churches and colleges, organizing commercial bodies and fraternal societies, and pushing on with brain and brawn and pen until Pullman cars traversed the one-time wilderness on eight great overland lines.

While this is not a book of statistics, the historical references are believed to be correct. The main purpose has been to record some of the humorous and thrilling events during many years of pioneer travel, leaving out most of the heartaches and disappointments, the excessive fatigue and hardships, and giving more of the rainbow glow to an adventurous life on the frontier.

We shall ever have a kindly feeling in our hearts for the many friends on the frontier who smoothed our thorny way by generous and thoughtful hospitality. They threw such a rosy glow along the sparsely settled highways and made so homelike the widely separated settlements that the retrospect is colored by their kindness. In looking back, we are glad to linger over the humorous, to separate from its crude surroundings the picturesque element, and to endeavor to perpetuate the romances of the miner and prospector, the cowboy and the bullwhacker, the stage driver and the freighter, who with gaudily decked Indians made the frontier a galaxy of fascinating pictures. It was a land where eyes often ached with straining from horizon to horizon for the sight of a cabin, and where the heavy rattle of the stage-coach and the howling of coyotes were the only sounds that broke the silence of the vast expanse. Yet even that great silent anthem of Nature was entrancing in its immensity. Strenuous and trying as the life was, it had many compensations; it afforded experiences and a fund of reminiscences that may interest those who have followed our trail in the luxurious ways of modern travel.

C. A. S.

Spokane, Washington,
June 7, 1911.

CONTENTS

Contents

ILLUSTRATIONS

Fifteen Thousand Miles by Stage

Fifteen Thousand Miles by Stage

CHAPTER I

BEGINNING THE STAGE-COACH HONEYMOON

THE wedding bells had pealed merrily over the little village in northern Illinois, the marriage ceremony was over, and amid laughter and tears the guests had departed. There were many misgivings thirty-three years ago over a life to be spent away out on the Far West plains and mountains. People east of the Mississippi really believed such a life meant only hardship and danger, rubbing elbows with the slayers of Custer, the broncho busters, gamblers, and rough elements generally. Even the few better advised pictured it a mere existence among cattle barons, cowboys, miners, and freighters, forgetting their own earlier days in the now middle West where their pioneering had met with charms and fascinations they still loved to

I

recall. The multitude of friends thought it little less than a calamity in 1877 that a girl should choose as a life partner one who would carry her out into that mysterious and unsettled country.

A dear old uncle, the local printer, was so sure of an error in copy for the wedding invitation that he changed the name of the bridegroom to suit the general supposition that a suitor less liable to roam in savage lands was to have first place. When the engraving had to be changed to suit the bride instead of Dame Rumor he said the father must have lost his usual good judgment to allow such a wedding to take place. He did not know that the dear old father's tearful consent had been the most forceful opposition to the nuptials. As the one most interested I knew the struggle in his heart was between his love for me and my happiness.

It was not particularly reassuring that the tall, boyishly slender bridegroom had come with the halo of a hero, fresh from the Sioux battle-fields. He had been with General Crook's command against the hostile Sioux and Cheyennes, with Sitting Bull, Crazy Horse, Dull Knife, and Little Wolf as Indian leaders. The newspapers had thrilled the village with tales of Indian warfare in which this newcomer had participated and now the younger generation stood in open-mouthed wonder and their elders in awe and homage due one who had come unscathed through such experiences. I must confess the opposition and these thrilling recitals did not leave me wholly without misgivings. One incident of that Sioux war, however, will give an idea of the manner of man I was to follow into an unknown future: He had not gone as an enlisted soldier with General Crook, but as a civilian to report the war news to the New York *Times*, Chicago *Tribune*, and the *Rocky Mountain News*. He wore civilian dress, but General Crook said: "It mattered not what the coat was; Bob was every inch a soldier, always the first man to the front when the battle call was on, where he could get his news in the most reliable way, and he never failed to work his rifle as well as his pen."

In the famous battle of Powder River where forty-seven were assigned to charge through the Crazy Horse camp and stampede the savages on to Major Moore's much larger force which was to be in ambush, Bob was one of the forty-seven mounted on one of the best of the "Egan Grays." The "Egan Grays" were the pick and pride of General Crook's cavalry, commanded by Teddy Egan, and on this occasion Captain Teddy remarked that Bob would not be at the tail end of the party so long as he stayed on that mount. The forty-seven brave troopers surely did awaken the camp on that terrific charge. Teddy Egan's horse was shot in the neck, Lieut. John G. Bourke's bridle rein was shot out of his hand, Hospital Steward Bryan's horse was killed under him, and in a few minutes

" Bob's stampeded mount fell over a precipice and broke its neck "

troopers were being killed and wounded, and Bob's stampeded mount fell over a precipice and broke its neck. The camp was so much larger than Major Moore had counted on that he refused to take the position assigned him or let any more troops go to the rescue of the forty-seven, believing every man in the attacking party would be killed.

The battle raged for hours in the heart of the Indian village which was destroyed by fire at the first onslaught. Early in the fray all hands dismounted, using dead horses and logs as breastworks of defence, while fighting to the death and waiting for the rescuers who did not come.

The soldiers with Major Moore heard the incessant firing and could even see the terrible battle from their safe vantage ground on neighboring bluffs and begged to go to the rescue of their comrades. Fearing a mutiny at his refusal, the commander said he would have the first man shot who started to the Indian camp. Finally Col. T. H. Stanton, of the pay department, like Barbara Frietchie and her flag, stepped from the rank and said, "Shoot me if you will, but I am going to help our comrades. Come, boys, how many of you will go with me?" Out sprang eight men only who dared to disobey their commander, but away they flew yelling like a band of Indians and calling loudly to the boys in the battle: "Hold on, we're coming." Down the mountain they flew, making such a din with their yelling and their rifle volleys that the Indians were deceived in the number of the party and took to their ponies and their heels in a panic. Help had come none too soon, for twelve of the forty-seven were already past the fighting stage, and lay dead and wounded by their rifles.

The brave Colonel Stanton was never shot as threatened by the timorous Moore, but a long and spirited court-martial followed in which Major Moore was condemned, while a little later Colonel Stanton was made Paymaster-General of the United States Army.

Teddy Egan said when we met in later years that the success of that day was due not a little to the coolness and good marksmanship of Pard and Lieut. John G. Bourke, an officer of General Crook's staff, both of whom were commended in general orders by the Secretary of War for exceptional gallantry.

It was thus just after the close of the Sioux war that Pard was made a prisoner by a pale-faced maiden, as the western newspapers expressed it, but it was a case of captive leading the captor, for back they went to the same trackless wilderness where he had fought with sword and pen for first news.

In 1877 there was but one transcontinental railway across the desert West, the combined Union and Central Pacific road from Omaha to San Francisco. There were no railroads north or northwest of Utah, and but a short branch west of St. Paul.

In those days the frontier was no myth, but it was there with its dangers and hardships still to be endured. Hundreds of thousands of square miles were still marked upon the school

Omaha in 1877

maps as "unexplored regions." Stage lines, hundreds upon hundreds of miles in length, traversed lands that were otherwise unexplored, to reach outposts and *entrepôts* of the great frontier. Wyoming, with its vast area, greater than all the New England States combined, had but a scattered population of 20,000 people, mostly distributed in a thin fringe along the line of the newly built Union Pacific Railroad which traversed the southern boundary of the territory. The middle and north sections were given up to roving tribes of Indians, with here and there on the plains a few reckless cattlemen, whose herds had so recently displaced the myriads of buffalo, and in the hills a few adventurous gold-

A buffalo herd holding up a train

seekers who kept themselves fortified from the red enemy. The only nucleus of any considerable number of whites off the railroad was away up in the Sweetwater country at South Pass, where some two thousand people had more firmly established themselves and their rich possessions.

The venture of Brigham Young in peopling and reclaiming the Salt Lake Valley was still fresh on the page of history, but the Salt Lake Valley was but a gateway to the great Northwest. Brave, restless, pioneering spirits pushed on in the same way as their forefathers had done, but there was the satisfaction that civilization was creeping more rapidly behind the pathfinders.

It was small wonder that old friends looked solemn and that tears streamed down parental cheeks when a daughter was going to such an unknown life and country. Few girls realize what they are doing when they leave the shelter of a loving home life for a man who may only be full of promises he cannot fulfil.

The dear old father, who had reluctantly given his consent to a marriage that would take his beloved daughter so far from home and friends, packed the boxes for the new home with the generous bridal gifts and home linens and cemented them together with his tears, which he tried dextrously to hide by a

" The real home for many years was in the saddle or stage-coach "

cheery voice: "I say, mother, I made our new son promise to put in a hundred bushels of potatoes every fall, but if he stays in Wyoming I think he will have to rustle some when its credits now are only wind and Indians." "Well, pa, don't worry," mother replied, "It does seem a long ways to be from home if things don't go right, but so long as daughter can sing as she does now she will never go hungry, for they do say there are churches in Cheyenne just the same as here. Everybody says our church won't know what to do without their 'sweet singer.' But you know a girl always thinks she knows more than anybody else about the man she wants to marry. She weaves a halo about him that makes it pretty hard for him to live up to, but sometimes he does it. You know she is a pretty good judge of human nature and maybe he'll surprise us all some day by living up to her ideal. He don't seem to know much about women, but he does seem dreadfully fond of our girl. It was really funny last night to hear him tell Rev. Hutchinson, the minister, that the bride-to-be wanted the word 'obey' left out of the ceremony because there is Woman's Suffrage in Wyoming, and suggest, 'If you don't want to leave it out entirely, just put it in my part, for I've been running wild so long I just want to be obliged to obey somebody.'"

That was not hard to believe when he raised his voice in full, round tones with an "I will" or an "I do" whenever the minister made a slight pause in the marriage ceremony. In answering at all such impressive pauses he could not fail to answer in the right place and give the impression that he was in dead earnest in the matter. The incident caused a perfect round of merriment and the funereal restraint common on such occasions was replaced by a burst of applause for the nervy man from the West.

Pard had just published a two hundred and fifty page book on the resources of Wyoming, and while at Omaha en route to Cheyenne after the wedding he was urged by General Passenger Agent Thos. L. Kimball to create and take charge of a publicity department for the Union Pacific Railway Company. His book on Wyoming was the kind of a book that they wanted written on every State and Territory their lines reached or intended to reach, and they also wanted to know the resources of all the country west and northwest, that they might know where and how to extend their railroads to commercial advantage. It was an undertaking of great scope, and would require travel almost without end.

Pard's ambition knew no bounds, but it required much consideration before accepting the position and he then required that I be allowed to accompany him on all his journeys. He would not take me so far away from friends, then leave me alone in a desolate country, and he never did.

Instead of a home in the windy city of Cheyenne, as had been anticipated, it was only a sort of home station for repairs and an occasional few days' rest, and the real home was in the stage-coach and saddle for many years that followed.

At Omaha, we were guests at the Grand Central Hotel which was then located where The Paxton stands now.   It was burned a few years later, and thus was obliterated a place where we had the first startling episode of an eventful life.   A terrible storm came up one night, such as are often experienced along the Missouri River bottoms.   The lightning flashed in blinding fury and the thunder roared like a thousand cannon.   Wakened by the com-

First home of Platte Valley Masonic Lodge No. 32. On Old Oregon trail. Built 1870

motion I went into the sitting-room to close a window.   Pard heard the noise, and thinking it was a burglar, he softly crept into the room, lifted a chair above his head, and approached the spot whence came a slight rustle; he was just ready to strike the intruder to the floor when a flash of lightning revealed my white-robed figure at the window gazing at the storm.   The chair fell from his hand with a crash, and he was limp with terror at coming so near a domestic tragedy.   It was only the timely lightning that kept him from felling me to the floor as he was sure he had left me in bed.   A curious coincidence might be stated in the fact that at that very time Omaha was greatly excited over a trial for murder of a man who had shot and killed his wife in mistaking her for a burglar.   Such events seemed to be in the air, and we decided to wear bells on our toes when we made night raids thereafter.

In Omaha at that time we were often guests in the home of General Crook where, with the General and the officers of his staff, Pard lived over and again the experiences of many an Indian battle-field, and they had many a good joke to tell on one another. It gave me a new insight into a warrior's heart, for while they laughed and joked over many a heartrending episode, it was only to cover the tear in the eye and to hide the depth of the heart-thrust such incidents gave each and every one. That little early experience served me in good stead oftentimes afterward and taught me to be lenient to some seemingly blusterous individual who might only be struggling for mastery over his deeper feelings.

Farnum Street, the main business street of Omaha, had not yet been paved and it was an odd sight to see the teams and wagons get stuck in the mud on that central thoroughfare. Even horses drawing light buggies shared the same fate, and a few months later our own carriage stuck fast en route to the railroad station and we missed the last train that could carry us to our friends in Chicago in time for Christmas. People had to tie on their rubbers, or leave them glued in the clay soil of the crossings.

CHAPTER II

CHEYENNE

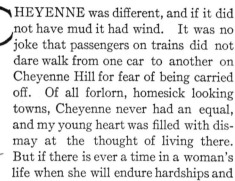

CHEYENNE was different, and if it did not have mud it had wind. It was no joke that passengers on trains did not dare walk from one car to another on Cheyenne Hill for fear of being carried off. Of all forlorn, homesick looking towns, Cheyenne never had an equal, and my young heart was filled with dismay at the thought of living there. But if there is ever a time in a woman's life when she will endure hardships and make sunshine out of shadows it is when she first leaves the home nest to follow the man of her choice. There was a lot of good in Cheyenne that could not be blown away, and memories still cling lovingly around the raw old place. Hon. E. A. Slack and wife had been East for our wedding and that fact alone gave us a little home feeling in the town. Mr. Slack was managing editor and owner of the Cheyenne *Sun* and Pard had been a hand at the case and at the desk in association with the editor before the experience in the Sioux war.

There were many hard things said and rough jokes sprung on Cheyenne in those days. For example, one evening at the theatre in Denver the villain of the play was advised to leave the United States and go to Cheyenne. Cheyenne was the chief outfitting point for a chain of small military posts, Deadwood and the Black Hills several hundred miles to the north, and it was between an outgoing and a returning freighter near there that the dialogue took place about the famous load of twenty barrels of whiskey and one sack of flour when one said to the other, "What in —— are you going to do with so much flour?"

For laundry work we paid $2.50 per dozen pieces, and pianos

rented for $15 per month. That seemed enormous then when fresh from the $3 rental price of Chicago, but prices for every-thing from bread to hats seemed extortionate.

The present United States Senator, Chas. E. Warren of Wyoming, was then an enterprising drygoods merchant of Cheyenne, and that he was a man of resources even regarding small things was made manifest early in his career. He had been married several years before a little daughter came to them,

Deadwood in 1876

the same daughter that made life such a joy to her father after her mother was taken from them and whose recent marriage caused such a social stir at our National Capital.

When the little miss was to make her first appearance among friends in the East the Warren store was searched for all its best materials for baby's outfit, and money and work were lavished without stint on the little darling's tucks and ruffles. But a great heartless railway company made such a mysterious disappearance of the trunk containing all the dress parade ward-robe, that when the little family arrived at its eastern destination the trunk was missing and could not be found anywhere. The little miss had to meet all her relatives and new-found friends in ordinary store clothes. Senator Warren struggled for years to find some trace of the missing trunk, but without success, nor could he secure any reimbursement until he thought of a unique method which he at once put into execution. He placed a watchman in the railroad yards of Cheyenne with instructions to report the arrival of the first freight car bearing the name of the road upon which he travelled. In a day or two the watchman gave the necessary information. Senator Warren at once went before a local magistrate and sued out an attachment upon the freight car. Then he wired to the railroad officials stating what he had done, and awaited results.

In less than three hours came a dispatch saying that a check for the value of the missing trunk had been forwarded to him, and asking him to let the freight car proceed upon its way. Then the suit was withdrawn. And now comes the sequel to the story in the fact that the trunk has recently been found after all its years of hiding in some obscure and remote storehouse. It was found after Miss Warren's late marriage, and its contents may yet make a mother's heart glad, as even the cans of condensed milk were intact.

The second railroad from Cheyenne south to Denver was completed at noon on Sunday, Dec. 4, 1877, and the first train on this new Colorado Central road was run on the following Tuesday, with Mr. Phelps, the local passenger agent, Dr. Gordon of Cheyenne, Pard, and myself as the first passengers over the road. The time schedule to Denver was five hours, but we were seven hours in reaching Boulder, only half way, and changed our car twice. The car we started in was the one that carried Abraham Lincoln to Washington after he was elected President of the United States, and the same one that carried his body to its place of burial. I was never able to learn how that car became a common carrier of the windy desert. The outside was painted a bright yellow. Inside a long seat ran the whole length on either side of the car with upholstered cushions, and the upholstery was continued up the sides of the car between the windows. It was a great contrast, however, to the luxurious cars of the present day.

There were nearly as many churches in Cheyenne in '77 as

there are now, but I hope there is less rivalry. The divine head, Rector Thompkins, of the Episcopalian diocese, was so angry because I preferred to sing in another choir than his, that he rode in the same Pullman car in a section opposite my own all the way to Omaha without seeing me. At another time his choirmaster, one Mr. Wells, sought revenge at a public meeting where we were to sing a responsive duet. We had our places on the platform and I had carried my part and paused for his response. He simply stood there with his eyes riveted on his music until the audience thought I had made a complete breakdown. It was a terrible moment, but fortunately his part was not difficult and I took it up and sang it myself, and after that first part I did not allow him a chance but sang both parts to the end. The table turned on him so completely that he looked like an apoplectic when he turned to his seat, and he was exposed to most cutting criticism by the musical fraternity.

Without a spear of grass, without a tree within the scope of the eye, without water except as it was pumped for household use, with a soil sandy, hard, and barren, and with never-ceasing wind—that was the raw Cheyenne in the late '70's, in marked contrast to its parks, shady streets, and well-kept lawns of to-day. That was the place of my early bride days. What a transition from the green rolling hills of northern Illinois, with all its forests, its fruits and flowers, and rich harvest fields, and its clear flowing rivers.

In all my girlhood the one thing that I wanted to avoid in my life was to be a pioneer. So often had I listened to tales of my elders of " '49 and spring of '50" etc., that it had made me say many times that I would never be a pioneer and be called the oldest settler in a town or country, or one of the early ones in any State history. Yet, there I was at the very threshold of a new land where I was to be the first woman in many then unexploited regions, and the title of "old settler" was to be indelibly and forever attached to me and mine.

The matrimonial venture did not lead me to the duties of a matron with home, children, and windows full of flowers, but our launch was pushed into the sea of adventure paralleled by none save that of my own Pard, whom I followed for thirty years wheresoe'er he blazed the trail, until we were captivated by the soughing pines of Spokane.

Soon after our arrival in Cheyenne, the locality was visited by the worst hail storm in its history. In our house a hailstone went through a window, then through a cane-seated chair, hitting the floor with force enough to bound back and make a second hole through the cane seat. The city looked as if Fort Russell had turned her batteries loose on the town, for there was scarcely a north window left unbroken. Many of the stones measured seven inches in circumference, and our enterprising landlady gathered enough hailstones to freeze several gallons of cream and then gave what she called a hailstone party.

Old Fort Russell was the pride of Cheyenne and its Sunday concert was the event of the week. Everything on wheels moved to the fort and if there were not wheels enough to carry all who wanted to go, the surplus would walk out over the hard, sandy road rather than miss the harmonies that floated out through the bright, clear air.

Cheyenne afforded my first glimpse of army life, and Fort Russell was a fair post to compare with any on the barren frontier. In the first place, a plains fort is no fort at all; it is simply a collection of houses and buildings set down on the prairie or on the crest of some high bluff, with no bastions, walls, stockade, nor defence of any kind, and might better be termed a small settlement than a fort. Select a fairly level piece of ground, say 400 yards square; on two sides build substantial quarters for the officers, and on the other two sides rows of barracks for the enlisted men. Erect stables, guardhouse, post-trader's store, a club-room for officers, another for enlisted men, install hospital for the sick, with capable doctors and attentive nurses, a bakery, reading-room, gymnasium, and bathing-rooms, and the picture is complete. At regimental quarters a good band was always stationed, and, once or twice a week there were hops and dances for both officers and enlisted men. At the post exchange light wines, beer, and cider were sold at almost cost prices, but in some cases no whiskey under any pretence was allowed for sale within the limits of a garrison. In the billiard rooms a nominal charge of five cents a game was made, the receipts merely sufficing to pay the attendants and keep the place in repair.

Very raw material is taken for soldiers; they are men of all nationalities and all climes. They enter the army as bright as meteors and as verdant as unripe cucumbers, but no matter how ignorant or green a recruit may be at the time of joining, he usually leaves the army well satisfied with his five years of discipline and experience, his erect figure and fine marksmanship. The bump of fun is exceedingly large in the average soldier of the line. Young men in the prime of manhood and of fine physique generally look on the term of enlistment as a sort of lark, and propose to get as much amusement and fun out of the five years as possible. Their devices and tricks for getting out of drill and other duties are as varied as the boys themselves. In time of peace, guard duty is about the hardest service in the army, and to this the soldier is eligible one day in every six or seven. Any man in any company, whenever he feels so inclined, if not detailed on some duty, can amuse himself by knocking over jackrabbits, bagging sage hens, quail, and prairie chickens galore, or missing as many shots as he wants to. Tours of detached service are simply picnics, and no man would stay in a garrison if he had half a chance to get out over the prairie for service of any kind. But with all the cleverness at entertaining themselves and having jocular sports about the fort, the life is a tedious one, and to an ambitious man it becomes almost intolerable. The call to arms is hailed with joy, not because it means war, but because it means action and a change of scene and events.

The light air of the mountain country makes people energetic and full of vim, and the climatic influence is especially noted in school children where every eye gleams in a nervous tension unknown in lower or southern climes. Sometimes it may tend to make children too precocious as was the case during one of President Harriman's more recent visits to Cheyenne, when Frank Jones, the young son of Chief Clerk D. A. Jones, of the Master Mechanic's office, was sent to the private car with a telegram for Superintendent McKeen. Pushing his way into the private car of President Harriman, the lad said: "Hello: I got er telegram for McKeen." "You mean Mr. McKeen," interposed Mr. Harriman. "Yep, I guess so; th' head cheese 'f th' motive department." Mr. Harriman smiled and took the telegram and had it sent to Mr. McKeen. "What do you do," he asked the lad. "I 'm one 'f the directors 'f th' Union Pacific." "What?" exclaimed Mr. Harriman. "Yep, I direct envelopes over t' th' Master Mechanic's office," was the laconic reply as the lad left the car. He left Mr. Harriman and the other magnates in an uproar and the joke no doubt followed Mr. Harriman for some time.

There were many idlers in Cheyenne in spite of the life-giving air, but I never saw them stand in knots and make remarks about passing ladies. If a woman chanced to pass a saloon where a lot of men were lolling about the entrance, she could pass quietly along without hesitation for every man of them would be out of sight before she reached them. I saw that happen so often from the windows of the hotel that I knew it was not simply a chance circumstance, and that ladies were shown a deference by those outcasts of society that proved them not lost beyond recall if the right influences were used. Social conditions of the West were entirely new to me and it required time to adjust myself to the more democratic gentility which is the outcome of a concourse of pioneers.

It was a difficult matter up to 1877 to draw social lines in Cheyenne, but in every growing town there comes a time when its four hundred will draw the reins of exclusiveness. That four hundred is generally considered the upper tendom, but there are places where the lower tendom will swarm away from their betters, leaving it an easy matter for the others to draw the social lines as tight as they please. In the early days the bad elements of Cheyenne were so large and unsavory that they clung together and poured out their disapproval of a higher life in no unmistakable terms. But those in the better way conquered and in '77 the social status was no longer quivering in the balance, but was governed by such as our now noted United States Senator, Chas. E. Warren, the Hon. E. A. Slack, Judge (later United States Senator) J. M. Cary, Luke Voorhees, and others who have risen to prominent places in the affairs of our nation and who were educated up to their great usefulness right on the windy plains of Cheyenne.

Cheyenne and Wyoming were little less known for the strength of character and cultivation of their ladies than for their notable men. It was no wonder that Mr. Slack, editor of the Cheyenne *Sun*, was such a gloriously fine man, for he had a mother who was an honor to our country.

She was Mrs. Esther Morris, born in 1814, at Spencer, Tioga

County, New York; her grandfather, Daniel McQuigg served as captain under General Sullivan in his expedition that drove the Indians out of western New York. He was one of the first twelve settlers in Tioga County. Esther was left an orphan at the early age of eleven years, and she was ever a warm advocate of right. She took a stand for justice at an Abolitionist meeting held one night in the Baptist Church of her native town, when she was but twenty years old. So incensed were the pro-slavery advocates of the community that a prominent citizen declared that if the ladies would leave the church the men would tear it down. Esther stood up in her seat and said: "This church belongs to the Baptist people, and no one has a right to destroy it. If it is proposed to burn it down, I will stay right here and see who does it."

She married Artemus Slack at the age of twenty-eight, after she had made a comfortable fortune for herself in a commercial enterprise. Mr. Slack was then engaged in the construction of the Erie Railway, but when he died several years later he was one of the chief engineers of the Illinois Central and left her a large grant of land along that line.

In 1845 Esther Slack was married to John Morris or Peru, Illinois, but it was while settling the Slack estate that she realized the great injustice of the property laws in their relation to women, and she resolved to devote her life to the betterment of such conditions.

In 1869 she joined her husband again at South Pass, Wyoming, and it was there she was made the first woman Justice of the Peace in the United States, if not in the world. Mr. Morris objected to her acceptance of the office and made a scene in the court-room and she fined him for contempt which he refused to pay. Then she promptly sent him to jail. It was a good illustration of her determination of character.

She tried more than fifty cases and never had a ruling reversed on an appeal. Her court was world famous and from her success there she took up the work of Woman's Suffrage and carried it to a successful completion in Wyoming.

When I knew her best she was more than fifty years old, but young in heart, and her powers of conversation though blunt and often cutting, would have given her a conspicuous position anywhere. The charm of her personality was in her cheerful disposition under all conditions. It was as natural for her to look on the bright side of things as it is for the flower to turn to the sun that gives it warmth and life, and her faith in the eternal goodness of God made her old age one of joy and cheerfulness. Those in trouble always found in her a kind friend and wise counsellor.

Another Cheyenne debutante was Miss Estelle Reel. She was a teacher in the school there and we became warm friends. She has developed into a sphere of usefulness attained by few. She went to Wyoming for her health after her education was

Miss Reel's savage wards

completed, and as she became well and strong again she took up educational work and passed from teacher to county and State Superintendent. She became very much interested in the leasing and disposition of the State school lands, with the object of securing a good school fund, the result of which was that the State has now a satisfactory school fund and the best system of schools possible. She made her trips throughout the Territory by stage or on horseback, and often crossed long stretches of the lonely prairies alone.

Her successor as State Superintendent was a man. "Why

did you not select a woman?" she asked of the political leaders. "Well, this man is the father of eleven children," was the reply, "and we concluded a man who is doing so much for the State is entitled to as much consideration as a woman who seems determined to remain an old maid." Miss Reel laughed merrily and told her political friends that she had no desire to compete with the man who had eleven children.

Miss Reel has been for many years the Government Superintendent of Indian Schools for the United States, and she is thoroughly absorbed and interested in her work. The Indians call her the "Big White Squaw from Washington"; they love and adore her in the true Indian way of wanting to give her their children.

Even Pard had a political bee buzzing in his bonnet when we were married, and he had been assured of the Territorial Secretaryship of Wyoming if he wanted it. The incumbent of the office was then a Mr. Morgan who, with his wife, were almost our first callers, and I cannot forget how unhappy I felt all the time they were in the house to think that we were being urged to usurp the places of such charming people as they were, and it gave us both a distaste for politics that we have never rallied from, and within a few months from that time when the bubble was about to burst upon the people Pard resigned all claims to the office and decided to remain with Jay Gould's interests and take up the line of work as it had been outlined at the Union Pacific headquarters in Omaha. That meant the penetrating into all the unwritten lands of our great West and Northwest and dipping a pen into every interest that could be made a feeder for the great railway system. How much of the vast influx of settlers has been due to Pard's facile pen and untiring energies none may ever know, but we have watched the flow of immigration until it has become a tidal wave of humanity sweeping over the broad western domains and obliterating every vestige of the pioneer trails. The trip from Ogden to Helena and on up to British Columbia in an automobile or by steam car is a lark nowadays, and so it is all over the land where the creaking, lumbering old stage-coach rattled along the rutty, rough highways in the '70's and '80's of the nineteenth century.

We had many misgivings about the success of so vast an undertaking and though we never discussed failure we planned constantly for steps of progress and were always met with joy and compliments whenever we entered the home office at Omaha. The company soon considered me such an inseparable and indivisible part of Pard that they never made out any transportation for him that its counterpart was not made out for me whether on their own road or requested of another.

Circumstances often compelled us to make trips separately, but we generally met on the road somewhere. I well remember a trip west after our first Christmas back in Illinois in '77. It was in the dead of winter and Pard had gone ahead to make a quick trip to Salt Lake. I was anxious to reach Denver at the same time that he returned there, and to do so I had to battle against the home people for starting out when the whole western country was snowbound. One old northwestern conductor, J. J. Donnelly, swore most vociferously that I "would never get through in God's world," and when it was too late I began to feel repentant for my wilfulness and to think that the wishes of others should have been given precedence. The cars of the train leaving Chicago were miserable shells; either the good cars were stalled in snowdrifts or the railway company did not want to send them out, and I was the only woman on the train. We were twenty-four hours going sixty-five miles and butted snowdrifts all the way. The second day out the weather mellowed and rain began to fall, then a freight wreck delayed us some six hours and we had to transfer to another train sent to our relief. The change was made by walking along the track through the wreckage of freight cars and wading ankle deep and more in slush, and before Omaha was finally reached I was in the fourth car, having changed for a worse one every time, until there was not only no sleeper, but only one passenger coach on the train.

From Omaha west we started out on the Union Pacific train well equipped again, and with many belated passengers, but at Ogallala the train was held forty-eight hours by floods and one thousand feet of track that had been washed out had to be rebuilt. The town swarmed with cowboys and renegade gangs of bandits who laid a plot to hold up our train at a station just west of Ogallala. The telegraph operator at that station was A. G. Smith, now the secretary of the North Coast Railroad Company; he was bound and locked in a small side room in the station, but as he often slept in that little room he had fitted up and connected a little battery so that he could send out a message at night from there if he so desired, for he was always anticipating just such an experience.   When our train was ready to go on west it was a combination of several trains and the bandits hoped for a rich haul, but the imprisoned operator worked one hand loose and got a message into Ogallala just before our train pulled out, and in spite of the signal to stop,

" The bandits hoped for a rich haul "

our train flew past the greatly incensed hold-up band.   Then they heard a second section coming not four minutes behind us and when the whistle blew for the station the robbers were in a state of great anticipation, but unfortunately for them the second train contained the sheriff and a posse of deputies who captured several of the bandits whom the court sentenced to many years' imprisonment.

I was heartily glad to reach Denver after my week on the road, but I soon learned that Pard had also been delayed and he wired me to come on to Laramie in Wyoming. I arrived there in the evening and he was to reach there early the next morning. It was a bitter cold night and I was glad to be off the train and have a good warm room, but when I was ready to retire I noticed for the first time that the room was lighted with electricity, and how I was to get rid of that light and have it again in the morning was a problem that set me guessing, for as yet our city hotels were not so fortunate as to have electric lights. I hunted all around the room for some instructions but found none. There was but one large lamp and it hung by the bed so I had none to experiment with and I looked long and lovingly at the projecting flat button above the glass bulb wondering what it might do to me or to the light if I tried to turn it, and I wished it would talk. Finally, after locating the call button for the office in case I should need help, I nerved myself up to an experiment, and the joy that it gave me to see the light come and go was supreme. I tried it many times during the night, and when the morning call came for me to get up for Pard's early train I turned on the light again with the joyousness of a child, and thought how strange it was that my first experience with those lights should be in a place that Eastern people considered as out of God's jurisdiction, so far away did the Laramie Plains seem to people using oil or gas. Later electric lights illuminated nearly every small town, not only streets and stores, but the homes long before Eastern homes had the luxury.

Once in New York a friend asked if it did not seem good to get back to a city having the luxury of gas, and when I said the electric light was a little strong sometimes but that it was preferable to gas he looked as if I had lost my reason or had no regard for the truth. He had been West! Oh, yes, he had been as far west as Buffalo, but there were no towns in New York lighted by electricity and he did not enjoy my expressed sympathy for users of gas who had travelled so little. In later years, after his mind opened up to the advantages of the great West he often referred to that moment of humiliation for himself when he thought I needed pity and sympathy for living outside of New York, and had the tables turned on himself.

Laramie was then the home of Bill Nye. He edited the *Laramie Boomerang*, which brought him into prominence as a humorist. Bill Nye was a funny man with his pen, but not with his tongue, and it was seldom he could give quick, bright repartee in speech. Once in his home town his wit did come in a sudden flash on an occasion when he went into a bar for his favorite beverage. As he put his foot up on the rail and leaned over the mahogany, a stalwart stranger gave him a shove that aroused the funny man's ire. Turning about and indignantly scoring the great bulk of humanity beside him, he said he would give him just two minutes in which to apologize. The great six-footer eyed Mr. Nye's diminutive form from his bald head down to his shiny boots and back again, taking nearly the limit of his time in the scrutiny. Then, without a gesture or smile, he simply said, "I apologize" and walked out. The manipulator of cocktails let go his breath with a noisy "phew!" as he asked Nye if he knew who that man was. Mr. Nye replied that he did not and did n't care as he had apologized. The man behind the bar was so excited he could scarcely articulate, but he bawled out: "Why—why—why, that man is John L. Sullivan; now what would you have done if he had not apologized? I say, what would you have done?" "Well," said Nye, as his eyes widened with the thoughts of his miraculous escape, "I would have extended his time!"

Before the railroad was finished there was a tri-weekly stage between Cheyenne and Denver, which were rival cities for many years, but the location of Denver gave it every advantage as an outfitting point for miners, or as headquarters for tourists for scenic delights and its climate was ideal. Two or three rail routes have been built between the cities hoping for a closer relationship but the topography of the country made railroad building difficult and unsatisfactory, and two of the roads have alternately been rebuilt and blended until the Denver Pacific and Colorado Central have each lost their original lines. The only rail route from Omaha to Denver was through Cheyenne until the Julesberg cut-off was built which is now called the Denver Short Line from Omaha. Denver people also had to go through Cheyenne to reach Ogden just as they do now, and there seems to be no better way of surmounting the Rockies than the route through the Laramie Plains.

There were but few times in our years of pioneering that we did not live at hotels and the few exceptions developed some peculiar conditions. We felt especially favored at one time by being offered some charming rooms and board in one of the most aristocratic families of the place, where we could go and come at will, and the condition was charming for it would be like going home after an arduous journey. On our first return, however, there was an extra fine pair of blankets, a wedding present, missing from our bed. It was a pair that had been accidentally left out when our goods were stored away and they seemed safest to be in use. The bedroom in our absence was used as a spare room for guests, and when I enquired about the blankets no one knew anything about them. I asked who had occupied the room, and was told that one guest was a Baptist minister from Laramie and another was the president of the State College of Colorado at Boulder. We knew both parties well, and they were so far above suspicion that it made the joke on them a laughable one, but we never found the blankets and we soon after learned that one member of the family was a noted kleptomaniac who did many curious things. On one occasion she took out her false teeth, dressed in a disguise, and went about town begging flowers from those who were fortunate enough to have blooming house plants. Her excuse was a sick loved one who was passionately fond of flowers, and although she was recognized by two or three they said nothing to betray her, but gave her the flowers in pity for her own weakness. On one occasion she arranged the flowers very tastefully and sent them to a funeral with the request that they be left on the grave. After the ceremony was over and the cemetery was lacking in visitors she brought the flower piece home, rearranged it, and sent it that same night as a wedding gift. She also found it convenient to unpack and use my silverware and other wedding presents, and to give away my gowns when I was absent and then we decided to look for home comforts elsewhere.

There was one place in Denver where the landlady's mother was insane, and oftentimes I would have a strange feeling of a human presence when I believed myself to be alone, and would turn about to find the crazed creature standing grinning behind me. I grew more afraid of her every day and finally locked my doors every time I entered the rooms. After that I would often see the knob quietly turning or hear a little click at the lock as she was stealthily trying to enter. It was a beautiful suite of parlors and the location was ideal, but they were no compensation for such occult companionship, and we went back to the Windsor Hotel, satisfied to remain there while in town.

It was a keynote of progress to see every new hotel in Denver built a little farther uptown. The old American House down on Blake Street was the most fashionable hotel in town in 1877, and it elicited as much surprise and pleasure as the Brown Palace did in later days. The Windsor, the St. James, the Albany, Wentworth, Glenarm, and others out to the present site of the Brown Palace have told the trend of progress, and there are but few people now who remember Blake and Larimer streets as the principal shopping streets of the city.

The night of the opening of the Tabor Grand Opera House was an event in Denver's history not to be forgotten. The city celebrated two events in one, for the first passenger train on the Denver Short Line arrived the same evening, and brought in the Nebraska Press Association. Accompanied by a party of friends, including Mrs. David Kimball of Omaha, I made that first through trip. At Julesberg we were met by Pard and John Arkins of the *Rocky Mountain News* and Tom Dawson of the Denver *Times*. Since that time Mr. Dawson has been Senator Teller's private secretary in Washington and is now the head of the Associated Press which sends out all the Washington Congressional dispatches.

The members of the Nebraska contingent included Fred Nye and Mr. Woodbridge of the Omaha *Republican*. Mr. Nye was very short and Mr. Woodbridge was very long, so one said he brought the other along for use as a fire escape. The entire party occupied boxes in the new theatre and the curtain raising was delayed an hour for the belated new train to arrive, and the city guests to get their dinner, for all trains then stopped for meals or waited for the end of a run.

CHAPTER III

IT was past the middle of November when we left Denver on a bright Sunday morning to enjoy the glories of Clear Creek Canyon and to penetrate the mysteries of the Black Hawk mines. I felt especially interested in this trip because it was there and at Central City in 1871 that Pard had worked at the printer's case so arduously, and made a record far beyond his co-workers in the number of "ems" he could correctly set up in a given time, always working early and late that he might supply his invalid father with help for family needs.

The wonders of Clear Creek Canyon are not so unknown to the world now, and do not need minute description. The narrow-gauge rail line was considered a most wonderful achievement in engineering, with its towering cliffs on the one side, and the torrents of rushing waters on the other. We crossed and recrossed the rocky gorge, reviewing the frowning cliffs and foamy depths, gaining a glimpse of our engine as we rounded some sharp curve, or rolled under a projecting shelf that threatened to fall upon the baby train. On and up we went, wrapped in a halo of sublimity, *en rapport* with the grandeur of nature's arts, and dumb with admiration and reverence. What halcyon days those were, with all the vigor and enthusiasm of youth to summon to the appreciation and praises of such exciting travel.

In the party for that day was a retired banker from Boston,
a man genial and companionable, who entered into the spirit of
enjoyment with great zest, but he amazed everybody by asking
if we were *west of Omaha*. When he saw the consternation de-
picted on the several faces, he said he really did not know where
he was, that he had bought a round-trip ticket to the Coast
including several intermediate trips, but he did not know how
far he was along although he had spent several days in Denver.
Our train was carrying a "Pinafore" company up to the

In Clear Creek Canyon, Colorado

mountain towns that morning, and as it was waiting at the
forks of Clear Creek for the down express we heard an altercation between a man and his wife belonging to the company
which suddenly culminated in the man rushing from the car
saying "Good-bye"; he sprang to the platform, and, before
any one realized his intent he stepped up on to the framework
of the bridge and jumped into the creek. The water was very
high and the current running with a fall of a hundred and fifty
feet to the mile. He made frantic efforts to save himself, but
to no avail, and even his body could not be recovered. It was
a great shock to the company with whom he was a general
favorite as their "Dick Dead Eye." It seemed impossible that
he meant to do more than frighten his wife, for he was such a

clever, good-natured man, always doing something to entertain the company. The distracted (?) wife offered $25 reward for the return of the body if covered with the new suit of clothes which he wore when he was drowned.

Ever and anon dark holes in the mountainsides would prove the love of man for gold, and his untiring efforts to draw out the very vitals of our mother-earth. Mother Grundy beamed upon us as we whizzed past, while the donkey pictured in the pinnacles above had more the appearance of wishing himself nearer that he might enjoy his hereditary amusement of landing all intruders at the foot of the hills. The "old frog" seemed ready to begin his evening melody as soon as the shadows lengthened, but he looked as contented as though he had not been sitting bolt upright on his stony hind legs for ages and criticised by every passing man, woman, and child.

The high, towering cliffs were as grand and majestic as though the storms of centuries had not fought and striven to

Mother Grundy, Clear Creek Canyon, Colorado

crush them to the earth; and who can tell how many centuries
they may yet hold their mighty sway over the dark shadows
of the canyon with its mass of human habitants.   The unruly
waters of the creek went rushing and seething over the rocks in
their wild race to the sea.   The mountains, the pictured rocks,
and the roaring waters wove around us such a spell that the
cry of the brakeman for Black Hawk seemed like a sacrilegious
intrusion into the sanctum of our deepest and purest thoughts.
But the spell was broken and we descended to earth to find ourselves still of the earth with human beings round about us.

When we made the first trip up this canyon the track was
laid only to Black Hawk.   While the Central City station was
only a mile farther up the gulch, the rail line had to circuit
about and zigzag for four miles among the gold mines on the
mountainside to make the grade.   Workmen were busy all
along the distance hurrying the work to completion.

The altitude of Central City is 8300 feet above sea-level or
nearly twice that of Denver.   There was no hotel in Black
Hawk, but at Central City the "Teller House," built by our
good friend Senator Teller, was as fine as any country hotel
in the State.   Most streets of Central City were not over twenty
feet wide, and the houses looked like bird cages hung on hooks
jutting out from the mountainsides.   Nearly every house was
reached by a flight of stairs, and though it might be two or three
stories high on the lower side, there would be an entrance on a
level with the top floor on the upper side.   Pard pointed out
one rickety building where, in 1871, his dextrous fingers picked
type out of the case at the rate of seven dollars per day, which
amount, however, he found harder to collect than to set the type.
But the more thrifty looking Central City *register* Office, where
Col. Frank Hall did the newspaper business on a cash basis,
furnished many a remittance to Pard's sick folks at home.

The Hill Smelting Works were then in this canyon, and
covered four acres of ground.   Professor Hill (later Colorado's
United States Senator) took great pride in explaining the remarkable twenty-seven stages of treating the ore before it was
lumped into the beautiful stacks of bullion piled on the office
floor.   Fifty-two tons of ore were treated daily and that was
considered a large day's turnout at that time.   Fifty cords of
wood were daily consumed in smelting the fifty tons of ore.

The expense of running the smelter was on an average of five hundred dollars per day.

The Bobtail gold mine tunnel was in the western part of the town. With lighted torches and rubber clothing we penetrated twenty-two hundred feet into the secret chest of mother-earth to see where she stored her wealth. We also visited other mines and scenic places, Pard to gather his statistics of productions, and

Tons of bullion ready for the mint

I to study the people and the social ways, and both to marvel at the wondrous handiwork of our great Creator.

Next morning by half-past seven o'clock we were on our way through Virginia Canyon to Idaho Springs, a distance of only seven miles, but wonderful in its scenic grandeur. It was over this route that the stage drivers made some memorable records on the last four miles, sometimes making that distance in twelve minutes. General Grant and his daughter Nellie were put through at a four-minute gait, and when the General protested against such speed the driver coolly said his own neck was as dear as anybody's and the General need not worry.

It was here also that Horace Greeley paid an extra fare to be taken to Idaho Springs in time to catch a train to Denver. There had been a cloudburst down the north fork and it had washed out the track below Black Hawk, and the great Horace had an appointment to meet and he needed speed. Driving like a madman down the steep grade was too much, however, for Mr. Greeley; he tried to call the driver down, while striving also to hold himself on the coach, but the man with the ribbons called to him: "Keep your seat Horace, you will be there in time. You won't have to walk."

The wind blew a gale, but over one mountain and another we sped along, passing Old Chief, Squaw, and Papoose mountains, swinging the curves and corners of the road, glancing nervously at the depths and heights and wishing we might moderate the pace as earnestly as Horace Greeley or General Grant could have done, yet with no more influence over the Jehu than the squirrels of the woods chirping their incense at human intrusion.

About midway of the canyon lived a peculiar hermit, in an old log cabin, and the man's possessions were chiefly his dog and horse. The queer old man would find a mine and sell it for some price, then get drunk and stay drunk while the money lasted. When he started off on his spree he turned his horse and dog loose on the hills to care for themselves. The dog would follow the horse all day and drive it to the barn at night, watch by the door until morning, when they would both start out together again. We saw the horse feeding on the mountain grass and his faithful attendant lying a few feet away, waiting for the master's return. No one could learn what the dog subsisted on, for he never left his duty to forage.

The trip through that famous canyon was one we had the privilege of paying well for, and we had our money's worth, if we were glad when it ended and were safe once more at the Beebe House of Idaho Springs. We hurriedly wended our way to the hot springs for a plunge, but when we learned that the "Omaha Board of Trade" had just been cleansed we turned our faces to a dip of less proportions.

On another trip in summer we made the ride over to Bear Creek which was full of romance and grandeur. A gradual ascent over a smooth road along the bank of Bear Creek was a joy not to forget.   Wild roses bloomed in profusion, sweet syringa, wild columbine, daisies, and purple flagg grew in confusion along the rocks and hedges.   The most remarkable flower to me was that of the soap plant, or soapweed, an un-

In the shadow of the Chief, the Squaw, and Papoose Mountains, the horse and dog awaited the master's return

romantic name given it because of the soapy quality of its root. The stalks grew about twenty inches high, and many had fully forty blossoms on a stem that looked like so many water lilies on a stalk.   These weeds were very plentiful and would make a

3

fine showing in any Eastern collection of house plants.   The leaves of the plant are long and narrow, with very sharp points, and are used extensively in the manufacture of paper.

The only defacement in this canyon was a frequent sign warning the followers of Isaak Walton that no fishing was allowed.   One cunning nimrod made himself famous by ingeniously reaching the head waters and wading down the bed of the creek.   A wrathy ranchman discovered the young man,

" He lured the irate landowner into a deep hole"

clad to the neck in rubber, coolly casting his fly and unmindful of all threats that the irate rancher could hurl at him.   At last the infuriated owner plunged into the water to drag out the trespasser, but the hook and line man only went into deeper water, and continued to pull up the speckled beauties.   He said he came with the water from the mountain top and had a right to stay with it, then deftly he lured the irate landowner into a deep hole, at the same time telling him that when he was wet enough he had better get out of the water.   It was a most exasperating condition for the landowner and he left the water and the river vowing vengeance in "blue hot air," as he went dripping into the woods toward his cabin.

While resting on the hotel veranda at Idaho Springs we were given a striking illustration of the fine discrimination and disgust for intoxicated men by the mountaineer's good transportation ally, the shaggy little burro. Half a dozen little boys and girls were hanging all over one of these sturdy animals which was apparently a village pet. He seemed to immensely enjoy their fun of trying to cover his anatomy at all points from his ears to his tail, and would cheerfully and safely carry all such little riders as could cling to him without saddle or bridle. A big drunken wretch who had been watching the fun from a nearby groggery, thinking to participate staggered up, brushed the children aside, and threw his burly frame across the burro. In an instant the sleepy little fellow was wide awake, those long ears flew back to the horizontal, the man was thrown and kicked half-way across the street, and with mouth wide open exposing a wicked set of teeth the insulted animal followed up his advantage until he chased his victim over a neighboring fence.

Georgetown, a few miles above Idaho Springs, was then the heart of the mining section, and there General Marshall provided us with riding horses, and with his son for a guide we made the climb to the head of Clear Creek, where the waters were indeed as clear as molten crystal. We could look down on the "Silver Queen," as Georgetown was often called, with her four thousand inhabitants, where she made a mere speck in the distant valley. We visited many a "prospect" and "salted" mine, but the point of greatest interest was the Colorado Central mine. At a depth of two hundred and fifty feet we took a pick and hacked out pieces of silver ore from a vein that averaged $450 to the ton. The top of this mine was at an elevation of 12,000 feet above the sea-level, and it was entered through a tunnel 1360 feet long at the end of which 800 feet of mother-earth hung over us. The tunnel also led to the underground hall where was held one of the grandest and most unique balls ever given. There were eight rows of lights extending full length of the tunnel, and the silver walls were draped in bunting from end to end. The ballroom, thus cut out of the heart of the mountain, and which was later the machinery hall, was a blaze of light and beauty, for many ladies from the capital city and other towns of the West came in their richest gowns and made the function one of the most beautiful, novel, and weird known in mining history.

To one reared on Illinois prairies the wooded hills and timber chutes were intensely interesting. Often a chute is several thousand feet long that the timber cut on the mountain can be run to the bottom with lightning speed. It rains every

Pack train waiting for a load

day in and above Georgetown, just a shower about noon. The shower was as sure as the strike of a clock all summer long, and its great regularity rendered irrigation or sprinkling unnecessary to crops or lawns. One man along our way had a four-acre patch of potatoes which netted him $2500 a year. The sun shines only about six hours for the longest day in Georgetown, then the mountains hide it and there is only a mellow twilight after 3 P.M.

There can be no more interesting trips in Colorado that those to Green Lake and Gray's Peak. The former is well named the "Gem of the Mountains" and it possesses rare charms for all lovers of the beautiful. It is but two miles and a half from Georgetown, and the road leading thither winds around in short curves up the mountainside until, at a glorious vantage point fifteen hundred feet above the city, one catches through romantic openings in the forest the first glimpse of the lake. The noise of the village is no longer heard, or has become like sweet music, as the turmoil, din, and rattle of a busy city blends in sweetest harmony to the aeronaut as he rises among the clouds. The lake is only half a mile long by a quarter of a mile wide, but every foot of its surface affords interest to its visitors.

With a good boat, one could paddle about in the water as long as he chose, or better yet, an oarsman would go along and pleasantly tell the romances of the locality. The petrified forest in the bottom of Green Lake is no myth, although it may not be exactly what scientists call petrification. The wood has reached that stage where it is very hard and can only be chipped by a sharp instrument. When the water is calm the stubby tree tops can be distinctly seen in the green deep.

The beginning of a gold mine

There were thousands of fish of different varieties in the lake, and other thousands of California salmon were in the hatching pond near the lake. It was well worth the trip to see the fish at feeding time. Fishermen were charged fifty cents per fish for indulging in their favorite pastime but the catch would be broiled for them without extra charge. Some of the fish were said to be so large and tame that they had been trained to pull boats around the lake.

Two hundred feet above the lake on the farther shore is the "Cave of the Winds," a weird place where rocks are piled in pyramidal form, the point of which is called "Prospect Rock," but it is between the lower ledges where the wild winds race and roar, which gives the place its name. From "Pros-

pect Rock" a good view is had of the "Battle ground of the
Gods" where huge boulders were thrown about and piled in
direst confusion by some mighty upheaval of nature in ages
past. Then a little beyond were the sunny waters of Clear
Lake, whose clear liquid depths were marvels of submarine
beauty, and where rests the head of the tumbling waters we
had followed up through rocky canyons. It was a pity that
so transparent and iridescent in its own dancing aerie it
should become so contaminated, heavy, and poisonous ere it
reached the valley by the washes from the mines and smelters
intervening.

To visit the summit of the universe was an inspiration not
to be neglected and Gray's Peak with its altitude of 14,341 feet
was then supposed to be the nearest point to heaven that one
could reach on horseback. It was the dome of our continental
divide, and its electrical summit had not sufficient terror to
deter us from scaling its dizzy heights. From Georgetown the
drive was a charming one. The carriage was luxurious and for
ten miles along the beautiful toll road to the Kelso ranch the
receding lowlands spread out in wondrous glory below us. Our
carriage was well loaded, for aside from having four people in
the party we had to carry our saddles for the ride to the summit.
We spent a joyous evening at the ranch before a huge grate
fire, where several fine dogs surrounding the fireplace made a
picture of comfort that any artist might have coveted.

We were seated in our saddles at the first streak of day
for an early climb to the summit to watch the sun chase the
shadows from the earth as the goddess of the morning started
her steeds in the air. Old Sol made a merry chase after the
smiling Aurora, but they were both lost to us in the mazy
depths of fleecy clouds before the noon hour had passed.

One Mr. Case, the Union Pacific ticket agent of Idaho
Springs, and my sister were with us and shared some peculiar
phenomena away up in the clouds that came wondrously near
leaving our friend Mr. Case on the summit, and gave us a
scare that put lightening in our heels to get down from our
pedestal.

Gray's Peak lifts its head from the main range as one man
of genius rises above common humanity, and above his up-
reaching fellows of ambition and talent, and then looks back at

his less prosperous comrades in compassion and beckons them on. Half a mile above Kelso's ranch a couple of miners dodged their heads out of the ground and inquired if we wanted a guide, but there was no need of their services with such a good trail.

Midway to the top we were enveloped in a blinding snow-

The top of Gray's Peak

storm which lasted over an hour. Then ever and anon a storm would break over us or go around just below us. Slowly we climbed higher and higher for several hours, giving the horses a rest every few steps as we neared the summit. Up, up, up we went, riding and walking by turn, until weary but anxious we seemed to find ourselves at the very portal of eternity, and we were rewarded by a glimpse of grandeur unexcelled. Far, far away the billowy mountains rolled, robed in green and gold, and pink and purple, dotted here and there with huge patches of snow, and anon a lakelet glistening in the sunlight.

To the north Long's Peak stood out bold and stern above its hoary rivals. Southward Pike's Peak loomed darkly in the sky, and on still beyond, the Spanish Peaks pointed upward in

twinlike grace, while away to the southwest the "Mount of
the Holy Cross" gleamed in virgin purity against its dark
shadowy setting of pines and weather-beaten rocks.   In the
east the plains stretching beyond the slopes melted away in
the far distant horizon.   It was our "Angelus" and with
wonder, awe, and reverence we bowed our heads.

Fourteen thousand three hundred and forty-one feet above

Copyright Detroit Photo Co.

Mount of the Holy Cross

the tide level, up where the sun bestows its first morning kiss,
and where it lends its soft halo of mellow lights until it passes
to the world on the other side, we could nearly span the continent
from sea to sea with the naked eye.   What a sublime pinnacle!

One such view of grandeur can afford food for thought and
study for almost a lifetime.   One's soul is thrown in such
close communion with nature and nature's God that it seems
but a step beyond to the great eternity.

The peak was covered with small, flat stones from base to

summit, making the trail a shifting one and affording only a loose sliding foothold.   Near the top is a large spring where one can refresh himself, and where comfort would dictate to spread the lunch, unless one carries timber along for a fire on the summit, where it is intensely cold.

The clouds were full of freaks that drew forth loud exclamations of wonder and surprise.   They would wind their snowy sheets around the base of the peak and intertwine among the lesser hills, then rise and fall full of rainbow splendor.   At one time a seeming wall reaching thousands of feet above us and extending to the base of the mountains slowly approached us.   It seemed that nothing could save us—that we must be crowded off our pedestal and dashed on the rocks.   There was no break in the moving mass, and nearer and nearer it came. We stood in terror and awe of what might happen, yet in defiance we awaited its approach, until with all the gentleness of a mother's arms we were enveloped in a sheet of blinding snow.   So softly it fell, so still was the air, that no one spoke, and scarcely had our senses begun to shape themselves to earthly things again than the clouds rolled on in their great white purity, leaving us numb with fear and cold.

The little cabin on the summit was half full of snow and ice, the glass in the windows all broken; even the roof had long since given way on one side from its weight of snow, and its fallen timbers confined the clear space of the room to one corner.   We clapped our hands, we danced, and jumped about to get warm, then we spread our lunch which we had brought with us.   There was not a sliver of wood to make the least bit of a fire, but we drank our cold coffee and ate our sandwiches with a relish that an epicure might envy.

Some one had evidently been there before us, and not satisfied with leaving his name and address on a stone slab, he added a further identification of himself in the statement that he was the "first d—— fool of the season."

While enjoying the novel experience of our surroundings we suddenly heard a crackling in one corner of the roof that sounded like a bunch of rattlesnakes.   Not stopping to think that snakes could not live in that altitude, we rushed madly from the cabin, looked upon the roof, and around the ground on the new fallen snow, but saw no evidence of any living thing. The men looked after the horses to see if they were securely tied and found them showing great evidences of fear. When they were gently patted to assure them of their safety, the men were subjected to such thrills of electric currents that they were nearly struck dumb. One declared his mustache assumed life, the other that every individual hair on his head stood up straight. In trying to point to the location of the first noise, flames flew from the finger tips, and every pat on a horse's body would bring out fire. It surely was an electrical storm that we had not been advised about, and there-

Lost to the world

fore knew not the danger we were in. When miners realize that one of these storms is coming on they lose no time in getting down to timber line, but ignorance was bliss and fortunately no more serious effects occurred than to have Mr. Case stunned enough to fall, and though he was soon restored we could not dispel the strange feelings that had so nearly overpowered the entire party.

The snow-storm that had passed over us had dropped into the valley and become black as night from which forks of ragged lightning sent its glimmering lights back to us. The storm clouds seemed to fairly bump against a mountain in the great abyss below, causing them to rebound and float back over the same locality again until they struck another mountain, then to be whirled through a canyon away out of sight.

We had been so absorbed in watching the grand panorama below that we had failed to see a second wall coming toward us. This time it was not the fleecy white of unfallen snow,

but a wall as black as the starless midnight. We saw the
lightning flash in it and clouds whirl among themselves as
they came steadily on.

The great black mass came floating toward us with tokens
of danger not to be trifled with. There was no need of words
for haste; we snatched our bridles, not waiting to mount, but
hurried down the trail, fairly dragging the poor horses who
stumbled at every step in their haste over the loose shale trail.
Over a mile was left behind when we stopped for a moment's
rest; we, too, tumbled and tripped over the rocky way intent
only on reaching lower ground. The lightning flashed and
the thunder reverberated round about us, echoing from peak
to peak. Then the storm began to break in fury. We
mounted our horses the first moment that we could make
any time by doing so, but we could not escape the torrents of
water that came pouring down upon us, and we raced madly on
until we reached the Kelso ranch. Tired and wet as we were,
we dared not delay, and quickly getting the horses into harness
again continued the race with the elements to Georgetown.
Such a cloudburst in the mountains is always a forerunner of
floods in the canyons and valleys below, and we must keep
ahead of it if possible. The roar of the oncoming waters was
like wings to our horses' feet, and we turned from the course of
the storm not more than three minutes ahead of the great
waterspout that tore up the road behind us and filled the
canyons with floods and débris. It was a race for life, and when
we turned from its course we sent up a shout of joy that echoed
far down the Georgetown street.

CHAPTER IV

TO SALT LAKE

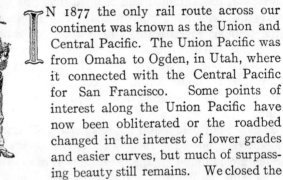

I N 1877 the only rail route across our continent was known as the Union and Central Pacific. The Union Pacific was from Omaha to Ogden, in Utah, where it connected with the Central Pacific for San Francisco. Some points of interest along the Union Pacific have now been obliterated or the roadbed changed in the interest of lower grades and easier curves, but much of surpassing beauty still remains. We closed the year by a trip to Salt Lake City and its environs, and were enthused over the novel life opening out before us as Pard's work progressed.

Full of the love of adventure, before leaving Cheyenne for Ogden we procured an order enabling us to ride on the cow-catcher or pilot of the engines whenever we desired. In fact our pockets were full of special privileges to go where we pleased and whenever we desired. The pass on the cow-catcher was one of the favors that I did not tell to my mother in my bi-weekly or tri-weekly records, sent to allay her anxieties and to reconcile the dear parents to the vacant chair at the home fireside.

We went over the summit of the divide seated in the lap of the engine, clinging to its iron supports with the tenacity of every muscle strained to its full worth. What a wild rush down the grade of ninety feet to the mile! Through tunnels, through snow-sheds, nodding a welcome and farewell at the same instant, and then two miles west of the summit, the train rolled onto the famous Dale Creek bridge, six hundred and fifty feet long and a hundred and fifty feet above the silvery thread of a stream. With bated breath we clung to the iron rail and felt the great throb of power behind us. The view was magnificent, but the wind blew a gale and seemed determined to carry us to total destruction, and in the midst of the intense effort to hold our position we heard the excited voice of the

Crossing Dale Creek bridge on the cow-catcher

engineer saying, "Hold on tight for it is sure death if you loosen your hold a d—— little bit." We had not drawn a free breath after leaving the bridge or turned for a look of thankfulness in each other's eyes before we plunged into a snow-shed and succeeding tunnel where not a glimmer of the track was visible, and the darkness of the moment was more appalling than when we could see the dangers around us.

Not a ray of light penetrated the black depths, the train creaked and the engine rumbled like muffled thunder, the end of all adventure seemed to press upon us in black inevitable surety.

"Fools will enter where
Angels dare not tread."

We thought the engineer had allowed us to plunge into that
terrible blackness in the hope that we would be dissuaded
from the further effort to ride on that pilot seat, but his own
pale face as well as the frightened manner of other trainmen
who rushed to the front as soon as we were in the daylight again
gave evidence of something unusual, and it was soon learned
that the guard who usually stood at the entrance of the tunnel
to give assurance that everything was all right, and to keep
the tunnel illuminated with lanterns, had been suddenly taken
ill, with no one there to help him or to share his duties.   The
train was well in the darkness before any one realized the
full import of the guard's absence, then the engineer did not
dare to make a stop in the tunnel.   The smoke of the engine
would have soon suffocated every one on the train, and he hurried on to open air with the chance and hope that the track
was all right.   We were glad to climb down from our exalted
seat and compose our nerves in a quiet nook of the Pullman
car for a while at least.

Leaving Laramie City, the soil assumed a deep reddish hue,
showing the presence of iron.   The rocks and minarets of the
mountainsides had most fantastic shapes, from massive castles
to church spires, pulpits, wigwams, skulls, and almost anything else that an imaginative fancy would help to find in the
picture.   It was breakfast time when the train pulled into
Green River station, a place as bold, barren, and cheerless as
one could wish to see, with its only pleasing features in the
great towering rocks and the rushing waters of Green River.

A short distance below Green River City Pard pointed out a
small wooded island in the middle of the river as being an
important landmark in connection with a thrilling twelve
hundred mile horseback ride of his in earlier days from
Denver through the wilderness a hundred or more miles south
of the Union Pacific road to Salt Lake City.   On the ride in
question Pard lost his partner, Abbott, by drowning, while
they were fording the river, the stream being very much
larger down at the point where the misadventure occurred.

Going on to Salt Lake alone after the sad calamity and

numerous other unfortunate incidents and close calls for his
life, Pard did not relish the idea of riding back to Denver
alone.   In his search for a companion he heard of a Scotch-
man, named Alex. Cochrane, who was intending to ride over

Green River Castle and the island where Pard and
Cochrane hid from the Indians

the same territory, but Cochrane having preceded him out of
Salt Lake they missed each other on the trail for several days.
When Pard finally overtook Cochrane and each had allayed the
fear that the other was a highwayman or a horse thief, they were
overtaken by a small party of Mormons who wished to trade
Cochrane out of his horses.   As the animals were finely bred
and great pets Cochrane demurred; but with evident determination to in some way get hold of the horses, the Mormons insisted on accompanying the gentlemen to their camp for that

night. About daylight a great commotion arose around the camp and Cochrane and Pard waked up to find themselves surrounded by a score or more Indians, or Mormons disguised as such, some of whom were taking great liberties with Cochrane's horses, such as riding them about the camp and patting them in a familiar way. On asking their Mormon companions what this meant, the latter replied that the Indians probably meant to take the horses. Our friends thereupon commenced saddling up and by dint of considerable coaxing and apparently not believing anything serious was intended, finally got their horses saddled and packs on. By this time one burly Indian was sitting astride a colt of Cochrane's favorite saddle-mare and, on being asked to get off, he refused to do so, saying he was going to keep that animal. As Cochrane and Pard leaped into their saddles, the former, being immediately opposite the Indian who was mounted upon the colt, put the spurs into his mare, and at the same instant pulled his revolver from its usual resting-place just inside his vest, and shot the Indian. The riderless colt sprang like a deer after its mother and then began a race for life.

There was a long chase punctuated by many lively volleys from the pursuers, several of which took effect in the leading horses, although none stopped the flight. The first safe rendezvous after the escape, which seemed little short of miraculous, was the little wooded island in the middle of Green River just referred to. It was here that Cochrane begged Pard to leave him, as they were pretty sure to be overtaken by Utah officers backed up by Indians. Considering himself entirely responsible, he did not want Pard to suffer with him. This Pard refused to do, and they proceeded on their long ride to Denver, using every precaution known to such an old California backwoodsman as Cochrane to elude their pursuers, and finally reaching Denver without further serious mishap.

Just back of the city of Green River the noted Castle Rock towers six hundred and fifteen feet above the valley. Its summit is crowned by a strange, decomposing, weather-beaten limestone whose outlines are like a huge turreted castle falling in decay. The whole country around Green River was most forbidding in its barren alkali surface. It looked as if the waters of the universe could scarcely cleanse it of its poison ash. It was from this unattractive spot that the Oregon Short Line first divided the arms of the Union Pacific and sent a helping hand across the northwest to McCammon and Pocatello and thence on to Portland. The real division point was a few miles farther west than Green River, at a point called Granger, but it was many years before the business was transacted or exchange made at the real point of diversion.

Forbidding as Green River was, it had a fairly good hotel, and was an eating station for all overland trains; it was far better to have transfers at Green River where waiting for late trains did not mean starvation as at Granger. The overland train then stopped at Cheyenne for dinner, Laramie for supper, and Green River for breakfast, and did not reach Ogden until a late supper time, making the time thirty-three hours from Cheyenne to Ogden, and nearly three full days from Omaha to Ogden, which has now been shortened to the rapid transit of thirty hours or less for the entire distance.

Soon after leaving Evanston we again took seats on

4

Devil's Slide, Utah, on the Union
Pacific Railway

the engine, much against the wishes of our new engineer for that division. It may not have been a rational thing to do because huge rocks of the disintegrating mountains were constantly falling along the track, and the vibration of the trains often loosened some overhanging walls of Echo and Weber canyons. But we could not withstand the temptation to chance the exhilarating dash, and once again in the open we wished for two pairs of eyes to make sure that no point of interest escaped the vision. The curves in the road were short and decisive, changing the entire view at every train length. High up on the mountainside "The Witches" were holding a session of consultation; they were queer formations resembling tall women, one in a pulpit above the others as if a presiding officer. The walls of rock were so high and craggy that only the proud eagle could find a resting-place among them. In that locality was also the famous thousand-mile tree, just a thousand miles from Omaha, and it bore such a placard in large letters to be read from the train.

Then there was the Devil's Slide, a wonder in itself, consisting of two walls of rock about six feet wide and from twenty to fifty feet high, running parallel for six hundred feet up the mountainside, with a space of only fourteen feet between the ledges. A ride down that slide in a toboggan would afford thrills and chills to satisfy the most ambitious lover of wild sensations.

The rocky cliffs rose from five hundred to a thousand feet on either side of the canyon, and the Weber River had made so narrow a channel that much of the railroad was built over the middle of the stream, but suddenly, as if we had made a flying leap over all difficulties, the canyons were left behind and the Great Salt Lake Valley spread its panoramic area over such vast estate in the foreground that the mind was lost in the expanse and in thinking, with Brigham Young and his apostles, that it was indeed the "Land of promise made to blossom like a rose." Even the old iron horse snorted with satisfaction as it halted on the edge of the heather land.

Salt Lake City was more of a curiosity in 1877 than in 1911. Brigham Young had but recently passed away and guards hovered over the grave held intact by a deeply cemented slab. But in spite of all precaution a deep-laid scheme to carry away the body came near being successful. Several men rented a nearby house at the base of the hill on which the cemetery was located. They dug a tunnel nearly to his grave before their plot was discovered and frustrated, and it was never learned how the dirt was disposed of that was taken out of the tunnel, as it had been secretly taken away and all traces covered up. What a curious sensation it was to feel

Copyright Detroit Photo Co.

Brigham Young's grave

that we were really in the realm of Mormonism. The land of tired women and wizen-faced, long-bearded men. The stone wall surrounding the most of Brigham Young's collection of homes was still intact; it was several feet in thickness and ten feet high, with an occasional cumbersome gate bearing a heavy padlock. His own office building, near the Eagle gate, seemed to be the only edifice denoting any comfort. His large easy chair, where he was wont to sit, and where Pard interviewed him some years before, still stood in its accustomed place on the front veranda. It was there he was so often seen in converse with his various apostles. Some of the gates were then standing unbarred and open, exposing much of the

grounds and many of the occupants.   It was indeed an iron-clad
prison during the life of Brigham.   The home of the favorite
Amelia was just outside the walls and across the street from
his office building, and there was but one finer house in the city
at that time.   Later she sold her life interest in the house for
$10,000.

The tabernacle remains unchanged in its general features,
with its seating capacity for 12,000 people and its fourteen
entrances, each from nine to eleven feet wide.   Its organ,
built in the building of native woods, was a marvel of its kind,
and afforded a grand accompaniment to the choir of a hundred
and fifty voices, just as it does to-day.

The new Mormon temple near-by, in the same inclosure,
was nearly half a century in the hands of the builders.   The
base of its foundation is sixteen feet thick and nine feet on the
ground level.   It is built entirely of granite brought from the
Wasatch Mountains and the cost has not been less than $15,-
000,000.   Its subterranean construction is a marvel of intricate windings and strangely constructed apartments.   Any
one imprisoned in that great vault would be lost to all human
aid except the jailer who put him there, and all the strange
tales of mysterious disappearances in that city of many saint-
less saints have ever been connected in my mind with those
great black echoless chambers.   It is there that the endowment
robes are put on never to be taken off, the robe of fealty to
the Church and its teachings that no member dare deny.

The endowment house of 1877 was within the Temple
Block, but it looked like an ordinary two-storied dwelling; there
was nothing about it to attract attention but its ever-closed
windows and blinds.   It was in the endowment house where all
marriages were performed.   Applicants for matrimony were
baptised in a room adjoining the main building the night before the ceremony was to take place, and they were then told
that the strictest attention must be given to every detail as
they went through the "House of the Lord" on the following day.

It required a service beginning at eight o'clock in the morning and lasting until three o'clock in the afternoon to sufficiently
impress the woman with the abject slavery to which she must
submit when she marries, and the man required the same time
to gloat over his power and witness her submission.

There they were anointed with oil and every part of the body blessed for its usefulness. They were given celestial names by which they were to be called at the great resurrection. But God is to call only the men, and the men must call the women. It rests altogether with man whether the woman he marries will ever be called to life eternal, and no one but the husband knows the celestial name of the wife; the wife is never to speak that name after she whispers it to her husband under a penalty of eternal death.

Mormon Tabernacle and Temple

It is in the endowment house where various robes are worn: the apron with the nine fig leaves; again the robe consisting of a long piece of cloth folded over and cut open in the middle to let the head through, then girdled at the waist. All wear caps and moccasins, and finally the real endowment robe is put on, with a sign of a square on the right breast and a compass on the left, and on the knee there is a large hole which is called the "Stone," but I do not know its significance.

These suits are always and continuously worn by Mormons now the same as then. It is seldom that a Mormon will take the robe off all at once, but as he slips one part off he puts another one on, for they are taught that no evil can befall them so long as the endowment robe is on the body.

There were no marriage certificates, and the only record was a list of applicants for marriage, and even that is denied by the Church. So a marriage ceremony might at any time be denied if it was likely to make any trouble for the Church. If it was desired, a polygamous marriage might have no proof, the bridal pair would then go alone in the marriage room, and there would be no witnesses to the final ceremony, which consisted of kneeling at a small table in front of the Bishop who asked a few questions, made a few commands, and pronounced them man and wife.

It is said that of all Brigham Young's fifty-six children not one was halt, lame, or blind. That he would take one of them and dandle it on his knee with a "link-a-toodle, ladle, iddle, oodle" the same as any other dad, and he was always particular about those who came to play with his children. If any young man tried to enter the family gate, he was put through a course of questions that implied a penalty equal to the Inquisition if he spoke falsely.

It was seven o'clock in the morning late in December that we started southward from Salt Lake to the valley of the Jordan and of Utah Lake. At the American Fork Junction where we took a dummy train into the mountains we notified the jolly German landlord to have a hearty dinner ready for a hungry party when we returned from exploring the canyon and it was indeed an appetizing trip. After two or three miles in the open landscape we entered mountains showing the wildest formations. Gigantic heights on either side looked as if the molten masses had been forced thousands of feet up in the air and suddenly cooled in all their irregularity of motion. The air was perfumed with the odor of the pines, stately cottonwoods towered above us, and the broad willows swayed over the running stream, while the maples colored the whole landscape with their bright-hued leaves still clinging on the branches. The Indian pinks, which are so charily cultivated in the East, grew in profusion, and in the wild rose season the canyon is a veritable bower of pink petals. But over all stands the grand Aspinwall Mountain fourteen thousand feet high, as if stretching his white head to kiss the clouds that keep him wrapped in robes of purity.

We passed under a hanging rock broader than our car and

as we emerged from under the threatened passage there loomed
in view a tall crag with a hole through it like an all-seeing eye
ever watching and magnetically holding in place that delicately
poised mass of stone that might cause much terror if it were
to fall. American Fork Canyon was one of the most noted of
the Wasatch range of mountains for snow-slides and several
miles of our way was under the sloping roof of snow-sheds that
hugged the mountainside.

Copyright Detroit Photo Co.

American Fork Canyon

Dale Creek, sixteen miles from the junction, had choice
features for a summer residence. There was a picturesque
old mill, falling into decay with its silent wheel, while a more
modern mill was turning out many thousands of feet of lumber
every day, and close by thousands of bushels of charcoal were
lifted from the smoking pointed pits. The active mill and
charcoal pits were not inviting features of a summer resort,
but the Oregon grapevine, covering the mountainsides, aided
in giving to the whole scene a richness of autumnal colorings
that held one's eyes entranced. It made one weep to see the
great glorious trees falling under the woodman's axe to feed the

clamorous mill.   Oh, with what wanton wastefulness the great
monarchs of our forests are sacrificed to man's avarice.

The little Dale Creek station was five thousand feet above
where dinner was waiting, and we were glad to hear the call for
the downward trip.   Nature's handiwork formed a grand panorama, but man was turning its glories to material use and destroying the enchanting site.   The havoc of trees almost made
us lose interest in the object of our trip to visit the "Emma
Mine" which was then one of the banner mines of Utah.

The conductor stationed himself at the brake in front of
our small open car having six cross-seats, and when he gave
command of "All aboard," he also gave the brake a fling and
with its release we went spinning down the road in a most in-
dependent manner regardless of other power than our own
momentum.   Words fail to express the exhilaration of such a
ride.   We seemed less a part of the majestic scenery through
which we passed than when we trailed up behind the decrepit
engine or the sinewy mules that carried us part of the way.
It was like unto a racing automobile of the present day running
on slender iron rails.   The mules that had taken us up were
given standing room on a rear platform and seemed to enjoy
the ride down-hill, even though they had to struggle for an
equilibrium.

It was in American Fork Canyon where we found the only
free school in Utah, for the Mormon leaders did not believe in
free schools, or in educating their people, except for church
work.

We called upon a Mormon Elder, who was also the postmaster and proprietor of a music store at the junction town.
His two wives occupied contrasting positions.   Wife No. 1
was on her knees, scrubbing the kitchen floor as we saw her
through a glass door, while wife No. 2 came in well dressed
and sat down to listen to our conversation.   She had eyes
like a startled deer as we plied the Elder with questions regarding his religion and its effect on their lives.   He made
his answers with surprising alacrity, and when asked if
the Bible advocated polygamy he scratched his head and said,
"No, but we adopt that law and the Bible backs us up in it."
He advocated his principles in a way to impress strangers
with the sincerity of his Mormon Christian character, but we

had hardly left his place before we learned much to his discredit that the courts and Uncle Sam would have to settle.

Our host at the junction hotel was a Mormon out of gratitude. He reached Utah a penniless man, and the Mormons cared for him and placed him where he could make some money. He had but one wife, but his statements were so liberal we thought he must have half a dozen at least, and when I began to fear that we might miss our train back to the city he said, with a sly twinkle in his Dutch eye, "Now, never mind lady, I'll get you there in time. Don't be scared, we have women enough down here now."

There were many things in the city of the Latter Day Saints that were of special interest. We were glad that circumstances often led us there whether it was to better prepare for a journey into the great Northwest, or to rest on the return when nature has endured its limit, there to sit by the side of a warm, bright fire and think of a long journey drawing to its close, reviewing a vast panorama of places, faces, and circumstances rising before the mind's eye in a most bewildered vision. In our long tedious journeyings I often longed for a season of rest. "God bless the man who first invented sleep,"—so said Sancho Panza, and so say I; that quotation often ran through my mind until its prosy tone took my soul away to float among the lilies of dreamland, while my head was left to roll at will against the hard casings of the windows, the rough ribs of a stage-coach, or by a sudden lurch to almost leave my body.

In 1881 Salt Lake City was much excited over Governor Murray's action in trying to exclude the Apostle Cannon from Congress by awarding the certificate of election to the Hon. A. G. Campbell. Extra tithings were vigorously collected and extra taxes assessed on the Mormon Church to obtain money for the apostle's use in Washington. It was the first direct blow at the Mormon life, and all pure-minded people took off their hats and bowed in acquiescence to the decree that crowned the effort for Mormon exclusion with success.

Although the city had but twenty thousand people, its buildings covered an area of nine square miles, with broad streets and large blocks containing ten acres each. East of the city, three miles distant, the Wasatch Mountains rise abruptly to a height of eleven thousand feet; they are covered with snow that knows

no melting.   On the west the Oquirrh Mountains, which are
almost as grand, unite with the Wasatch range some twenty
miles south of the city, enclosing the beautiful Jordan valley
with its fertile farms and fruitful orchards.

There was not a better kept hotel between Chicago and the
coast than the Walker House of Salt Lake City.   Major Erb, the

Copyright Detroit Photo Co.

Mormon Tithing House

genial landlord, had hosts of friends whom he made glad to come,
and sorry to leave.   The house was a four-story brick structure,
while the table was noted for its abundance of well-prepared
eatables.

There were no public schools, but every Gentile church had
one or more schools which it supported.   The Presbytery of
Utah, in the two years 1880 and 1881, had established twenty-
three schools in twenty-two Mormon towns, employing thirty-
five teachers, and schooling twelve hundred children.   The
Collegiate Institute in Salt Lake City was at the head with an at-
tendance of two hundred bright, promising scholars.   The
Congregationalists were backed by the "New West Education
Commission" of Chicago and had an academy and primary

school, and several schools in outside towns. The Mormons taxed each scholar twenty-five cents per week, and aside from that all citizens, whether Mormon or Gentile, had the regular school tax to pay into the Mormon purse which was kept closed to education.

Mr. Reynolds, the noted polygamist, who had been for two years in the penitentiary, was released in 1881 and again lionized

Copyright Detroit Photo Co.

Co-operative Store

by the Mormon masses. The Sabbath afternoon after his release he preached to a crowded house in the new church in Temple Block. Every available corner was filled with the followers of his creed and the scheming leaders. He cried down all teaching and schooling save the doctrines of the Church and the Mormon faith. He said his imprisonment had not made him "love his wife less or respect *them* less." He instantly noticed his blunder in using the plural and added that he meant his family.

Amelia's palace had long been unoccupied because of a ghost that haunted the place, and the superstitious people gave it a wide birth. Amelia, having sold her life interest in the place, built a new palace on her father's grounds. Brigham's grave was no longer guarded; in 1881 the old guard died and the vacancy was never filled.

Many miners swelled the population in town in winter simply to be on hand to move at the first bidding of the most exciting mining field in the spring, and in '81 they made a grand rush for Wood River in Idaho.

Park City, on the Union Pacific Railroad, was drawing the most local attention. The Ontario mine there was one of the largest in the West. It produced $1,500,000 in 1880, and it was the bulwark of the mining industry in Utah.

The Hot Sulphur Springs in the outskirts of the city were not much improved, but they formed the favorite winter resort for the citizens, and street cars were run to them at short intervals. Fort Douglas was not as attractive then as now, and the guns were trained toward the city as the point most likely to need punishment.

The Salt Lake Theatre was a little gem of the Doric style of architecture, with fluted columns and massive cornices. It had the usual dimensions of parquette and dress circle with three balconies and four private boxes and could seat nearly two thousand people. The city had just planned to have the electric light, and gas stock was falling below par.

Salt Lake City was fortunate in those pioneering days in the possession of a splendid circle of strong, public spirited men, such as Judge Goodwin and Pat Lannan of the *Salt Lake Tribune;* Governor Murray, with Col. N. E. Linsley and Col. E. A. Wall, foremost among mining men; O. J. Salisbury of stage line fame, and Walker brothers, the bankers and merchant princes, to shape the destinies and ceaselessly push the development of the city and surrounding country. The four Walker brothers, though in different lines of business, had the unique system of keeping one common bank account, on which all drew at will. This continued for many years even after they were all married.

I made a trip into Salt Lake in 1883 from San Francisco in company with my sister and her daughter and Mr. W. H. Babcock, now General Agent of the Lehigh Valley Railway Company, and his wife. Pard had preceded us by a few days and was to join us again in Zion City. After leaving 'Frisco it was learned that some of the passengers were taking our party for a Mormon family, and we decided to carry out the little play for their entertainment. There were two or three who shifted their positions whenever possible to hear some of our conversations, which we took pains to make interesting by having some little jealousies, or in talking about the different places of residence, and which one was to go on East with W. H., etc. As we neared Ogden we drew him into that discussion and he said, "Well, now, whose turn is it to go?" Of course, we mentioned the wife by her given name, and then he added: "That ought to settle the matter." He wanted to know what he brought us the last time he went East, and what we wanted this time; also, which one should go to the ranch, and which one to the house in town, and many other questions that made it difficult for us to hold our facial expressions. We had the passengers pretty well wrought up and their remarks were quite as amusing to us, such as "They look so intelligent, too, don't they?" "I would like to tell them what I think of Mormonism." "Isn't it funny how they divide up?" "He seems to think a lot of that little girl," etc. We have often wondered what direful tales they had to tell their friends when they reached home, about that "real" Mormon family that seemed so happy, and did not dare to quarrel in the presence of the Mormon Master.

About noon of a late August day after our arrival in Zion City we were attracted by loud words and cries on the street and saw a big burly negro in an altercation with a restaurant keeper named Grice, whose place of business was just across the street. The difficulty arose over work and wages, and the negro Harvey grew so insolent that he had been ordered out of the establishment. He came out with threats of violence and flourish of a pistol, daring Grice to come out on the street. Grice first telephoned to police headquarters and in obedience to the call Marshall Andrew Burt, the most popular officer of the Territory, who had been Chief of Police of Salt Lake City for nineteen years, and Water Master Charles H. Wilcken made their appearance. Mr. Grice started out with them to find the negro and they had not far to go. On the first corner stood Harvey with a rifle at half cock in his hands. As soon as Grice called out, "There's the man" Marshall Burt advanced to arrest him. The street was full of people but Harvey raised his rifle and fired directly at the officer.   Marshall Burt fell, with a cry, and died within a few minutes.

Officer Wilcken was thus left alone to fight the maniacal negro. As the rifle could not be used at such close range, the negro drew his revolver and shot the officer twice, but they

The Hermitage, Ogden Canyon

were only flesh wounds and he knew he must overpower Harvey or more people would be killed.

Those on the street were so panic-stricken that they did not realize the officer's great need of help. Finally Homer J. Stone stepped into the fray, and they soon succeeded in throwing the negro. When he was once down, people by the score were ready to tramp on him; and in spite of Officer Wilcken the man was fairly kicked to the city hall which was close by. Within ten minutes after he was locked up it was known that Marshall Burt was dead, and a thousand infuriated people took possession of the avenue, clamoring for the blood of the murderer.

The door of the jail was broken by the mob and the negro was tossed out all bleeding and bruised. The air was thick with oaths and imprecations and the appeals of the wretch for mercy were unheeded. He was dragged a distance of seventy-five feet and strung up over a beam in the city hall stables. While still struggling, his body was lowered again and dragged like a mop over the sidewalk for two blocks. An express wagon was procured and it was the intention to drag the body from one end of the city to the other, but such an outrage was prevented by Mayor Jennings, who jumped into the wagon and cried out that he would shoot the first man who attempted any further indignity to the dead body.

The face of the polygamous wife that was turned to the Gentiles was usually a smiling one, for she dared not imply aught else than contentment to a stranger. If one visited a Mormon home often enough he might ultimately be ignored and witness a hair pulling scene without any restraint. It is not in human nature to submit to tyranny of one wife over another, and they were of the same flesh and blood as other women.

Mormon women looked at me in open-mouthed wonder when I asked Pard to do some little thing for me, and as he was always bestowing gracious and gallant attentions upon me they were constantly curious about us. It was not an uncommon sight to see a Mormon sitting on a fence watching his many wives working in the field, and more than once we heard calls to one and another to hurry up with their work. Gallantry was something that a Mormon woman could not understand.

It was supposed that our first trip would be a brief one, but duties multiplied until Pard was obliged to remain in Salt Lake City for some time. I had promised to sing at a concert to be given at a near date in Cheyenne and was obliged thereby to return alone. Of course, it was best to brace up my courage and go back, for Pard wanted me to help his old friends in their musical effort, and added that it would be doubly pleasant to be there when it became known that a certain appropriation was announced for his first book by the Territorial legislature.

After that was over I was to go on to Illinois for the holidays, and he would join me in time for Christmas. We had our first parting, and our first disappointments followed closely.

On my arrival in Cheyenne I soon learned that the concert had been postponed as my telegram had not been received telling them that I would surely be there, and also because of the illness of another one of the participants. Transportation failing to arrive, I did not get off for the East until Pard's return.

We went on to Omaha together, after a brief trip to Denver, but in going from the hotel to the depot in Omaha we became so deeply mired in mud that it was impossible to extricate the carriage only in time to reach the station as the train was crossing the Missouri River bridge. That was the last train to reach our home before the Christmas gathering, and it seemed like the last straw in the load of disappointments. Youth is often deeply hurt, but it is so elastic that it bounds back into the happy line again with very little encouragement, and a message from home saying Christmas would wait for us made us forget every other annoyance.

CHAPTER V

IN THE COLORADO ROCKIES. ESTES PARK

FTER our Christmas festivities we spent several months in Omaha where Pard published a monthly paper called *The New West Illustrated* in the interests of immigration; it was devoted entirely to the Far West's attractions, its stock-raising, and its wonderful mineral productions. In the early summer we went again to the mountains. With an atmosphere at once cool and invigorating we were made to feel as if treading on air. Ascending from the city heat to the world of eternal snows, so strangely high and wonderful, we moved along the zigzag road from summit to summit, thinking always that the next pinnacle would fairly afford a view into eternity itself, and it was a surprise to look down into a valley for our destination.

Estes Park is a veritable Eden nestling on the north side of Long's Peak, twenty-five miles from Loveland or Longmont. The stage ride was one of grandeur from the very first turn of the wheels, up, up, up, along the zigzag trail until the day was nearly spent; then just as the sun was slipping away for the night we emerged from a dense wood to the face of a precipice, and there, down a thousand feet below were the fifty thousand undulating acres of this grand mountain eyrie.

It was an entrancing sight with its green fields and meandering streams surrounded by rocky walls thousands of feet high, up into the very domain of the snow king. The hotel and little ranch homes dotted the park with life and old Long's Peak seemed to stand as sentinel and guard towering over all in grandeur and dignity.

The crack of the whip sent the tired horses galloping down the steep grade to the MacGregor ranch, where there were many people on pleasure bent, some in tents or small cottages, and some in the main home building. Mrs. MacGregor was an artist possessing rare merit, her decorative work around the house proved her ability with the brush, while our host was a retired man of the quill. The refined atmosphere of the home was most attractive. Among the guests was Sol Smith Russell's favorite brother, who was enjoying his honeymoon up among the crags. There was also one Colonel Jones, a lawyer of much renown from Texas. We sat around a big camp-fire one night telling stories and conundrums, thinking the children had all gone to bed. Suddenly a small boy rolled himself into the arena and called out, "Say, why are Colonel Jones's feet like a camel?" The Colonel was the prince of the party; in his fastidious toilets he was always immaculate and a picture of a man perfectly dressed, and he added to that a charming individuality. All eyes were turned on him, and we waited breathlessly for the boy's answer, which was drawled out in regular Missourian tone, "'Cause they can go so long without water." It fell like a sudden cold shower on the assembly, and though all eyes did turn toward the genial limb of the law, every one present wanted to apply a shingle to the lad where it would do the most good.

Mr. MacGregor had about twelve hundred acres in his ranch, from which the table was supplied with fresh vegetables, eggs, butter, cream, and other tempting viands. The cool breezes coming down from the snowy cliffs and ringing in sweet cadences through the pine trees were fairly hypnotic in their influence to hold travellers in that enchanting spot during the heated term of the lowlands.

There were days of exploring that kept up the excitement for the venturesome. Lily Lake was especially interesting. Midway up the side of Long's Peak, the lake contained hundreds of acres so thickly covered with lilies that the only water visible was along the shore line. Instead of being the more common white lilies they were of a deep orange color, and the odor was also of that fruit. The water was deep close to shore, and it was dangerous to ride our horses in after them, but Mr. Bradley of Boulder, Colorado, performed the perilous mission with surprising coolness. When he was reaching down from his horse for the few last flowers to complete his armful, his horse suddenly went off into deep water and down out of sight,

Lumber flume by the romantic wayside

but by the time others started to the rescue the gallant rider came up from the depths triumphantly holding his bunch of lilies.

An irrigating ditch taken from Lily Lake was dammed every night by the beavers and every morning a ranchman had to ride three miles to tear down the dam. It was a good illustration of the industry and persistency of that energetic water worker, who so zealously keeps up his work under most adverse conditions, and it is a good example for imitation by the human race.

Midway to Lily Lake there was another small body of brackish water called Mary's Lake, which was noted for a

peculiar variety of fish which inhabited it. When grown they
are about a foot long and have much the same color as a trout,
but they have four legs and wallow about in the soft muddy
pools. They also have a covering over the head like a hood,
and when they are jerked out of the water with a hook they
squeal like a pig.

Estes Park

Mountain sheep
are fond of this brack-
ish water and in the
days of 1878 they
came every day in
large numbers to
drink. We saw sev-
eral fall under the
hunter's bullet and
many mountain
cabins were adorned
with the horns of
these wary cliff
climbers. Their
horns differ from the
domestic sheep in
being much larger
at the base, some-
times five or six inches in diameter; they are curved as if to
enable the sheep to fully protect his head and to do the trick
so often accredited to him of rolling down a precipice without
breaking the points.

In Willow Park we were invited into a spring-house for a
drink of milk, or of water from a fine spring which was harnessed
to do the churning by means of wheel and shaft. On one side
stood a freezer of ice-cream, most tempting to warm and tired
scenic enthusiasts, and close by were saddles of two fine elks.
There was scrupulous neatness in every pan and board. We
noticed our young men making goo-goo eyes at several responsive orbs, and fearing that we might permanently lose several
of friend MacGregor's boarders we hastily mounted our horses
and led the way at a gallop down the mountainside.

Another day we were on our horses in the early morning to
explore the mysterious depths of Black Canyon, with its thick

growth of pines and black and gloomy shadows. None but an experienced woodsman would have known that we followed a trail, but the confidence in Hank Farrar, our guide, was absolute, and we plunged recklessly wherever he led. I rode a cross saddle which was not as popular as it is at this advanced age, and my costume was long trousers and short skirt, with close fitting bodice. Then with a long skirt strapped to my saddle I could quickly change my appearance when I dismounted. I always carried such an outfit throughout my frontier experiences and oftentimes it was the only suit I could carry. On some long trips where we had but one pack animal there was no way to carry anything but food and blankets except what I could have strapped to my own saddle.

We followed the Black Canyon Creek, and as we went stumbling up the mountainside the creek went tumbling down its headlong course as if trying to equal the gaiety of our cavalry brigade. Three miles up the canyon the Black Falls at eleven o'clock in summer time are crowned with rainbow colorings. There was one fall of twenty-five feet and then after many lesser falls the whole river seemed blocked by a huge boulder, perfectly smooth and gently inclined, but the waters struck the rock and leaped over it, falling a hundred and fifty feet in a great unbroken sheet shimmering in the sunlight. On either side of the river the ride through the canyon was in a dense white pine forest whose lofty tops are never cheered by the merry songsters, for no bird but the eagle lives at such an altitude. We climbed on up to Emma Lake, ten thousand five hundred feet above sea-level, and there we stopped for our noonday rest, and luncheon in the warm sunshine, which was most grateful on this July day. We gathered flowers close beside a snowbank, and in a little cove of a smaller lake still higher up some half dozen of the party paddled about on a huge cake of ice. Some of the most ambitious ones scaled heights from which they declared they could see all of this continent and part of Europe, but we smothered them in snow before they could further slay their reputations for veracity.

I used to think that the snowy range was a chain of mountains entirely and perpetually covered with snow; it was a disappointment to learn that the term implies only fissures in the higher ranges where snow never melts, and that few peaks have the surface covered all the time. The "Mount of the Holy Cross" in Colorado, derives its name from two fissures cutting a mountainside at right angles, forming the shape of a cross, and in which the snow never melts entirely away. The red shadings of the cross are made by infinitesimal red animalcula so numerous as to color the snow. The snow line in Colorado in summer is about 11,250 feet above sea-level.

The return from Emma Lake was somewhat more eventful. One stream my horse absolutely refused to leap across. It was too deep to ford and too wide to step over. My "Daisy" would curl herself up for a leap, then suddenly decide that she liked it where she was, and would turn about and nibble the tufts of grass. It required the help of a rescue party to give my horse some unmistakable demonstrations of our earnest intentions to get home, before she would bound over to the other side, and then she cantered victoriously on to lead the rest of the party as if she had been the first brave horse to cross. Night came on and we were still eight miles from home.

After pushing along vigorously for two or three miles, the guide held up a warning hand and faced about, but we were not prepared for his announcement that we were off the trail. Whoever heard of Hank Farrar, the guide, being off the trail? It seemed like some joke he was playing, until he dismounted and made several side trips into the woods to get his bearings. He led us at last over rocks and fallen trees and through "cut-offs," until hope seemed to vanish from every face and a night on the mountainside, without food, shelter, or blankets was momentarily growing to a certainty, when suddenly he called out "All right, I have found it," and we knew "it" was the trail, and we were merry in an instant, although it was too dark to see the glad light that beamed in every eye.

Mr. MacGregor had become anxious for our safety and we met him coming to us with lanterns and a basket of food. He said he knew we would get in all right, but some of our friends were decidedly uneasy. After a good supper every one was glad of the experience of being lost and rescued, and camp fire stories of the trials in the dark woods grew quite thrilling.

The next day there was a total eclipse of the sun. Slowly but surely the darkness spread over us and the useful smoked glass revealed something coming between us and the sun, leaving us a little more in the shadow as the moments passed. A strange, weird light enveloped the mountains, and an uncanny essence pervaded the whole atmosphere. The dogs barked in savage fear and their hair stood straight up along their backs as they tried to find some place to hide; some of the poor creatures cried as if they were being whipped, some howled, and still others bayed in mournful tones. The chickens cackled and sought their places to roost, the roosters crowed, and all the

Hank Farrar, the park guide

feathery kingdom were chattering over the unseemly hour of night. The huddled people felt a sort of ghostly presence as the weirdness of the surroundings deepened. A sharp quick cry of "Look! look!" caused every one to lift his glass and double his energy to see what more gruesome details were to send the creepers along the spine. The last rays of the sun were being hidden from our view, and the little rim of light seemed to be intensified a thousand-fold as the rest of the sun passed into the shadow. For two and a half minutes the obscurity was total. The corona was grand beyond description, and they who climbed to the near summit of Long's Peak and looked beyond the limit of totality had an experience that seldom falls to lot of man, but all were glad when it was over and the day came on again with a greater glory than we had ever felt before.

A strangely pathetic incident was that when night really did come, and all that had been so strangely weird had again become normal, the feathered flocks of the barnyard absolutely refused to go to roost until after ten o'clock, as if anticipating a second deception, the roosters crowed and the hens kept up an incessant cackle, until with almost one accord they filed away to their respective low branches of the trees, still scolding and chattering as they settled themselves for the night.

It required a day or two of quiet before any one felt like making other explorations, but as the uncanny feeling fled,

A busy day

the plans were made again to follow our trusty guide through Horseshoe Park to the cascades of Fall River.   Thus do we all forget strange and unseemly conditions when the skies clear and health bounds in the veins.

We had to leave our horses at the entrance to the Fall River Canyon and climb over rocks and fallen timber for miles on foot. There was a wild cataract of immense volume tumbling madly over grotesque rocks in a width of one hundred and fifty feet, at the head of which, some miles farther on, a perpendicular fall of one hundred feet gave an impetus to the motion that lent to these two miles of cascades a force uncontrollable. Were all the grandeur of the main fall and cascades confined, old Niagara would have to yield the honors to her western peer up here under the protectorate of the snow-clad peaks of the

Rockies. When we thought of the many marvellous bits of scenery hidden in the remote nooks of uninhabited places in our loved country, we could but wonder if they would not some day be revealed by railroad invasion to the travelling public as scenic wonders of the world, and be made accessible with less discomfort than was then possible.

The Earl of Dunraven owned the largest part of Estes Park, and it became a favorite resort for many of his countrymen.

Along the banks of the many streams throughout the park were numerous bright tents, betokening camp life. A Boston party were reminders of the Aztecs in their barbaric costumes. They looked as if they had spent a winter in reading yellow literature and then concluded that a camp trip to the Rockies necessitated costumes of outlandish design. One stripling wore a pair of schapps, a six-shooter strapped around his waist, his blue flannel shirt decked with white braid and brass buttons, and he crowned it all with a large sombrero trimmed with tinsel cord.

His sweetheart was attired in the same unconventional way, with the gayest of gypsy colors. Her feet in brogans, not ornamental, were swinging below her too short gown of navy blue. Her skirt and waist were profusely trimmed with scarlet flannel and brass buttons, and finished with a long fringe made of the same flaming flannel. A gay red sash girdled her waist, a bright red bow tied the braids of her long black hair and her shapeless hat had the same gaudy ribbons flowing to the breeze. Such were two of the party, not more conspicuous than their companions. It must have been a surprise to them to see people in civilized dress in the camps about them.

The wonderful scenery about the park is more seductive than the Garden of the Gods, and as we turned our backs upon its enchantments, the sun never shone more brilliantly, the flowers never blossomed more beautifully and the waters never chanted more hypnotic music, all luring us to stay. But the high stone walls and pinnacled buttresses of the highway soon hid the charms and left us to the plain, practical, and unpoetic experience of chuck-holes and sidling roads in the ride down to Longmont and the iron horse in waiting. We longed for the trout supper, the crackling camp fire, the soughing of the pines, the mellowing lights of evening time, without the smoke of factories to dim their lustre, and we longed for the quiet hush of the night and the faces grown dear among the Bohemian experiences.   But all were now engraven on the tablet of memory and new conditions with new faces were again around and about us.   We had a long trip ahead of us into Montana, and we hastened on to Salt Lake City again and then to the northern border of Utah which ended the rail route.

CHAPTER VI

TO MONTANA IN 1878 THROUGH THE BANNOCK WAR LINES

"SAY, if you fellers ain't got no guns you better git some for you may need 'em 'fore you strike another town o' this size." It was Jake Farson, the stage-driver, who spoke thus to two travellers preparing to take the outgoing stage. Everybody around the little Mormon settlement of Oneida, on the north border of Utah, in 1878, knew Jake Farson as well as the people did all along the stage route from there to Fort Benton. He was a little taller than the average, with keen, penetrating eyes, a firm mouth, and determined expression of countenance that such men have who push to the frontier. His hand was wide across the knuckles and his long fingers ended in broad cushions which touched every buckle and strap of the harnesses after the stock-tender was through with them. "Don't know how derned soon we may have to get into a race with them red devils, and I want to know where all the weak spots is in this here gearin'," said Jake, as he minutely tugged at every part of the outfit.

The Bannock war of 1878 was at its height and no one knew what terrors might befall an unprotected stage at any hour of that five days' trip between there and Helena.

James Randolph and Pard heard the conversation with far different feelings. Randolph was fresh from New York, without any knowledge of the dangers of such a trip and evidently viewing the situation as a huge joke. He said his revolver would do for him as he displayed a tiny toy, while refusing to provide himself with any more burdensome firearms. His haughty manner and curt speech made him and Jake enemies at the very start.

Pard was made of different stuff.   He had been with General
Crook through four Sioux campaigns, and the horror of it all
rooted him to the spot for a time, while trying to clear his mind
for action.   He knew what Jake Farson said was only too true.
It had been but a few weeks since General Crook had written,

Copyright Lee Moorhouse, Pendleton, Oregon
Chief Joseph

forbidding the crossing of the Blackfoot country to Helena at
that time, but it was thought that we had waited long enough
for the danger to be past.   The papers were not publishing
any further accounts of the war, and Pard did not know what
news was being suppressed until now when about to start out
in the thickest of the trouble, with his bride of only a few months.
To take her into such dangers seemed an impossible thing for

him to do, yet there he was, sent on an important mission for a great corporation, with plans laid out for months of exploration and hard endeavor on which depended his future life work.

He went back to the little structure graced by the name of hotel, which had seemed such a crude, crowded cabin, where every available square inch was made to do service of some kind, without being partitioned off on the first floor or under the low gabled roof above.

As he caught a glimpse of the tallow dip glimmering through the window with all its homely surroundings, he could but feel a sense of security and comfort compared with what might await the party on the long, desolate road to the north. It was a trip of five days' and nights' continuous travel to reach Helena, Montana, in an old Concord stage-coach that was already piled to the roof inside with mail and express, leaving only cramped space between it and the one rear seat left for the three booked passengers. He looked through the window into the dimly lighted room and saw the cheery face of his young wife as she watched the packing of a lunch box, and warmed the heavy wraps by the glowing fire; how could he tell her of the danger ahead and much less take her along with him, but he suddenly resolved to tell her the conditions and then send her back over the lonely desert to her home friends, while he continued the journey alone.

With this clearing of the dilemma he opened the door to hear her say, "Well, Pardy, old boy, here is a wondrously fine fried chicken for the redskins if they get us before we can eat it." The resolution in her face and voice showed no sign of retreat for her, and every effort to persuade her to return was met with a laugh that made resistance useless.

It was nine o'clock when Jake drove the six bronchos up to the door for the trio to get aboard, and fill the last available inch of space afforded them. Mail and express had been held back for a number of days because of the danger in sending it out, until the accumulation was so great that it could not be properly cared for, so now the heavy load added a new danger. It compelled slower travelling, and if the stage should be attacked by the savages it would also prevent the free handling of any weapons for defence.

It was not a very merry party that was pulled along into

the black night, and the very shouts of good-will that followed close on the rumbling wheels seemed like a wail marking the departure to where none return.

The long bags of mail were under the two seats in front, as well as over them, and left no way of stretching out the limbs or feet, or to do other than sit in a perfectly straight position day and night for five consecutive suns.

The first night the drive was comparatively safe and, adjusting themselves to their positions as well as possible, the three passengers talked a while on the dangers and possibilities

Eagle Rock Bridge.   First one built across Snake River

ahead of them, and then one and another began to nod like sunflowers in a breeze. Occasionally one would waken and squirm for a new position, only to settle down again in the same old uncomfortable way.

When the night wore away, bringing a glorious sunny morning so full of hope and promise, it dissipated all fears as had the darkness generated them, but Pard knew there was no time for a cessation of alertness; his well-trained eyes watched the horizon with the keen instinct of the red warrior. The day wore slowly on and when the sable shades began to envelop the earth again, there also came a greater realization of helplessness, and a cold fear filled my heart.

To be in the heart of a wilderness, to know that it holds the brutal redskins waiting for prey, and from whom no mercy could be expected should they attack the party, was enough to give grave thoughts to all and to wonder what a day or a night might develop.

Just after dark the driver reined up at a small cabin where dwelt a solitary stock-tender. The stage station contained four stalls for animals, and a combination parlor, kitchen, and sleeping apartment ten by ten feet in size. Over the door, outside, huge characters read, "Hotel de Starvation, 1,000 miles from hay and grain, seventy miles from wood, fifteen miles from water, and only twelve inches from h—ll."

The walls of the room were decorated with pictures cut from police publications. Over the door, inside, in charcoal letters a foot in length, were the words, "God bless our home," and in another place the notice, "Wanted—A nice young girl for general housework. Apply within." The host's duties were not only the care of the stage horses on one side of the thin board partition, but he was also the cook and general utility man on the other side. The supper table stood against the partition and as the travellers were gathering what information possible, while trying to eat some of the coarse food, the horses were stamping and pawing in discontent and plunging against the frail barrier of boards between them and the dining table so violently as to suggest their kicking the dishes off the table,

The host's news was far from reassuring. The stage ahead of us had been attacked by the Indians and burned. The driver was killed and the horses stolen. There were no passengers, or they, too, would have been killed or captured. It seemed necessary to adopt some plan of action in case of an attack, and Pard looked at the driver with a knowing scrutiny and asked him if he would stand by the party if trouble came. James Randolph looked up with a puzzled expression on his face and asked what was meant by such a question, as he could not see how the driver could do anything else than share the fate of the others. Pard said he believed the driver was a fair man, and would not desert us, but he had known some drivers to "cut and run" in a time of peril, which means that they would cut the traces, mount one of the horses and start off with all of the horses leaving the stage and passengers to their fate.

Jake Farson had been changed off down the road and this driver lacked the frankness and firmness of speech and purpose that characterized our first jehu, and when the question was put to him so frankly the blaze of blood was apparent rising beneath his swarthy skin, and his answer was evidence enough that he had his own safety in mind when he drawled out that he would stay with us as long as he could. Randolph instantly lost the indifferent air that had characterized him from the first, and with fire in his eyes he turned a withering glance upon the sniveling driver, saying, "Now, you mark me, this man and his wife shall keep their eyes out on either side of the coach, and mine will be riveted on you, and the first move you make to desert us will be your last, for by the Holy Church, there is a horse apiece for us, and if one goes, we all go." With that bold thrust he left the table and lit a cigar as he sauntered out of the cabin leaving no doubt behind him of his sincerity.

The night was a perfect one, the moon hung full and resplendent, and the stars twinkled as merrily as if looking down upon a land unknown to carnage and bloodshed. The stage-coach was not the popular old "thorough-brace," but had been changed to what was known as a "jerky" with sides and top of canvas, and a boot fore and aft to resemble the regular coach in all but size and comfort. Some of the mail bags had been left along the way, but the smaller coach made still more cramped positions.

It was often lamented that necessity made it needful to crowd into so small a space, but now, by shifting the mail sacks, it served well to reflect the shadow of the driver on the canvas so clearly that his every movement was discernible from the inside. The first part of the night wore away at last, and midnight brought us again to a lonely station, where no change of horses was waiting because the tender said the Indians had run them off, but more likely he was afraid to go out in open ground to bring them in.

He coaxed and begged the driver and passengers to remain with him, for Indians were seen on the road ahead at five o'clock that afternoon, and death surely awaited any white man who dared venture on.

A council was held, but the poor shack that would be the only shelter was a burlesque for safety. It was the only protection gained by staying, and the Indians would burn the occupants out of that in a very few minutes, if they could not

lure them out in any other way. As a last appeal the trembling
stockman finally exclaimed, "Well, if you will not stay for your
own sakes, for God's sake stay for that woman you have in
the stage there." Pard exclaimed, "That woman is my wife,
and we will abide by her decision; if she says to wait, we will
wait." Advancing toward the stage, they found me expectantly
and anxiously watching their faces, and I read the inmost thoughts
of each of them by the mellow light of the moon and the sickly
rays of the lanterns. It was a desperate situation left for me
to decide, and perhaps the fate of all hung on my answer. In
spite of their care to speak in low tones I had heard the most

"Indians were seen on the road"

of their conversation, and after a little more explaining I said
that to go on with the stage there was one show of getting away
if there was time to mount the horses, and the moon was so
bright that anyone coming toward us could be seen for some
distance. If we stayed there with all the horses gone there was
no hope of escape. So it was decided to move on, with the poor
stock-tender violently gesticulating and declaring, with many
oaths, that it was a drive to death, and ended with "May the
devil take the lot of ye" as the last vent of his rage at being left
alone again.

Randolph decided to take a seat on the box and share the vigil
of outlook, as well as to watch the mistrusted driver. A signal
was arranged whereby the inside passengers were to instantly
get out and mount a horse if an attack seemed imminent.

We listened to the grinding of the wheels in the deep sand,
and watched the clouds of dust roll into the coach, enveloping
us in gray cloaks until we looked like hooded monks. Our eyes
and ears and nostrils were full of the fine alkaline ash that cut
the tender skin like an acid. We listened, too, with bated breath

6

for every sound. If one spoke suddenly it would cause a response of—Hark! The breeze flapping a curtain, the horses' hoofs on the stones, the lurching of the coach, all seemed to make a different noise than when our eyes could penetrate the distant shadows in the light of day. Once the driver stopped and climbed down from his seat. Quick as thought Randolph drew his revolver to fire, but heeding a second impulse, he jumped off the stage only to find a loosened tug which the jehu was calmly hooking up. But our companion expressed himself in no unmistakable language that Mr. Driver better say something next time he got off the perch, or he might not be able to fly up there again, for there was to be no foolishness on that trip.

Every curtain was rolled up to its limit, in order that we might see as clearly as the moonlight would permit. After every sudden and seemingly perilous rousing all would grow quiet with a sort of dulled consciousness that could hardly be called sleep, but a stupor that comes to over-excited nerves, only to jump to action when the slightest agitation occurred. Thus the night wore on, while the sage-brush shadows seemed ever to conceal a dusky form, and the rumbling coach on the rocky roadbed sounded like the roaring of Niagara to our overstrained ears.

It was indeed a night of fear and horror. The Indian fire signals that lit up the horizon at several different points were felt to be the telling of our whereabouts, and we might be going straight into a deathnet of their weaving for all we knew.

With a good repeating rifle across his knees and eyes fairly bulging from their sockets, Pard's tense vigil that night will never be forgotten, and I knew I saw an Indian every time the breeze swayed a sage-brush; every shadow gave me the creeps. Never was a morning sun so gladly seen to redden the eastern sky, and dispel the black shadows of the night and suspicion. The poor tired horses, doing double work, seemed to partake of the courage the new sun gave, and quickened their pace as if sharing the joy of release from the goblin hours of darkness.

It was nine o'clock when the stage rattled into the corral of one of the home stations. The place was fairly bristling with soldiers and armed men. A high stockade surrounded the corral and portholes were manned with lookouts and guns. It was easy to see why the ride had been free from attack, as these trusty messengers of Uncle Sam were known to be in that vicinity, and the Indians ha₁ fallen back from the road and given the signal of the soldiers' arrival by their many fires, thus allowing the stage to pass unmolested while seeking their own safety.

How glad and thankful we were for the courage given us to make that night ride and reach such a haven of safety. But

Courtesy of Lee Moorhouse, photographer, Pendleton, Oregon

To-ka-map-map-e, Squaw of the Battle of the Big Hole[1]

the sensation of peace and rest was not of long duration. Our government and our people are generous and resistless in the civilization of the great West, and the United States mail must move onward. Accommodations were ten times over-strained at this little fortress by the more remote settlers seeking

[1] At the Battle of the Big Hole, when General Gibbon engaged Chief Joseph, this squaw was captured and tied on a horse behind a soldier who was ordered to take her to Gibbon's Headquarters. She succeeded in getting her hands free, took a knife out of the soldier's belt, killed him and made her way to Joseph's camp.

the refuge of safety, by freighters with their wagon-loads of costly goods, waiting for a day of surety to go onward, stage company officials, stock-tenders and drivers, and a few travellers who would not venture farther; but now, in addition, were the newly arrived troops.

It surely was a place devoid of all comfort except that gleaned from a table well laden with pork and beans, bread, and black coffee, all of which better satisfied a hungry stomach than all the dainties of a rich man's table, though not the viands an epicure would select.

The gleam of the soldiers' guns in profusion gave a sense of security and so stimulated the desire for adventure that it was decided to continue the journey at once, hoping the first flush of excitement given by the arrival of the soldiers would open the way for a safe run through to Helena. We, therefore, ate our breakfast and listened to tales of woe and fear, and watched the faces of those who kept silent.

As we climbed into the stage again there was much muttering and some loud imprecations on our foolhardiness in deliberately riding out to sure death or worse. The day was a perfect one, cool and crisp; the clatter of our horses' feet and the rumbling of our coach wheels were soon the only sounds to break the great silence of an uninhabited country. I say uninhabited because there were no homes dotting the great highway in 1878 as there are now, thirty-two years later. The stage company's stations were from ten to twelve and twenty miles apart, and once in twenty-four hours there was what was known as a home station, where supplies were stored and where there was some pretence of defence from the frontier enemies.

One of the home stations on this line was kept by a Mrs. Corbet, who made herself a terror to travellers, and no one passed her place without adding a bit to her already notorious history. She was very tall and large of bone, and claimed to be a cousin of "Long" John Wentworth of Chicago, who was one of the sterling characters in that city's history. It was reported as not an uncommon thing for her to go out with pistol in hand and command stage passengers to go to her table and eat meals that she had prepared for them at one dollar per. Not having been informed of her peculiarities of entertainment, we decided to enjoy a remnant of lunch from our own basket, and when we had finished we went to the door for a drink of water, and were informed by a shrill voice from some obscure place that if we wanted water we could go to the river and get it. We gazed at the limpid river flowing at the base of a steep declivity, and thought it better to go thirsty than take any chance of having the stage go on without us. As we drove away from there the driver told us that Dame Corbet was sick

Mrs. Corbet lifted him by the ears and put him out

that day, else she would have been out after us. He then related how, "a spell back," a couple of Montana gentlemen had stopped there for dinner and one of them having called for coffee was quite incensed at its quality, and asked the waitress if she called that "stuff" coffee. He had not seen Mrs. Corbet, who was standing in a near doorway, but she walked up behind him, lifted him by the ears, compelled him to put the price of his dinner on the table, and then she put him forcibly out of doors. Some of our first callers in Helena were given this story, with a few additional flourishes, and while they seemed to enjoy it as if it were a new one, I later learned that they were the identical two gentlemen of the coffee episode, but they had the courtesy to spare my chagrin, and listened as attentively as if they had never heard the incident before. It may not be fair to tell their names, but one of them has since been the U. S. marshal of Alaska, and figured in the story of "The Spoilers" by Rex Beach.

That third day's ride took us off the Indian war grounds and our spirits rose according to our thankfulness and hopes.

At the last station before reaching Helena the driver who was to take the stage through was taken ill, and much to our joy we saw that Mr. O. J. Salisbury, one of the owners of the stage line, was to handle the ribbons. At the previous station we had taken on a young lady who was to teach in a country school near Helena; she was a newcomer from the States and had stopped at intervals of her journey through fear and weariness until that day; she had gained the seat with the driver and held it until the end of the journey. In the parlor of the Cosmopolitan Hotel the new teacher made me her confidante, and the things she said about Mr. Salisbury, "stage-driver," were intensely amusing. After she had exhausted her adjectives in describing him, and her surprise at his conversation, she ended her story by saying that he almost proposed to her as they were driving into town, and if he was a stage-driver she just wanted to see him again. When she was told who he was her surprise and chagrin knew no bounds. Later, when he told his side of the story, it was doubly amusing. He was a most extraordinary man in intelligence and good looks, and he had played rather a practical joke on her, which she soon realized, but she was not allowed to be the only one to feel the force of the joke, and to his dying day Mr. O. J. S. held up his hand in self-defence when he saw us coming toward him. Knowing him well, we learned his side of the escapade before telling him what the fair school-ma'am had said of his lovemaking, and the blending of the two would make quite a readable romance.

We reached Helena about one o'clock of the fifth night out, and in spite of the lateness of the hour many people had gathered at the Cosmopolitan Hotel for the latest news, as the telegraph wires had been cut by the Indians, and also for the excitement

of seeing the stage arrive and unload. It was the chief entertainment of the town for the four and twenty hours. Tired
mentally and physically from the long perilous trip, there yet
seemed much buoyancy in our movements as we emerged from
among the dark depths of the old coach, and with a sense of
security and safety quite exhilarating to our benumbed muscles,
we made our way into the bright hotel office. But I am sure
I was asleep before my head fell on a pillow.

The house was only a two-story brick building, the rooms
were large and airy, and the second story was on a level with
the street in the rear, so that an entrance was made on either
street. No one thought of locking doors, and when we asked
for a key to our door we were given our first "tenderfoot laugh,"
although they did hunt up a key, which we never used after
the first night.

It was the first experience with a Chinese "chambermaid,"
but he went about his business in such a methodical way that
it was enjoyable to watch him about his work. Chinese servants
were about the only kind to be had in Helena, but they were
loyal helpers in any capacity, as we learned then and later by
personal experience.

We had a good long sleep into the day following our arrival
and arose rested and renewed to get a daylight view of the town.
Our first caller that day was the Hon. Robert Fisk, editor of
the Helena *Herald*, who began immediately to lay plans for
our enjoyment, and to open the way for us to gather material
for various publications and to have the resources of Montana
made known to the world at large. He first arranged for a drive
to the Hot Springs about four miles from town, which was
delightful in spite of the very rough and rocky roads. There
were practically no improvements at the springs, but some very
crude rough buildings that served as shelter only for the bath-
ers—quite a contrast to the elegance there now, which has
made Helena famous. The water contains soda and sulphur
and it was hot enough to boil eggs.

We were most generously entertained by the townspeople
who have made history for Montana, including the Fisk brothers,
Col. W. F. Sanders, Col. Sam. Word, Colonel Broadwater, Captain Mills, and many others, who have closed their careers, but
will live ever in the hearts of the Montanians.

The scarcity of fruit seemed like a famine of luxuries. Oranges were a dollar apiece, apples were seventy-five cents a pound, and the hardy pears were twenty-five cents each. There were no tramps, no beggars or burglars, no objects of charity in the town—doors were always left unlocked and one could not help feeling a sense of freedom unknown in the more "civilized" cities along the rail routes. It seemed a pity to propose a railroad to such a happy community, yet the thought of the long distance to the steam horse made one prefer even the bold bad burglar, if one was an adjunct of the other. We would have felt especially shut out of the world while the wires were down had we been given time to think about it.

Typical home stage station

Messrs. Schwab and Zimmerman, the managers of the hotel, made us feel at home in ways seldom offered in these later days of touring, and their tables were full of tempting viands. Many of the army officers' families made the Cosmopolitan their home, and during the prevailing Bannock war the officers' wives were there, living in the dread expectancy of fatalities to loved ones at the front.

There were some queer-looking individuals in the dining-room, and I can never forget two women who seemed to view life and their personal appearance with grave seriousness. They were most angular in figure, tall, slim, and stiff, with long slim features that could not be raised into a smile. Each tried to outdo the other in little "spit curls" from the middle parting of the hair down to the lobe of the ear, and each was so prim and precise in every move that one could easily believe they were automatons. I do not often smile at another's appearance, but they fascinated me and I could not keep my eyes from them.

Those were days when men in the army besought their

friends to bring out sisters, cousins, and aunts, and they were sometimes weird specimens of the sex, but even such could reign as queens, dance, ride, and flirt to their hearts' content, and marry, too, which does not always follow in these later days.

The frontier was a fact and not fiction in the '70's. A woman in the far West was a blessing sent direct from Heaven, or from the East, which was much the same in those days. Almost everywhere away from the more favored ox freight lines the modes of living were crude and often far from tempting.

The furniture of a stage station might be all homemade, but attractive and comfortable, but usually it was stiff and scarce, and the seats only boxes and kegs which had yielded their contents to an uninviting table. There was seldom a cloth to cover the pine board tables, but that was better than the much soiled colored ones that in some places seemed to do service for a whole season.

The bottles of condiments, with the addition of an old caster of cruets filling the centre of the table, wore their fly-specked paper wrappings, and were made worse by dirt and greasy hands; the cups and plates were of the heaviest and coarsest ware, glasses were thick and lustreless, if there were any at all, the snout of the cream pitcher (which never knew cream) would be gone, the sugar bowl cracked, and over all in season a swarm of flies settled and buzzed and fought for more than their share of provender.

Yet people lived and thrived and waited, for in the wake of all this toilsome, dreary pioneering development and prosperity must come. With the coming of the dainty matron, the real homemaker, the whole western world brightened, and it was no wonder the great and glorious pioneer cried for a mate. Neither must we forget the occasional oasis of even those early days where everything was spotless in its cleanliness, and the tables were loaded with the choicest viands of the most dainty housewife's handiwork.

Helena of thirty years ago was a busy town; the buildings were mostly two-story bricks. The Government Assay building was an attractive structure in its surroundings of trees and grass, and on the inside we were shown through the whole process of the works and examined scales so delicate that even a pencil mark would change the balance. I wrote my name on a piece of paper that had already been weighed and found the writing to add just $\frac{1}{264}$ of a grain. I am curious to know how much less weight it will have when affixed to this manuscript.

The brewery of Helena made more money than the mint in those days, but in a way quite different.

Captain Berthoud had just been put in command of a party of some twenty men to make a survey of Yellowstone Park. He offered us the protection of his party as we desired to go through that country. General Miles, with a party of soldiers, also invited us to go with him as soon as the Indian outbreak was quieted. But the Indians did not quiet down, and we had to wait two years before we could safely make the trip into that great wonderland.

Indian war dance

CHAPTER VII

BUTTE. VIRGINIA CITY

FROM Helena to Butte the old stage line went via Deer Lodge, then south through Silver Bow. The sun shone beautifully when the start was made from Helena, but only a few miles had been left behind when it began to rain and the storm grew in intensity for the rest of the way to Deer Lodge, where a delay of a day was made for the storm to spend its fury. However, the second day later it still stormed when the trip was continued. The mud was deep and clung in heavy pads to the coach wheels and clogged them in the chuck-holes, until our six horses were undone in extricating the stage and pulling the load over the divide.

While waiting for a change of horses at Silver Bow, Pard sauntered into the stage station where he found a copy of his book on Montana. Not averse to landing either a compliment or criticism, he asked the man on duty whether it was something worth reading. "Yep, that's a great book, by a feller who's got 'em all skinned on drawing the long bow." "Well, do you mean the man really lies in his descriptions or figures?" anxiously queried the author. "Well, now, stranger, you see it's like this. You can read that thing through from beginning to end, and you can't put your finger on a single gol darned lie, but the fellow what writ that book has the darndest way of telling the truth of any man you ever saw."

By ten o'clock at night the stars came twinkling out to light us into the thriving little mining camp of Butte at an altitude of fifty-eight hundred feet above sea-level, up where the sky was blue and the air then was pure. It was in days before the smelters sent forth their sulphurous fumes and changed the atmosphere to that ascribed to a much lower region. But trees never grew around that section, and with no water the town must be lacking in the charm of shade for many years to come. They say in these later days that trees would not grow because of the acid fumes in the air, but they had refused to grow ages before the smelters were ever started.

Our first visit to Butte was as brief as we could well make it. The hotel was most objectionable, and was overrun by creepers and crawlers to a degree beyond endurance. The stay was rendered quite charming outside of the hotel, however, through the courtesy of H. T. Brown, proprietor and editor of the Butte *Miner*, and his wife, who invited us to occupy a room in their own home while in the town. It was a gracious favor, which was more than appreciated. When writing to my friends from the hotel I cautioned all of them to examine the letters carefully to see that nothing crawled out of them.

We were offered two of the choicest lots in the town if we would locate there, but they seemed pretty dear at the price asked. The offer was left open for two years, but there was no change of heart with us, and we lost our one chance of a fortune through Butte real estate.

At that time clocks were kept an hour ahead of time, so that servants, workmen, miners, etc., would get up early and put in a day's work.

Across the street from the hotel was a wholesale liquor house and several retail places for the fiery beverage. There was also a dry-goods store, a hardware and jeweller's establishment, and down the street a little way an Odd Fellows' Hall and a couple of banks made a good showing.

Butte had aspirations to be the pride of Montana, leaving Helena a wall-flower who had had her day. It was in the days of the "Alice," the "Moulton," "the Original," the "Lexington" and some thirty other mines that made a lively camp, and things were doing. Hundreds of smaller mines and prospects drew a population like a magnet draws the steel, and the charm is ever invincible to those who have once been under the spell.

A lively mining camp illustrates the love of man for a Bohemian life. The professional man, the college graduate, the society favorite are all to be found, with manners as reckless and debonair as their garb. When they came from the far East the Missouri River was known as the dividing line between restraint and freedom. At Omaha one was said to throw his Bible and his manners into the river and don his schapps and leather belt of cartridges, to which was attached his bowie knife and revolver; then with a canvas coat and a slouch hat and an old brown pipe he swung into a mining camp with an air of intimidating every-

In days that are gone

body in it, and a bravado of manners that visibly fell at the first words of a bull-whacker who recognized the tenderfoot on sight. There was never any use for a tenderfoot to try a disguise; the "earmarks" were as visible as his nose on his face, and his attempted bravado would make him the butt of every joke.

It is a strange condition of man that he must progress or he must go backward; he cannot stand still. The white man keeps his inherited love of life in the open air with its easy swing and lack of conventionalities. It is no wonder then that an Indian taken from his free life and graduated from an Eastern college will return to the agency of his fathers, hide his civilized clothing in the brush, mount his pony and with a pal who lies in waiting, dash off to the old tepee with an unsuppressed whoop that gives vent to his untrammelled joy.

There were fifteen brick business blocks in Butte in 1878 and the growth of the mining interests and the town has been a history the like of which is unknown, but Butte is to-day the same forbidding spot of barrenness, without trees or grass to temper the glaring sunlight, and people live there only to make their "pile" and go elsewhere to found a home.

Butte consumed eight thousand dozen bottles of beer in 1878, and one million cigars. It also furnished many historical characters, but there were few men more widely known than Judge A. J. Davis, a wealthy bachelor, whose estate was finally fought over through many terms of court until the most of the fortune clung inseparably to the lawyers who had the case in charge.

The judge went to Butte with a modest fortune which was replenished by mining enterprises until it reached fabulous dimensions, but in spite of his horde of wealth he loved it all down to the very last penny, and when he had to let any of it go without a promising return of threefold, it had to be drawn from him by some strategic move. His avarice and his extortion was a byword in the whole country, but it had no effect upon his itching palm. On one of our later trips into Montana, when we had learned to know the judge and his ungenerous character, we asked the stage-driver if old Judge Davis had married. "Married!" exclaimed the jehu, "Married! Why that there old fellow is just too d—d stingy to even divide his affections."

Montana is in itself a veritable panoramic park. The Crow Indians had a saying that the Great Spirit only looked at other countries, but lived in Montana all the year. The Sioux Indians deem it an honor to die in Montana, where it is so beautiful everywhere, and only a step to the happy hunting grounds of the Great Spirit.

Only one other State or Territory has such innumerable clear streams running through grassy woodlands or taking the serpentine trail through myriads of canyon fastnesses. The forests, noble in size, had clean-swept lawns beneath their sheltering branches, and everywhere the rich alluvial soil offered such diversity of industry that it was well called the Mountain Paradise, as the name implies.

The names of some of the rivers are somewhat startling, but were doubtless given under the same curious conditions

that have named places and things elsewhere. There was
Crazy Woman's Fork, Big Hole River, Stinkingwater, Hell-
gate, Badwater, Ruby, the Gooseberry, and the Owl, besides the
great triple-headed Missouri, the Yellowstone, the Powder, Big
Horn, Belle Fourche, and the Rosebud, with their hundreds of
tributaries that altogether make Montana the second best
watered domain of all the great States.

A store of the frontier

One night on Big Hole River about six miles from Glendale
we were delayed and lost the connection out to Salisbury on
the main overland route to Virginia City. The stage thorough-
brace broke and we had to wait for a new one to be made and
put in, and we did not reach the station until several hours late.
The inn was only a rancher's cabin, and a small one at that.
There were twelve or fourteen men to stay there over night;
Mrs. Bowe, the inn-keeper's wife, made a bed for us without
any mattress on the floor in the living-room, to which we added
our own blankets, and slept the sleep of deep exhaustion on
the hard side of the board floor. There were two sick men in the
house, and the daughter of the house was also ill. One of the
men had erysipelas in his head and face and it was swollen as
full as the skin would hold. When trying to do a little something for his comfort he showed his gratitude by the tears that
trickled from between his swollen eyelids, while he tried to be

mirthful and said the doctor had made a Bannock Indian out of him by painting his face and neck with iodine.

Pard went fishing that night even after our late supper and caught a fine lot of trout which we enjoyed for breakfast. Then he went off next day, leaving me at the cabin to put in my time roaming about, reading to the sick, or scribbling away at one of the tri-weekly letters to my mother, or to some of the newspapers who kept up a call for "more."

There was much strife between the two of us lone travellers for news. Pard was a veritable Corliss engine at pumping up statistics of the various products and prospects of every foot of land. The periodical *New West Illustrated* came out with astonishing regularity and filled to the brim with just such information as emigrants were searching for in view of new homes. Then came the special book, *To the Rockies and Beyond*, followed by *Montana and the Yellowstone Park*, and the rhythmic jingle of *Where Rolls the Oregon*, meaning the great Columbia, with its headwaters of Snake River, from its source to the sea. There did not seem to be much left for me, except just little, every-day things as they come and go in frontier lands.

But that all people could not see with Pard's optimistic eyes was evident later in the fall, when a wagon-load of tired travellers stopped for the night on Red Rock divide, just before reaching the new little settlement of Salisbury. The wind was blowing cold from the north, and the snow was coming down in blankets. Everything was wet and soggy, and dreariness overspread the party of immigrants who were trying to make a camp by the roadside, and the oncoming darkness only increased their discomfort.

The landscape was a vast panorama stretching far away in unlimited grandeur, and in fair weather that same summit was often called "Inspiration Pass." But now it huddled under its snow covers and lowering clouds, a dreary desolation, void of life. A woman sat on the wagon tongue from which the horses had been led away to hunt for their supper at the end of a lariat. The children were tired and cross, and the little one in the mother's arms fretted to be free and stretch its tired limbs without restraint. The men had tumbled out the mess box and made a shelter in the wagon box and under it for the night's rest. The wet canvas cover of the schooner flapped loosely and noisily as it opened and shut to each and every gust of the storm, and betokened a weird and restless night for the weary mother.

Our stage delayed for a few minutes to give the belated wayfarers some needed counsel. We peeped out at the side of our closely buttoned curtains and contrasted our own comfortable corner of the stage-coach with the flapping, bedraggled skirts of the woman on her way to the new land of promise. The driver told them to go on down the hill a couple of miles farther and they could get a better place for the women folks. Then a sharp, shrill voice piped up from the wagon tongue saying: "If this is Strahorn's paradise, as his book calls it, I just wish that he had to live in it, that's all, but I wish I was back in Missouri whar we 'uns come from," and then she burst into tears. She did not know that the man "what writ the book" was enclosed in that stage-coach, or she might have said more. We drew our heads in from the window and felt a heart full of sympathy for the poor tired family, but we learned in after years that their whole love was given to their Montana home, and old Missouri was like a bad dream to them.

We are often told that adversity is the only teacher who can develop the talent lying dormant within us, and Pard had graduated in that school of hardship while in the Sioux campaign of 1876 and spring of 1877, when sleeping in pools of water without a tent, and then on winter campaigns with but one blanket, and mercury freezing in the bulb.

The desolate, homesick woman put Pard in a reminiscent mood and he related to the companion passengers some of his own experiences as a campaigner with General Crook in the Sioux war. From tales of personal sufferings in lack of food, blankets, and shelter, he told of the literary talent that was pitted against him in summing up war news during that campaign and getting letters and telegrams out to their respective papers. For instance:

"There was Jack Finnerty of the Chicago *Times*. I have always had a notion that he stepped out from some place in Lever's novels; he was brave to rashness, and devoted to the interests of his great journal. Joe Wason of the *Alta Californian* and the New York *Tribune* was always on the skirmish line after 'pints'. His red head shone like the danger signal of a freight train, but in spite of his red head he was one of the bravest fellows I ever knew. There was T. C. McMillan of the Chicago *Inter-Ocean*, and representatives of half a dozen other papers who campaigned for seventeen months on that expedition, and whose readers never imagined while reading the reports at a comfortable breakfast table and growling at the dashed correspondents because they did not make fuller reports, that the "dashed correspondents," dressed in rags, soaked through with rain, and almost crazed with want of food and rest, had written what they could on a cottonwood chip or piece of flat stone, and often at the risk of life from stray bullets."

Those were days of hardship and peril that made this night of storm and this woman's distress a paradise if she could not see it through the snowflakes. The snow increased in its blinding fury, the driver could no longer see the road, nor tell where to drive. Gen. Charles A. Warren, a noted figure in the history of Montana and Washington, was one of the occupants of the stage. He was a man of strong build and a nature inured to the mountain hardships. When he saw the serious condition we were in, he at once leaped from the stage and with one companion broke the road ahead through the drifting snow to guide the horses into a safe route over the mountain and through the dark ravines. For hours those brave ones toiled on, refusing to yield their places to any one else until the valley road insured our safety. We have met the old general many a time since then and he laughingly refers to our night trip over the "Paradise Road."

A faint glimmer of lights through unshaded windows betokened the little town of Salisbury at last, and we were at rest until another day dawned, and we branched off for the gold-famed city of Virginia.

Gulch gold is not the only thing that has made Virginia City famous; it had been for several years a rendezvous for the thugs and highwaymen that kept the territory of Montana in a state of fear and terror until the Vigilantes Association was formed to rid the country of the despicable oppression.

It was during our first trip to Virginia City in 1878 that the first man was hung by order of the court. The sheriff who was to perform the duty arrived on the same stage that we did. He had explained the affair to us en route, and said no one would be admitted to the hanging except those having written invitations. And what was our surprise on the morning following our arrival to receive one of those "written invitations" to be present at that first legal hanging. It is needless to say that we did not accept the courtesy and at the awful hour we were as far away from the scene of action as it was possible to be.

Finding the gold that made Virginia City famous

Our headquarters were at the Madison House, the chief hotel of the city, kept by Mr. F. J. Farrell, but there was not much to delay us in Virginia City. Two or three days would have given us ample time to visit the famous gulch mines and for Pard to gather his statistics and such information as he required. But the time had come for all stage lines to put on what was called "winter schedule time," which meant no travelling at night, but stopping and starting at seasonable or unseasonable hours, according to the distance to be made and the condition of the roads. Sometimes a stop would be called at four o'clock in the afternoon and a delay until the next morning at seven, or it might be a stop at eleven at night with a call to go on at three A.M. Here we found a new phase, for not only would the stage stop at the half-way station over night but it would stay there over Sunday. There was no regularity about anything but the discomfort. Travelling on passes and in the interests of the transportation companies, we were always expected to smile and look pleasant whate'er befell us, but there were many moments when we wished we were paying our fare and had the privilege of free speech. If there is any one thing that my Pard does more freely in his later days than to pay railroad fare, I don't know what it is. We were never required or requested to restrain our speech, but we knew it to be an unwritten duty, and we lived up to it. If we do a little complaining now it is because we know we could not suffer all those hardships and inconveniences in our maturer years, and we wonder how we endured them then.

The novelty and excitement of travelling as we were then doing was a wondrous joy in spite of all unpleasant conditions. As soon as it was known in a community what the import of Pard's mission meant, every door was opened to us, and we were not only entertained by the "four hundred" in their homes, but every facility was placed at our disposal for promoting the interests of the work. It was a rare opportunity such as no two other people ever enjoyed, and we appreciated it to the full in spite of its hardships. We came in contact with the very best people and formed lifelong friendships that have ever been dear and sacred.

CHAPTER VIII

COLONEL SANDERS AND THE VIGILANTES

 HEN we left Virginia City to go back to Helena we had the charming companionship of Col. W. F. Sanders. It was an all night ride, but he made the time so intensely interesting in telling of his experiences during vigilante days that no one ever missed the naps he might have caught had there been the usual stage load. The colonel was one of the earliest pioneers of Montana, even when it was called Idaho, in the earliest '60's.

The Territory was in the hands of men who feared no penalty for their crimes, and it was rid of them at the hands of men no less lawless in their taking off, but working to accomplish what the laws could not. The discovery in the fall of 1863 of more than one hundred bodies of victims of the road agents finally aroused the feelings of the law-abiding citizens of Montana to a pitch of frenzy. They felt that the mysterious disappearance of many other men was to be traced to the bandits. Scores of miners who had set out with large sums of money for various places had never been heard of and had never reached their destinations.

Colonel Sanders had taken up his residence at Bannock City when it was only about a year old, and Virginia City and Nevada City close by were just getting on the map. There were no livelier settlements than these on the face of the earth. The craze for gold had collected there California gamblers and cutthroats, Mexican desperadoes, deserters from both the Federal and the Confederate armies, fugitives from justice of a dozen countries, and last and least in number were a few honest miners and peaceful immigrants. There was little government and no law except a limited quantity of the home-made article.   It was here that Colonel Sanders became prosecuting attorney.

Murders occurred daily, almost hourly. Had there been the most perfect system of legal procedure, time would not have permitted of the orderly trial of offenders, so frequent were the crimes. Alder Gulch continued to disgorge its treasures in a steady stream, and the very excess of its bounty excited the most selfish passions of men.

Rude courts were established and the guilt or innocence of offenders was submitted to regularly chosen juries, but the swag-

Col. Sanders's Pullman car to Bannock City—1862

gering outlaws would boldly force their way through the lines of spectators into the presence of the qualified twelve men, announcing their determination to have revenge upon every one connected with the case for any verdict other than ac-quittal. Witnesses and jurors, under these circumstances, were afraid for their lives, and justice had miscarried until the outlaws, seeing the blanch of fear everywhere, were in supreme control. In the early stages of this reign of terror some of the road agents had been tried, found guilty, and condemned to death by unanimous vote, but before the hour of execution arrived the renegades would have the citizens so terrified by threats that motions to reconsider would result in liberating the outlaw again.

The sheriff, Henry Plummer, was himself at the head of one of the worst gangs in the Territory. Plummer's gang was the only well-organized band of men in the community, and consisted of about two dozen "bad men" and a large number of spies, scouts, and outside correspondents. These were the road agents who prompted the writers of dime novels to do their worst. In action they wore black silk handkerchiefs over their faces, and their secret service system told them of every expedition worth robbing.

Individually the members of Plummer's gang were murderers who put small valuation on human life. They killed for vengeance, or even for "luck." They fired at women to frighten them, and killed Indians for no reason except pure wantonness. Plummer was said to be the quickest and surest revolver shot in the mountains. He could shoot with either hand, and according to report could draw his pistol and empty its five chambers in three seconds, making every bullet tell. He came to the gold camp with a record of three murders in California and had taken part in an attack on a Wells Fargo bullion express.

When Sam T. Hauser, late Governor of the Territory, started east with a load of treasure, Plummer gave him a red woollen scarf to protect his throat from chill. The red scarf was to inform Plummer's men that the wearer was the victim they awaited. This was the gang that engaged the attention of Colonel Sanders, and the movement which brought about the hanging of twenty-two of them, including Plummer. It was the first work that followed the formation of the Montana Vigilantes, of which Colonel Sanders was the active head.

On one occasion when Colonel Sanders was going from one town to another he had to spend the night at a little out-of-the-way place and sleep in the same bed with George Ives who was a notorious bandit. He was out looking for Ives at the time, but Ives did not then know the colonel by sight, and that fact was all that saved a tragedy then and there. In the few months preceding the uprising there had been a reign of terror in which no man felt that his life was safe. Ives had made life a terror in Virginia City. He ordered a barber's chair to be taken out in the middle of the street, and with a revolver in each hand demanded a shave; when the tonsorial work was done he drew out a long knife, and with two dexterous strokes the barber's ears dropped in the dusty street. "Just for luck" as Ives said. He was once sent to buy two mules from a German named Nicholas Thalt, in the Stinkingwater Valley—and murdered the German to save paying for the mules. He was caught redhanded and a crowd of citizens dragged him to Nevada City. Ives did n't worry any over his arrest, but this time the miners were aroused and sent for Colonel Sanders.

The trial took place in the open air before a huge bonfire late in the afternoon of December 21, 1863. Citizens came from

Highwayman waiting for his prey

miles around to attend the trial. The judge sat in a wagon. Colonel Sanders had a clear case against Ives, and he made the most of every bit of evidence. The jury, which was composed of the better element of miners, found the prisoner guilty and the prosecutor moved that he be hanged at once. Then for a few minutes it was a question whether Sanders or Ives would be the first to die. In the crowd were many friends of the prisoner and of Plummer's gang. The arrival of Plummer with a rescuing gang was momentarily expected, and part of the mob made an attempt at rescue, but it was repulsed. A pole was swung out of the window of an unfinished house near by, and in fifty-eight minutes after he was convicted, the body of Ives swung on a rope from the end of the pole. That was the beginning of the campaign against Henry Plummer's gang.

"Laughed at for his foolishness and shot dead by Slade"

The Vigilantes were made up of five men in Virginia City, three from Bannock, and one from Nevada City. It was a secret tribunal which worked for twenty years. In less than two months after they were organized they had hung twenty-two members of Plummer's gang, including Plummer.   They never bluffed, and when any one found a little white card which measured just seven by nine inches, bearing the numerals "3–7–77" in heavy black ink pinned to his tent or posted on some of his belongings, he knew it was a warning to get out of the country, or the second night thereafter he would be hung.

Probably the most notorious desperado, next to Plummer, was Slade; perhaps Slade was the worst of the two; at any rate he was a terror to the people in all localities.   Mark Twain tells in *Roughing It* how he ate at the same table with Slade, at the latter's station on the Overland Mail route in Wyoming, but the author says he was so agitated that he remembered nothing of Slade's personal appearance, except that he had very high cheek bones.   As a matter of fact, Slade was a large, well-made man, as active as a panther, and possessed of enormous strength.   He was skilled equally in the use of firearms and in rough and tumble fighting, and he enjoyed one form of fighting as much as the other.

Slade was a division agent on the Overland at Julesburg in 1862.   He was a terror of the most dangerous kind: a man who would resent an insult or affront, either real or imaginary, on the instant if he could, but later at all hazards.   His vengeance was most atrocious, and ended in death to his victim.   One of his first acts of treachery was when in charge of an emigrant train from the Missouri River to California.   He had trouble with one of his wagon drivers and drew his gun, but the driver had his out first, and Slade knowing himself to be in danger said it would be a pity to shoot, and they would throw away their guns and fight it out with their fists.   This the driver agreed to and threw down his gun, only to be laughed at for his foolishness and shot dead by Slade.

He was made agent of the Overland Company because of his fearless daring.   The company had been robbed of horses, and its coaches had been held up repeatedly, but Slade soon put an end to such offenders by following them to the death. He had been one of the most daring highwaymen of them all until he was employed to clean them out, and he moved on west as places required such settlements as he was wont to make. It was deemed safer by the company to keep him in their employ than to have him one of the desperadoes at large. He succeeded in stopping depredations on stage stock and stage company belongings, but it was done by his own bloodthirsty violence. He was his own judge, jury, and executioner. It was a work that delighted his soul to the marrow. At the time Mark Twain met him, Slade was said to have killed no less than thirty men.

It was at this time that Slade had his celebrated quarrel with Jules. Jules was the founder of the little town of Julesburg, Colorado, one of the most important stopping points on the Overland trail, near the junction of the North and South Platte Rivers. He and Slade had a quarrel and Jules "laid for" his opponent, posting himself behind a saloon door, with a double-barrelled shotgun. As the unsuspecting Slade came in the door Jules emptied both barrels into his body. Slade fell, literally riddled with lead. It was thought he had no chance to live, but, after weeks of suffering, he regained his health, and started gunning for his enemy. Jules had taken the alarm and left the country. He remained away several months, but finally, believing he could best Slade if they should meet again, he returned to his old haunts along the Overland Mail route. Slade, with a little party of friends, rode out and captured Jules. Then, according to the popular version, Slade tied Jules to a corral fence and spent the day in target practice, shooting off his enemy's fingers and ears and other members of his body, yet not killing him until night, in spite of his pleadings to be put out of his agony.

Slade's record as a killer became too strong for the company to stand. Passengers were terrorized, though, as has been shown, there was then no reason for any passenger to fear Slade because his thirst for battle was satisfied by fighting those of his own kind, but the company discharged him, and Slade moved to Montana, when the Virginia City excitement was at its height.

"Our organization was the simplest thing in the world," said Colonel Sanders. "We would turn to one of our members and say: 'You are a pretty square sort of fellow and we know you to be straight as a string; you shall be our judge.' And to another: 'You are a heavily built chap with lots of grit; you shall be marshal.' I was district attorney because I had a smattering of law, and it was upon my affidavits that all warrants were issued.

"It seems strange in these days to think of constituting a court in such an offhand way, without the slightest vestige of federal authority, but we did it, and our court was respected by all the citizens of Virginia City, that is, most of them. After a while, when they found that we were not hanging so frequently as before, the lawless element seemed bolder and more aggressive again.

"The leader of this tough part of our later population was Slade. He had a dozen satellites, and it was a favorite diversion of theirs to spend a night in a disorderly resort, and then set it on fire. He had been carrying on in this characteristic manner, going from bad to worse. It is related of him that his favorite trick was to go into a barroom and ask a stranger to have a drink. The stranger would comply, and, when about to drink his whiskey would be knocked insensible by a terrific blow from Slade's fist. After knocking one man down in this way, Slade would step up to another and ask him to have a drink, and the performance would be repeated as long as there remained anybody in the room to be knocked down.

"Slade overstepped the mark, however, when he tore up a warrant that was being read to him by an officer of the law. Slade had shot up the town the day before and the officer was seeking to arrest him for that offence. Still drunk, Slade tore the paper to pieces. As the marshal pulled out the document, Slade, quick as a flash, sprang at him, jerked it out of his hands, and then pointed a revolver at the judge's heart. It was all done in a second.

"'Now,' said he, 'I 'm about tired of this business. I am not going to be drained any more, and I am not going to recognize your authority; nor shall I pay that $400. I shall hold you responsible for my personal safety, and if any of your committee attempts to touch me I will blow your heart out.' The officer remained calm and made no further effort to arrest Slade, but the news spread like wildfire. The miners held a mass-meeting and decided that Slade had gone too far in thus flouting the newly established law and order of the camp."

As Colonel Sanders left the court-room after this scene he

met a member of the Vigilantes Committee and dispatched him
to a camp about two miles away for all the boys to come in for
they were needed.   They came from several camps, for the news
spread fast, and a court was called to vote on what should be done.

Over 15,000 miners voted to lynch Slade, according to the vigi-
lante process, and this great procession marched down the gulch,
captured the desperado, and informed him that his time was up.

" The old stage-coach rattled over the great, lonesome highway "

Slade weakened when he saw the array against him and wept
like a child, but his hour for penitence was past, the noose was
slipped around his neck, the barrel kicked from under his feet,
and law and order ruled in the great Northwest.

Just think of listening to all these talks at the midnight
hour and in the early dawn as the old stage-coach rattled over
the great lonesome highway miles and miles from human habita-
tion, and talking over the incidents with the very man who was
the ring-leader of the law and order court.   Think of the awful
hours of suspense that the wife endured while he was going
about the towns with a dozen or more men as a body-guard,
while some of these exciting things were being enacted.

It was little wonder that he had wanted to be present at
that first hanging in Virginia City which was the result of a
legally arrayed court and jury according to the law of our
Federal Government. He dropped the yoke of responsibility

then, and the lives and the property of the people he knew would be thenceforth protected through the proper channels. But what a great brave heart and soul he had to bring order out of chaos, peace out of carnage, and happiness from the great unrest. He has been an honor and a glory to his country, and Montana should give him a monument the highest in its realm.

At the time Colonel Sanders went to Bannock City it was scarcely more than a spot on the earth and was still in the domain of Idaho, but in 1864 Congress passed an act providing for a new Territory to be taken from Idaho, to be called Montana, and also that a part of southeastern Idaho should be restored to Dakota. Montana's first Legislature convened in Bannock in December of that year. Sidney Edgerton was the first Governor and Thomas Francis Meagher was Territorial Secretary, with George M. Pinney as United States Marshal.

One of the first acts of the new Legislature was the repealing of the statutes of Idaho and adopting common law, also providing the codification of Territorial laws. The Code Commissioners were Wilbur F. Sanders, William H. Miller, and George W. Stapleton. A common school system was adopted and an act passed making it a misdemeanor to carry concealed weapons. The vast number of criminals who flooded that region of the country paid no attention to the law of the courts, and the need of the Vigilantes Association was imperious, but with all the watchfulness and stern rigor of the few members of the law and order league it was fifteen years before a man was hung by the neck through a legal court of action.

Colonel Sanders had ways of his own in accomplishing his ends. He never wanted to be thwarted in his undertakings, and many good stories could be told on him. He called on us in New York City, when he was United States Senator, and invited us to attend the theatre and see the play of *Esmeralda* on the first double stage used in the city. We were sorry to decline such a courtesy, but an old Sioux war campaigner was to call that evening to talk over the war days, and subsequent times. Pard was delighted with the prospective visit and could not be persuaded to ignore it. The colonel left us saying he would come again as something might deter the caller, and he still might hope for us to go with him.

The first guns were hardly fired on the old war path of the Sioux trail before the colonel came in again. He sat silent for a few moments, then in his own brusque way said: "Say, stranger, I have asked these good folks to go to the theatre with me to-night, and they refused because you were coming; now, can't you come some other time? They don't come to New York often and they ought to be out every night."

The episode was as surprising as it was humiliating, yet it was characteristic of his blunt way of carrying a point.

At another time when railroads were finished through Helena we stopped there for a few hours in passing through Montana, and when Pard went up to see Colonel Sanders he found court was in session. The colonel, who was trying a case, saw Pard enter the court-room. He jumped to his feet and said: "Your Honor, Bob Strahorn is in the court-room, and we all want to see him; I move this court be adjourned for about fifteen minutes," and it was.

When Colonel Wilbur Sanders died, in 1906, Montana lost its brightest star, its great war-horse, and the bravest man that ever gave his life to his State. One forgets the eccentricities of such a man in his achievements, and the whole Northwest mourns his loss as irreparable.

CHAPTER IX

DIAMOND CITY AND HOT SULPHUR SPRINGS

WE were having a real cozy time in our easy chairs by a warm bright fire in the Cosmopolitan Hotel in Helena, commenting upon the events of the day, and tracing an outline for future travel, when the poetry was all taken out of our souls by the report that our stage for White Sulphur Springs would leave at four o'clock the next morning. Then we tried to sleep, but when we need sleep it is often the hardest to obtain. However, we were ready on time, and for once be it known the stage was punctual to a minute.

These springs are located some eighty miles southeast of Helena and were then the best improved springs in the Territory. Any one who is familiar with Montana knows it to be rich in mineral fountains of rare merit, in whose waters many an invalid has found welcome healing properties.

The soft red light of morning began to illumine the eastern sky, and the sun shamed away the frost before we were hardly awake to the knowledge of our speed. Twenty miles from Helena the Missouri impertinently crossed our pathway, and with my slow wits I did not see how we were to cross. The driver whistled away as unconcerned as possible and drove on a little pier that extended a short distance over the water; but the little pier proved to be a ferry and we were soon adrift, kept in position by ropes and cables; the ferry turned so that the current struck the stern, and we were soon pushed by its force to the other side in safety. Scarcely a ripple betrayed the swiftness underneath. We had a two hours' wait at the river so we procured a boat and launched out for a morning sail. It was like meeting an old friend to see the grand old Missouri River again. The water at the place where we crossed was some forty feet deep, and clear as crystal. Our spirits rose as we advanced, and every glad song of early days that could be recalled was sent up to the blue vaulted sky, while peal after peal of our

"Twenty miles from Helena the Missouri impertinently
crossed our pathway"

joyous laughter went echoing along the moss-covered rocks which rose hundreds of feet on either side. It seemed almost impossible that we could be in the heart of Montana, so far, far away from the Illinois home, and yet enjoy so many happy days.

The first village reached on this trip was Diamond City, which was once one of the most thriving towns in Montana. It was located at the head of Confederate Gulch, which had

8

yielded so richly of precious metal.   In 1865 over a million and
a half of the yellow dollars were washed out of that gulch between
Diamond and Virginia City, and one pan yielded one thousand dollars, which fact was wholly without precedent.   Miners were still
at work throughout the gulch and made good wages.   Diamond
City once stood on stilts as the dirt was all dug from under the
buildings by the seekers for gold, but at this time the houses stood
on ground again as the vacancy had been filled in by tailings from
the mines above.   Confederate Gulch derived its name from
a part of that left wing of Price's army which took refuge there
after the Civil War.   That noted "left wing" divided itself and
part went to Montana and part to Idaho, and it did not require
much knowledge of human nature to pick out its members.

Diamond City was the county seat of Meagher County; a
dozen years before its population numbered several thousand,
but in 1878 it had only about three hundred.   The restless surging mass had moved on to other fields for gold and left only a few
late but earnest workers still washing out the sands.   The
Rocky Mountain Husbandman was a spirited sheet published
in the interest of all that the name implies.

Above Diamond City we observed the syphon wonder of boiler
iron pipes.   It led the water down the mountainside hundreds of
feet and up the opposite side nearly an equal distance, from
whence in ribboned ditches it skirted the mountains and poured
down upon the gold diggings wherever needed.

The hotel was a miniature one kept by a jolly Irishman by
the name of Nixon.   It consisted of just three rooms; the sitting
room was about ten by twelve feet and contained a bed and
table and a few chairs.   The kitchen and dining-room was also
a combination about the same size, and the second half story
was one room containing a number of beds.   Adjoining this
building was a long, narrow lean-to used for a store, hotel office,
and post-office.

Pard had been in the office but a few minutes when a man of
dishevelled appearance rushed into the room where I was waiting for supper.   He came to me with both hands outstretched,
as if he would embrace me, and all the time exclaiming how glad
he was to see me; he grabbed both my hands as in a vise and
great tears rolled down his cheeks.   I had not recovered from
my surprise and fear when he explained his joy at seeing one

from his own home, and that *one* the daughter of their dear old family doctor, dear old Doc. Green, who had saved the lives of so many of his family in his earlier days. The sturdy pioneer had been in Diamond City a number of years, and mine was the first home face he had seen since leaving his native place. He said it was "a joy like the meetin' of his own sister or mother whom he left in 1866," and his big Irish face beamed with a smile that would not lessen while we were there, and all he could give was free as air, from his smile to his hospitable board and the con-

The arrival of the stage is the event of the day

tents of his store. That I did not know him made no difference. I knew well enough the section of country near my home town called "The Island" which was wholly an Irish settlement, and I was his "old Doc's gurrel," which was enough to make him glad and happy. When we bade him good-bye he loaded us with such good things as his little store had in stock and the principal edible was dried buffalo and deer meat.

When we left Diamond City we turned from the main road to visit Hell Gate Canyon. It would seem as if that name possessed some magic power over these Rocky Mountain people, for so many defiles and fastnesses are favored with that suggestive title. We could form no idea of the awful grandeur of this place until quite within its portals. High on the right was a dark ominous hole, a seeming ingress to a cave. This was known as the Devil's watch tower. It is said that once a mountain hermit lived within its black shadows. A few shreds of old rope still hung from the dizzy peak above, and from the mouth of the cave protruded a decayed log on which the hermit used to light in his wild descent to his home in the cliff. We could not see why the road should wind its way along so confidently for an impenetrable wall loomed up before us, but the babbling brook called us to search for its source, so we drove on. We were surrounded by high walls and confined in a space thirty yards in width by sixty in length. Another short turn to the left between these towering dykes revealed what before had seemed an unbroken wall now rent from base to summit leaving a narrow gateway but seven feet wide, and the entire space filled with a bridge affording just room to drive through.

We passed into another grotto of equal size ornamented with pines and picturesque needle rocks. The rugged walls were covered with vines and rock-birthed plants robed in richest autumnal garb. There were four of these rocky openings, not exceeding the first in width, and every one leading to new labyrinths of wonders. The left hand wall of the second entrance showed as plainly the face of a man as if chiselled by an artist. The chin rested upon the bridge but the forehead towered high above. Hieroglyphics of some wild race were traced on one of the mountainsides, and holes and endless caves for mountain beasts and birds were found on every side. Often near the summit would be seen full grown pines struggling to reach the snowy lofts, but below all was barren, stern, and forbidding.

It seemed strange how the scene changed into a wooded gulch after leaving the last enclosure. How thankful we were for the far sun to lighten such glories all around us. The more we saw of the finite the more we bowed before the infinite Creator in thankfulness that we lived to see so many wondrous works of His Hand.

Hot Sulphur Springs was reached late in the evening and we hastened to rest until the morning threw the sunlight over our tired dreams and signalled us to rise. The warm fire cheerily blazing made us forget how near winter was again. The hotel was a new one. Brussels carpeting covered the floor; a rich beaver robe was thrown in graceful negligence over a low armed rocker by the window; snowy curtains, a good bed, and writing tables made our room one of great comfort. One hundred guests could readily be accommodated by Mr. Spencer, the genial host from the Sunny South. The dining-room and kitchen were in a separate building in true Southern style.

There were several stores in the town, a post-office, saloon, and many little cottages. A strong odor of sulphur filled the air, and we were led by it to the springs. At least fifteen of these hot springs came boiling from the earth, while within a stone's throw were springs as cold as mountain streams. The hot steam poured from the windows of the plunge and single bathrooms, and after once bathing we had an intense desire to try them again and again.

Many remarkable cures have been effected by these waters, and the resident physician and owner of the springs, Dr. Parberry, is himself a living proof of their cure for rheumatism. Hon. James G. Blaine, had been a half owner of this resort, but was unfortunately induced to dispose of his share to the present owner. There were 120 grains of medicated matter in every gallon of water. A large amount of slimy matter collects in the bottom of these springs, and when this is taken out and dried it looks like thin sheets of sulphur and will burn brilliantly. This famous resort is located between the two forks of Smith River, both branches of which are filled with trout.

Smith Valley is really the home of the shepherd. Ranch after ranch dotted the hillsides and plains, while thousands of sheep were feeding on the rich grass. We saw some fine Cotswold sheep that weighed 300 pounds each. C. W. Cook and brother located in 1873 with 800 Oregon sheep and after five years they had 15,000.

Mr. Cook once had a tenderfoot apply for sheepherding, and as he seemed a likely lad a task was at once assigned him. He was fresh from college and boasted of his athletic ability so much that he refused a horse to care for the flock in his charge, although he was warned to allow no lambs to stray from the fold. Night came on, the bell wether came in leading the woolly flock, but the tall wiry boy came not. Several hours passed, when anxiety for his safety started a searching party to the rescue. Hardly were the ponies saddled when the new boy loomed up in the mellow starlight carrying a jack-rabbit on either arm. Out of breath, tired and footsore, he told of his chase and final capture of the runaway lambs. He was ridiculed and laughed at until Mr. Cook put an end to the persecution by challenging any one of the crew to match the race and bring in another pair of jack-rabbits unharmed and with whole skins, as these had been.

A good story of western pluck is told of Q. O. Proctor, now located about a mile from the springs. Three years previous he did not have a dollar. He, therefore, rented twenty cows;

" It measured upward of nine feet from the nose to the tip of the tail "

from the milk of these cows he began the manufacture of cheese; he was soon enabled to buy the stock and add more; his business steadily increased; in 1878 he had 300 head of cattle and had made 10,000 pounds of cheese which he readily sold for twenty cents a pound. His buildings, vats, presses, fixtures, etc., were of the most improved plans, and he kept everything as neat and clean as a dainty matron's kitchen.

Rich gold, silver, and copper leads had been discovered near the springs and were to be extensively worked as soon as the requisite machinery could be obtained.

This lovely resort is environed with blue mountains that abounded in small as well as royal game. Every sportsman was gladdened by seeing the fine fresh game which he brought back, served *à la mode*, on the table at the hotel.

Dr. Parberry and Pard spent a day in hunting deer. It was on the 19th of September, our first wedding anniversary, and I was on the down end of the teeter board of spirits that day, but when they came home with several saddles of venison hanging on their ponies, I forgave the trespass of the day and joined in congratulations over their success.

A monster mountain lion had recently been killed near the White Sulphur Springs, and our new found friend, Dr. Parberry, presented it to Pard who shipped it at once to Thomas L. Kimball, General Manager of the Union Pacific road, where it was to be mounted and kept at the headquarters of the company. This royal beast is one of the largest of its species ever shot in Montana. Its weight was 312 pounds, and carefully skinned and stuffed it measured upwards of nine feet from the nose to the tip of the tail. It is a trophy of the lion tribe that can nowhere be excelled in America.

White Sulphur Springs has never had a railroad intrude into its secluded eyrie, but has been reached up to the present time by the tri-weekly stage from Helena, but a $2,000,000 syndicate has now begun operations to open up the medicinal waters to the world and make it the most popular resort in America. Work is being pushed on a rail line to make it accessible as soon as the Grand Hotel can be completed. It is to have a line from Dorsey on the new Milwaukee route, and the Helena Glendive cut-off of the Northern Pacific will also go to this famous resort. The sleeping populace of White Sulphur Springs has awakened to magical energy and excitement over this crowning reward for their patient waiting of a third of a century.

CHAPTER X

THE VALLEY OF THE WILD ROSE, DEER LODGE, AND MISSOULA

A SEPTEMBER ride from Helena to Deer Lodge and on to Missoula in the late '70's was a trip that idealized stage travel and made one forget the lack of civilization in a labyrinth of wild roses and clear running waters.

The old Concord coach was loaded inside and out and still there were some gloomy and disappointed ones unable to find a place to even hang on as the crack of the whip spurred the fiery bronchos into an irregular wild plunge and a dash through the streets out of the city to the great Overland road westward.

It is always an interesting part of travel to settle back in one's own corner and study the faces of the fellow passengers. It matters little whether it be on a train, a steamer, or a stagecoach, there is generally variety enough to make the effort entertaining.

The morning load was especially engaging. There was one woman with a young babe going to join her husband who had found a new home for them in this far-away country. Her bags and baskets took the room of two people and were piled on the laps of any who would hold them. There was another woman going with her brother to file a homestead on virgin lands, and still a third woman en route from Missouri to visit an uncle a hundred miles beyond Missoula, where thirty miles of the way was still only a trail.

She was going to revolutionize some things. She did not understand why people out there did not say "road" instead of "trail" and "horse" for "cayuse" and "jacks" for "mules," etc. She was quite chagrined to learn that a trail was not a road, a cayuse was not an American horse, and the poor little jack was a jack or burro and not a mule at all.

People who come West to teach ignorant people usually find that they bring more ignorance with them than they are able to dispel. Every part of a country has conditions of its own requiring words and expressions that are peculiar to itself, and inseparable from the locality where used.

In later experiences we found more real ignorance in the very heart of Boston than was ever met with on the frontier. People living in such far-away places are expected to be lacking in ways of the world, but we seldom found them so, and the dailies of San Francisco and the old Salt Lake *Tribune* were found with half a dozen or more popular magazines in many cabins. The people were posted on the topics of the day to wondrous wide extent and new arrivals were quizzed with a zeal unknown to those more favored with privileges to learn. There were exceptions it is true, but those seeking knowledge were in the majority.

The old McBurney House of Deer Lodge, kept by Aylesworth & McFarland, was a neat two-story brick house, with the Stars and Stripes ever floating above it, proving the loyalty and love of the country's flag by the genial proprietors of this hostelry.

It was a good rest to crawl out of the coach in which we had been so densely wedged and stretch our cramped muscles and take a stroll about town before enjoying a good supper. Then the load was made up again for an all night ride. Some of the passengers had reached the end of their journey, making less discomfort for those who must move on, but there were a couple of new ones.

A night in an overcrowded coach is never a joy to be anticipated, but it is a deal of discomfort to be avoided. Just as one loses himself in a moment's drowsiness the wheels either fall into a chuck-hole that will send one pawing air for something to grapple, or if the wheels strike a rock in the roadway it will stagger the whole coach and give such a lurching as will throw one's head nearly off the shoulders. Then some one gets cramps and every one must readjust a position to accommodate the peculiarity of that knotting muscle. As the night progresses and nearly every one is overcome with the stupor of fatigue some one becomes reminiscent and wants to tell a life history that should have been closed before that trip began. No one wants to hear it, yet no one has the courage or discourtesy to say so, and the narrator croons on until he has added to the record all the chestnut stories of a tenderfoot, and he himself has fallen to the foot of the ladder as an entertainer. We had one such who also related such thrilling Indian tales of massacres in that very canyon through which we were passing, that we fully expected some revenge to be taken on our own stage load of people by the watchful Indians.

One of the many fords

But mornings have a way of coming around about once in so often and so it came again at last, shedding a rich glow over the mountain tops and revealing through the dissolving night the beauteous landscape along some of the head waters of the Columbia River.

From Deer Lodge to Missoula we forded the Deer Lodge River seven times and crossed it twice on bridges. It was a veritable Lovers' Lane leading through bowers of wild roses; oftentimes the rose bushes arched over the stage road and joined their blooms in a wealth of beauty and untrammelled luxuriance, filling the air with their fragrance and our hearts with admiration and joy. It was an expanse of earth set apart for wild growth, not only of flowers but of wild berries and wild animals.

" That damn thing ahead of us is a bear "

From the seat with the driver there were views of long avenues ahead and most too often the glinting water in the distance betokened another fording of the river. Though clear as crystal it was deep and swift and when the leaders of our four-horse team reluctantly made the leap down the bank it always sent creepers up my spine. The water grew deeper at every crossing from the many lateral feeders of canyon springs, and my breath stopped and choked just a little higher in the throat, as I leaned forward with contracted muscles as if it helped the horses drag the burden over the rocky river bed.

Grand old pine trees, tall and stately, were gathered in forests on either side, with the ground beneath free of underbrush except for the rose and berry bushes in the more sunny openings near the streams. It was like one grand, continuous park, with the half dead pines covered with an inch of green moss, hiding all marks of death's decay.

A dark moving object ahead of us in the open roadway suddenly appeared in full view and the jehu pulled in the reins to get a steady look ahead. Then he exclaimed with a strong oath that "that damn thing ahead of us is a bear." He called to the passengers to get their shooting irons ready for there might be trouble ahead. Those inside thought of the dreaded Indian, and were greatly relieved to know it was only a bear that caused the call to arms. The horses reared and plunged from instinctive fear and we gained only a little on the king of the American wilds.

The driver lashed the poor brutes into a chase until there was grave fear that they would wheel suddenly backward and cause a serious accident. But the bear reached the river first, and by the time the stage reached the ford old Bruin was lifting his head out of the water away down on the opposite bank, where he emerged and shook his shaggy coat and scrambled into the brush.

It was the only spirited event of the trip, and early in the afternoon we were in the great Montana garden of the Hell Gate River. It seemed a curious name to give to such a beautiful stream, but it comes from the black and intricate passage through the rocky pass of the same name near Missoula.

Missoula was not of enough importance to have a place on the map, but it was a productive section that has since made itself known to the world. Peaches, pears, and melons—my, how good they were after a long famine of such luxuries!

Here Miss Libban met her uncle, who was overjoyed to see her, and at once began bestowing gifts upon her. He kept up a continuous flow of questions regarding her wants and wishes as he explained the necessary trip on horseback. The best horse he could buy was there with a good saddle, and some one engaged to make a riding habit while she rested a day or two from her journey. He brought a supply of sweets and fruits, and every time he showed his genial face he wanted to buy a new hat, a new dress, or gloves, or something, and so it was until they were started off. He was a man well known in Missoula, and one whose chief delight was in doing gracious things to make others happy. His generosity toward his niece was not a spasm of goodness, but as his friends said, "It was always his way." He was a man of wealth and spent it freely when he thought he could do good. His niece was the first relative whom he had seen in many years, and the dear old man was beside himself with joy.

The drives about Missoula were of intense interest because of nature's repose being yet undisturbed. The town was indeed a frontier village with only a few hundred people, and old French Town was made up of Indians on the alert for a new-comer who might be a prospective buyer of buffalo robes or other pelts which they had in stock.

French Town was but a few miles out from Missoula and it was near there that I went right into an Indian camp. It had seemed to me that filth and bad ways of living reached the limit of human ignorance at some of the stage stations, but this Indian camp was a prize winner. In Mexico and Italy it is a common sight to see friends doing the "work of love" in picking creepers from each others' heads and throwing them out without taking the trouble to kill them. But these Indians were not so wasteful, and as fast as the hand could work it plied between the head and the mouth, and the fat luscious creepers were eaten with a relish of true appreciation. We carried away for a paltry four dollars as fine a buffalo robe as ever came to market. It was nearly black, fine, silky, and curly, such as we see no more, but it was kept in the open air and combed and brushed and fumigated for a week before allowing it in close contact.

The little incidents from the lives of the people who have so courageously built up a remote settlement were always most interesting to me, and I was ever eager to listen to the strange experiences.

The editor of the *Missoulian*, which by the way was as creditable a sheet as could be published without dispatches, was driving about town with us one day when he called our attention to an attractive little vine-covered cottage and to a less pretentious one close by. He said, "There's romance for you under those roofs; one is rose-clad on the outside, and the other is rose-clad on the inside. This man with the vines had started a correspondence with a girl back East, and the letters must have been pretty good on both sides, for she decided to come out here and marry him, and he, therefore, sent her the money to defray her expenses. He built his house with all possible speed, but when the time came near to drive to Fort Benton to meet her his house was not finished, so he bought a team and carriage and sent a friend of his after her while he remained to garnish and trim and make ready the new home. It was three hundred miles to Fort Benton from Missoula, and the anxious lover counted the days and worked with a will.

"The messenger was on hand when the old river boat came steaming to the Fort Benton landing bearing its precious charge, who was soon singled out from the small number of passengers. He explained to her how glad he was that she had come, in fact he was so pleased with her that he forgot to say that he was not her lover but only a messenger to carry her to her new home. She had never seen her lover and why need she know that he was not the man. He went on with his own lovemaking with such good results that they were married before they left Fort Benton, and now they live out there with the 'clingin' vine' inside not a stone's throw away from the man whose wife she was to be. The philosophic bachelor thinks he was mighty lucky to get his team back. He keeps an immaculate house, and the girl may sometime repent at leisure her hasty marriage."

CHAPTER XI

ITTER Root Valley, like Hell Gate Valley, is one of the garden spots in Montana. Its name comes from the bitter roots that grow abundantly there and were much sought by the Indians for medicinal purposes and for concocting drinks.

The river of the same name is the purest, clearest stream we had yet found. It flowed swiftly and magnified its rocky bed so that at a depth of four or five feet the stones were more clearly seen than the ones on the bank. Trout were plenty, and so large that our angler wiggled about and threatened to hold up the coach while he landed some of the speckled beauties. Weeping willows hung low over the waters and down the wooded banks under the sheltering branches were many trails of wild animals in search of water.

Leaving Missoula we crossed the Hell Gate River, then mounted to the bench land, losing sight quickly of the little town in the basin. Two miles out we passed the military barracks and then speeded on up the valley. To one raised in the Mississippi Valley it was a funny thing to say *up* south and *down* north. The valley varies from six to ten miles in width and is sixty miles in length. The "jerky" stage made tri-weekly trips carrying mail and other commodities and an occasional passenger. It was expected soon to have the road opened to Bannock City and then regular freight traffic would open up and give the farmers a choice of two ways to ship out their products.

This valley was indeed a wheatfield and orchard. One farmer had 106 bushels of wheat from one and three fourths acres of land. Another had 820 pounds of tobacco from one

eighth of an acre. Still another served us with fresh ripe strawberries. We could scarcely believe our eyes when we saw the
bed from which they were produced. But there were the berries
in spite of the heavy frosts which had nightly occurred for some
time. The owner informed us that the berries were the richest
in November, although the vines bore fruit from early summer.

Copyright by Lee Moorhouse, Pendleton, Oregon

"On the opposite shore the jailers' tepees were pitched"

He also had the early varieties in abundance. This fact reminds me that a Mr. Curtis, of Helena, raised 15,000 quarts of
strawberries the summer of 1877, which he sold for fifty cents a
quart.

We drove off the main road to shake the limb of a stalwart
tree to which Peter Matt was hung for horse-stealing by the
Montana Vigilantes. It meant another star in the crown of
Colonel Sanders in ridding the country of criminal and lawless
control.

In crossing one of the tributaries of the Bitter Root River
called Lo-Lo we found the water impeded by a network of willow slips that were buried in the bed of the river and rose about
a foot above the water's surface. This proved to be a trap made

by the Indians for catching fish, and the trap in which the little fellows were struggling for freedom was quite a prominent feature as well as an ingenious puzzle.   On the opposite shore the jailers' tepees were pitched, and the keepers watched with fiendish delight the vain efforts of their finny prisoners to escape.   But the strange appearance of the Indians frightened our horses and made them canter off at a lively speed.   I really believe horses are afraid of Indians because of the odor of wild animals about them rather than the appearance of the Indians themselves.

Along the route we conversed with one Mrs. Carlton who had seven little children.   She did her own housework and sewing, took care of her children, made forty pounds of butter per week, and sold it for fifty cents per pound; she also cared for two hundred fine Brahma chickens, and helped to milk twenty-five cows.   Mr. Carlton was a steady, industrious ranchman and stock-raiser. The first question that always entered my mind when I saw such people was: How came you here?   But it was nearly always the desire for wealth and it was not uncommon to learn that the people had lived where we found them for several years, and they were well, healthy, and happy.

We crossed the river and rode for a short distance along the side of the valley when the home of E. W. Bass was pointed out to us.   Mr. Bass and his brother came from Missouri without means and secured a homestead from which they had become the richest men in the valley.   The mountains rose high on three sides of the home as if to shield the dwelling from the storm-king or other dangers which might beseige it.   Tall cottonwoods followed the walk outside the tidy picket fence, and over the arched gateway a thrifty ivy had coiled in graceful confusion.   The gravelled walk leading to the large two story house was bordered with trellised vines and roses.   To the left, on a high pedestal, stood a solid granite ball as symmetrical as if chiselled by an artist.   The ball weighed ninety pounds and was about fourteen inches in diameter.   It was found in a canyon near the premises in a whirlpool of water, where it had been ground to its perfect form.   To the right a pair of elk horns were posed as if still in proud defiance of the hunter's skill. Suspended from a staunch limb of an old elm tree a large swing made a tempting place to enjoy the shade and indulge in day dreams, or read the day dreams of others.   Through the arbor, covered with dense foliage, the path led to the flower garden where almost every variety of flowers known to grow in the country were found. The beds were bordered with verbenas of every shade; rich velvety pansies with their upturned faces gave a mute appeal for approval, while roses, geraniums, and mignonette filled the air with their sweet fragrance. Of course, special care had been used to keep that thieving Jack Frost from too early robbing them of their beauty. A clear stream went singing through the lawn and formed a picturesque waterfall that gave an effect that was simply magical.

The veranda was inviting, with its easy chairs and wood-bine shade, but we passed on indoors where conditions were equally charming. The piano stood open in the parlor. The pet cat was quietly sleeping on a wolf rug before the grate dreaming of cold winter's comforts. A sewing machine, scroll saw, more flowers, choice pictures, and a rich profusion of books, papers and popular magazines were still further emblems of the education and refinement of the occupants. The large bird cage with its happy family was quite an amusing novelty. It contained several gay canaries, with a southern redbird in proud command, which seemed to understand his responsible position, and chattered away as if the yellow songsters were contemplating disobedience to his orders. The storeroom was filled with rich preserves and jellies tempting to behold, the milkroom with pans of milk and thick cream, and the churn was running by a water-power that kept the dairy cool and sweet.

On every hand were tokens of the conveniences and comforts of a happy home that we did not expect to find in a valley seven hundred or more miles from the nearest railroad. I still have a rose and a few verbenas that were picked on that September day of 1878, holding much of their original coloring. The color was preserved by bleaching them in sulphur fumes before they were pressed, then when they were exposed to the air again and placed under a glass in a frame their natural color returned and remained.

Across the road the fruit trees were braced to sustain their loads of apples, pears, and plums, and we heartily enjoyed some luscious melons. There were vegetables to be taken to the Territorial Fair at Helena: solid potatoes that weighed two pounds apiece, and a squash that weighed over a hundred pounds.

We reluctantly turned from this little paradise, with its hospitable inhabitants, and continued the journey through that ever surprising valley.

Thirty miles from Missoula was old Fort Owen, built in 1850 in peculiar shape and irregular enough to command a view of all surroundings. The low walls massively built of stone were dotted on all sides with rifle holes. Indians would give such retreats a wide berth for the advantage was with the man on the inside, and an Indian never fights unless he has the best of his adversary. A family occupied a portion of the ruins and they

"We roamed among them for a while and found them filthy and indolent in the extreme"

looked more like prisoners peering out from behind the great walls than like free people. Near the fort was an old mill erected in 1851 by Father McValley, who made his own burrs and run them by hand power with only a capacity of one and a half bushels per hour.

A mile or two beyond was the town of Stevensville with but a few stores and a hotel and post-office. It was here that an Indian Mission was located in 1847. The priest said the Indians were very good while at the Mission, but when they returned from a hunt they had everything to learn over, even their prayers. About six hundred Flathead "non-treaties" were established in their tepees there, under the direction of Chief Shiloh. They were unwilling to give up the valley and had thus far refused any treaty offered them by our Government. Land was surveyed again in 1878 and offered them, but they would not take it. We roamed among them for a while and found them filthy and indolent in the extreme. I addressed an old squaw who hung her head almost to the ground and remained in that position, making stealthy signs to a papoose until another squaw appeared. They wore scarcely any clothing. To live a prisoner among such people would be intolerable; yet they claim that their tribe never killed a white man.

The Bannock war of 1878, which had caused our delay in crossing Idaho, was not alone a Bannock war, but it was a final attempt to unite all the warlike Indians and to totally annihilate every man, woman, and child of the white race on the Overland Route through to the coast. It was only by strategic and united work of the whites and some friendly Indians that the worst massacre of the age was averted.

A few miles beyond Stevensville was Fort Skedaddle, built of sod the summer before when an invasion by the Nez Percés was hourly expected, and men, women, and children were promiscuously huddled within the enclosure. It was a most appropriate name, for the people of the valley skedaddled to it in a hurry. When that band did pass up the valley they were two weeks in making the trip, but their chief said he would kill the first warrior who committed a depredation on life or property, so nothing was harmed.

All along our drive rich fields of grain were being cut, stacked, or threshed. Winter wheat was equally as great a success as spring wheat. Oats were yielding from sixty to eighty-five bushels per acre. Every one was charmed with this quiet, productive valley, and it was the first place in the Rocky Mountains where we had heard the cheery voice of the meadow lark. We stopped for the night at the upper end of the valley in just the neatest bachelor quarters you can imagine. He bade us welcome if we could live as he did and we were delighted. We were not expected nor did he usually keep travellers, but the room assigned us was in perfect order, and the snowy bed and gracefully draped curtains lent a bewitching charm to the scene. He declined all offers of assistance in preparing the evening meal, but soon spread before us a sumptuous repast that excelled many a fairer hand. He was as happy as a lord and wanted to live five hundred years just as he was, and then die on the spot. His living-room adjoined his little store, and was attractive for its orderly arrangement and neatness.

With all his tidy housekeeping and capability in his own kitchen Peter M'Quirk was not at all effeminate, but a manly fellow of fine mind; a knightly gentleman of education, but a voluntary recluse, who had his own views of life and his own reasons for his bachelorhood.

As darkness settled around us and the stars crept slowly out, we were called to witness a grand sight. Away over on the mountainside some stray Indian had set fire to the mountain grass. The red blaze ran in crazy lines from base to summit, now around, then over and across, silently eating away the verdure for the year. Indians say it only makes the grass richer another year. The sight beggared description. For miles and miles the bright glare was followed over the brow of mountains beyond, and as we were watching the beautiful lights, through the mazy curtains, from our pillows, our tired eyes closed in sleep, while our spirits chased on over the hills in the fitful glow, and mingled fires and flowers and bachelors and homey scenes in orchards and dusty highways in a strangely conglomerated dream until a new day dawned.

Seemingly isolated as this valley was it has become almost an empire within itself. Many notable Eastern people have built fine summer homes among the orchards and gardens of plenty. Marcus Daly erected a fine hotel in mid-valley, a few years ago, which is now being replaced by a $300,000 structure and equipment for an all-year-round resort.

Missoula was a stage drive of thirty hours from Helena, and then it was another long day's drive to the head of Bitter Root Valley. From Missoula we had hoped to go on through the mountains to Spokane Falls, which was only two hundred miles to the west, but the country that lay between was still an unopened wilderness, making it necessary to go back through southern Idaho and make a circuit of 1500 miles by stage via Walla Walla.

CHAPTER XII

TO FORT BENTON AND GREAT FALLS OF THE MISSOURI

 IT is one hundred and fifty miles from Helena to old Fort Benton, and owing to competing stage lines the through fare was but eight dollars. Of course, we adhered to the Salisbury line, which had tendered us so many favors, and from which nothing but a railroad could divorce us.

We left Helena early in the morning and spent the forenoon in passing through the noted Prickly Pear Canyon. The rich shades of autumn were constantly adding fresh attractions to the surrounding country, and nothing else could so grandly illumine the general landscape. Eighteen miles of this canyon road was built at a cost of $50,000, and in early days the toll was not less than eight dollars for single teams. But the cost had gradually grown less until it had reached the nominal sum of twenty-five cents. The picturesque Prickly Pear River winds around in many curves as it rushes in its mad course down this mountain hallway.

The "Shreckhorn" of the Rockies towered high and we fancied we could hear echoes of the Indian's fiendish yell reverberating from peak to peak of the craggy range. The rocky formation of slate made a lovely gray background for the deep scarlet and brown vines and mosses that filled every crevice. Standing out clear and bold was one solitary mountain of limestone. It threw up its hoary head in stately independence of its darker companions, and had no kindred for many miles.

Often there was scarcely room for the coach to pass between the abrupt wall on one side and the precipitous descent to the river upon the other. Every little while I held my breath and shut my eyes, fearing the next instant we would be hurled below, then anon the road would widen and with easy heart I gazed in ardent admiration on the water-chiselled rocks. Midway in the canyon was a park just large enough for a home-like ranch where the ranchman said he raised a thousand bushels of potatoes from two acres of land, and his oat yield was eighty-five bushels per acre.

Sun River Valley, midway between Helena and Fort Benton, is a large area taking in extensive grazing lands and hay lands along the river's winding way, and is one of the finest stock-raising sections of Montana. The stage made its usual

A round-up on Sun River

stop for mail and passengers at the village of Sun River. The night was a bitterly cold one, and being the only passengers, the thoughtful driver had showed us how to fold back some of the seats and make a fairly comfortable bed with blankets, buffalo robes, and cushions, on the bottom of the coach.

We were just fairly settled to the lumbering jolts, and drowsily lapsing into a sense of forgetfulness, when there was a tugging at the straps of the canvas door, and a cheery voice called out to know if there was room for another passenger inside. The question was too graciously asked to receive a rough answer, and with as gentle response as possible we resumed the sitting posture, and had seats properly adjusted that others might be accommodated.

There was but one newcomer, however. The man with the cheery voice was none other than Mr. Robert Vaughn, one of the cattle kings of Montana, who proved an interesting companion and gave much information about the great business in which he was engaged. Before we parted he made the offer of caring for as many head of stock as we would buy, and his pay would be one half the increase. We figured out a fortune in an incredibly short time, but just lacked the means to buy the first herd to start on, a circumstance that has kept many a man from making a fortune.

Twenty-five miles south of Benton the Highwood Mountain streams are alive with trout. It is called the happy fishing grounds of the north; no sooner does the hook drop under the

Ruins of Fort Benton at the oldest town in the State

surface than it is eagerly sought by the hungry fish. The twenty-four hours spent there were delightful.

Until 1850 Fort Benton was called Fort Lewis. The first steamer which succeeded in reaching Benton was the *Chippewa*, in June, 1859. The old fort was all there was of Benton at that time, and it was only twelve years since it had been deemed safe for a white man to be seen outside the old stone walls. One long business street now faced the levee upon which tons and tons of freight stood waiting to be shipped inland to numerous points throughout the Territory. The river winds as crookedly as ever between its rocky banks and on through an open meadow land of golden pasturage. No grain or produce of any kind was raised around this head of navigation. Now and then a timid tree that had been brought from its far-away home, tried to live, but it made feeble success.

The old fort which was a great object of interest was built as early as 1836, and was in a dilapidated condition. A miniature buffalo poised on the tip of a weather-vane was literally riddled with bullets. We halted in the court and looked around at its tumble-down apartments. The birthplace of Miss Nellie Clark was pointed out as being one of the brightest rooms. Miss Nellie was a half-breed, but since early childhood she had received kindnesses from all who knew her. She had been a thorough student in Eastern colleges, and was then a respected teacher in the Helena public school. She was playing chess at a ranch one day with her father, when they were attacked by the Indians and she saw her father and brother shot down by her mother's people. She often said it was a mistake to take her from her mother's people and educate her, for she was so often made to feel the bitterness of being but half white that there were times when she could scarcely endure and live.

The town of Benton is the oldest in the State. The old court-house and schoolhouse were under one roof, and wore a forbidding exterior. So little care was taken of the buildings a few years since that the cows walked in one stormy night and devoured many valuable papers. A new brick schoolhouse was being built on the little hill overlooking the river, in which apartments were reserved for court sessions.

It is strange how many people there were in this wide western country. From Fort Benton one might travel four hundred miles north, away in the British possessions, and every night find a white man's cabin with a welcome to a night's rest. A day's travel may not seem near to a neighbor, but there was little that could make the heart more glad than curling smoke from a cabin looming on the horizon at the close of a toilsome day without having a living thing in sight.

The Stars and Stripes floated in the breeze over the U. S. Custom-House. All bonded goods passed through the hands of the agent at Benton and were examined before going farther. Benton had then about six hundred inhabitants, but the number was rapidly increasing. Two years before there were not more than twenty white ladies in the town, but in '78 they numbered seventy. This little village had sent $600 to the suffering South during the cholera epidemic which was an average of one dollar for every man, woman, and child in the corporation.

We went aboard the steamer *MacLeod*, whose freight was being carried ashore, and where preparations for a new departure were being made. The captain hoped to make two trips from Bismarck to Benton that fall before the river froze over. It was a charming ride to the Teton River, six miles west of Benton, and there was afforded a glimpse of the Bear Paw Mountains, where during the gold excitement and the stampede the previous spring a number of miners were killed by Indians. These gold diggings, however, were on the Indian Reservation, and the intruders must have expected trouble. No man, whatsoever his color, will allow his home to be pillaged without resenting the intrusion. There is a wild fascination hanging over a miner's life, and he will follow the lead of the glimmering metal into anyone's domain and face any danger.

We were indebted to the princely generosity of Benton's business king, William H. Todd, for many courtesies while we were in Benton, and for a delightful trip to the Missouri Falls. Mrs. Todd came a pioneer from a home of southern luxury. She had a merry way of telling of her trials, as if they were of no moment, yet which many would recognize as monumental. She had never made a bed, never built a kitchen fire, or been taught any of the ways of housekeeping or cooking, but, she added, with a merry laugh, "I had one prize that I guarded very carefully, and that was a recipe for making coffee." She said she learned all she knew about housekeeping from her husband, who had been a most indulgent and successful teacher, and she had indeed become a perfect little matron.

Mr. and Mrs. Todd accompanied us on the novel excursion to the Great Falls of the Missouri, and provided everything necessary for convenience and comfort in camp, and ample protection against storms. We left Benton about three o'clock in the afternoon, leaving our best wishes for its prosperity, and sincerely congratulating the travelling public on the prospect of a new brick hotel, which would afford better accommodations than were possible to obtain then.

We drove back on the Helena stage road about twenty-eight miles to the home of a rancher and stockman named Kelly. It was the only house within twenty-five miles in any direction, and his genial, wholesouled nature gave every one such a welcome that it was helpful to forget the distance to any other place, and especially to one's own far-away home.

We spent the night at the Kelly Cold Spring ranch, and during the early evening sat out of doors, looked over the topography of the country, and gathered directions for the drive to the falls the following day. A little lull came in the conversation, and in the quiet moment a beautiful black and white animal came running around the corner of the house; whether it

Street scene along Missouri River at Fort Benton

was a young puppy or a big cat could not be told in the dim light, but I was about to try to pick it up in my arms, when I heard a deep stentorian tone of command from somewhere not to move a muscle.

The animal ran around under our chairs and about our feet with the greatest freedom. It seemed as if the cold chills running down my back would freeze me. When it scampered away, we made a rush for the door, and every one expressed gratitude at his escape, and laughed to think how near we came to being ostracized from polite society. Mr. Kelly said those animals were very numerous, but by being careful not to scare them they were spared annoyance.

I have had Indian relics from which the Indian scent could not be eliminated, but that animal was something that would give a stronger scent than the Indian smoke.

We started early in the morning, with instructions how to cut across that trackless waste of tall grass amid the coulées of the Missouri River to the Great Falls. It was the intention to make the trip and return that night. There was no wagon road or trail to follow, but Mr. Kelly said we could not miss the way. There are four falls within ten or twelve miles: the Great Falls, ninety feet high; the Crooked Falls, nineteen feet high, while the Rainbow Falls gracefully glide over a curve and down a perpendicular of fifty feet, and still farther up the

Indians of the upper Missouri

river arc falls of twenty-six feet. The Great Falls were but fourteen miles from Mr. Kelly's, as the crow flies, but we did not hit that trail. The country was dotted with little silvery lakes, and we travelled among them for hours but found no falls. The river banks were a succession of precipices and deep coulées which we followed again and again without success. We did, however, find a trail that carried us ten miles out of the way and brought us at last to see all the other falls before the great ones.

We found ourselves once at the mouth of Sun River, and three miles below we saw the Black Eagle Falls. On an island just below them stands an old tree, containing an historic eagle's nest from which the falls are named. Between these and the

Rainbow Falls is a spring remarkable for being the largest ever known. It boils up underneath the rocks and has a volume equal to the Sun River, which at its mouth is one hundred and thirty-five yards wide, with an average depth of four feet. The spring water is perfectly clear, and of a bluish tint. Even after it falls into the Missouri in full, deep cascades it retains its original purity for more than half a mile, when it is at last lost in the vast volume of the river's murky flood.

The Rainbow Falls excited intense admiration; it made a semicircle across the entire stream three hundred yards wide, in one unbroken sheet of foam, while the sunshine glistened through the spray in an intoxicating display of rainbow colorings. Only a hundred rods below the Rainbow Falls we came upon the Crooked Falls, nineteen feet perpendicular, the whole face of which is nearly a mile in length. It forms almost a circle, and then the precipice over which the water leaps suddenly turns at an obtuse angle to the right.

Thinking that we would return to these falls and see them again the next day we decided to go on six miles below and camp at the Great Falls. But alas for human hopes! We rode many weary miles and could not even hear the falls. Frequently Pard would sprint down a coulée, where we could not drive, to listen for the roar that did not roar. Once he ran into a whole college of rattlesnakes sunning themselves on the warm hillside; he did not see them until, in his haste, he sent one spinning down the hill, then he said there were a million rattlers in motion quicker than he could think. In fighting his way out he killed two or three of them, but fearing we would get out of the carriage he called excitedly that the falls were not there. We kept on long after the stars came out to light our way, when suddenly the horses stopped with a sudden backward motion that nearly threw us from the carriage. We had driven up to the very brink of a deep gorge: another step forward and we would have been dashed to the bottom. It was impossible to go on, and just as impossible to go back. If we were not lost our wigwam surely was lost, and no wood or water, and but little grass was within our reach. Fortunately we had picked up a long tepee pole in our wanderings, which we intended to use for an improvised tent, and we had a little water left in the jug that had been filled from the river above. Mrs. Todd never had such an unquenchable thirst as she had that day when water was unobtainable, and there was not much of it left in the jug.

We had brought only food enough for a couple of lunches, and as we now camped on the little hillock, we knew we must be very frugal for this was our second meal. We were likely to be in sore need before we found our way out to the ranch again, for lost we were good and plenty, and every one had a story to tell about such adventures, and how sustenance had been sought from trees and shrubs. One told how a Montana lady had made a rattlesnake pie, another said soldiers in old Mexico subsisted entirely on snake meat, and so we babbled on while we made a little fire with the tepee pole, and had a cup of hot lemonade with our lunch. We fastened a canvas cover to the wagon wheels, and with our blankets and robes we made a fairly warm place to sleep. During the night a little mouse sought our shelter and a few bugs. When they were safely under cover and engaged in a running race across our heads and hiding in our ears we heard the rain coming down pit-a-pat, and that seemed, indeed, a final stroke of bad luck. But the good morning brought us a clear, bright sky, and we hurried away from the dark depths where we would have been hurled had we attempted to go the few steps beyond our camping ground. We hoped to take our breakfast at the falls, but we travelled on until one o'clock before we found them. It was the easiest thing in the world to miss them, for they were between two bends of the river, and at least five hundred feet below the cliffs from which we finally spied them.

What a grand and glorious sight to see far out in that untamed land. The horses were unharnessed and fastened with lariats, and we climbed down the steep mountainside to revel in the full glory of the dashing foam. We spent hours in joyous admiration, in sketching and fishing, and climbing among the rocks and on the Devil's card table. This table is one flat rock about fifteen feet square and poised on a single pedestal scarcely a foot in diameter.

Immediately below this raging cataract is a noble cliff, water washed and worn, and which in high water stands out clearly as an island. In low water the river flows around it, making a sharp turn to the left, and at that season we were enabled to climb upon it as well as under it. In the latter place we found the ashes of a camp fire and some hairpins, which showed that other parties had been equally curious to visit this wonderful sight 4,000 miles from the sea by the river route.

The Great Falls extend only half way across the river, the other half is a series of cascades and rapids that take a final leap of twenty or more feet to the boiling chasm in the river bed. There is no foothold for man or beast along the stone walls on either side of this great aquatic display.

The scenery was so enchanting and the hour so late that it was deemed wise to remain all night on the bluff above, where we had left our horses, and make an early start in the morning for the Kelly ranch, hoping to find it with much less trouble than we had found the falls. We pulled ourselves up the steep slope by clinging to grass roots and shrubs and digging our heels and toes into the hard soil.

We were illy prepared for the surprise awaiting us in our camp. As soon as the men lifted their heads above the ravine their eyes went out to the place where the horses had been made fast, but they were not there. Not a shadow or trace of them was to be found; even the trail was lost in the hard dry grass. One was gone without his lariat, and the other one had taken his lariat along. How such a thing could happen without human aid was a mystery. Were Indians about, ready to pounce down upon us, were they bandits, or simply some one playing a joke on us? We had seen no one, not even a fresh trail in all our two days' pilgrimage, and yet the affair looked serious.

The gentlemen started immediately in pursuit. We did not have time to implore one of them to remain with us before they were out of sight. One of them had a gun, and the other a butcher knife that he had taken below to dress fish if he were fortunate enough to catch any. Mrs. Todd and I hunted up the hatchet and horsewhip and sat down on a robe to wait—two more forlorn individuals would be hard to find. We had some reason to think the horses were stolen as one lariat was untied from the animal's neck. Of course, we thought of Indians, half-breeds, Mexicans, and horse thieves all in no time, expecting one or more to appear every instant. We kept close to the brink of the precipice, and said we would jump over the cliff into the river rather than be taken prisoners by the Indians.

Our men met beyond a distant hill and after consultation Mr. Todd decided to go on until he found the horses or a ranch, and Pard should return to camp. All night long Mr. Todd wandered on his weary way while we sat on the bank feeding the camp fire to its utmost to guide him if he returned. The awful thunder of the roaring waters seemed like a field of heavy artillery; the weird light of the late moon on the white foam rendered it sublime, while the contrast of the black shadows in rocky outline caused feelings of awe indescribable and never to be forgotten. One lone sentinel at last was left to patrol the camp and to keep up a cheery blaze until day dawned and yet Mr. Todd did

Courtesy of Northern Pacific Railway Co.
Great Falls of the Missouri

not return. The moon was lost behind dark clouds and toward morning a light snow fell. Day came cold and damp and our condition was hourly growing more serious. All the forenoon we wandered about picking up fagots of wood and bits of dried grass that we might keep up our signal smoke for a rescuing party. Mrs. Todd exhibited most remarkable composure, and constantly expressed her belief that "William" was such a wonderful pioneer that he would surely bring our own horses or bring help. At noon we descended to the river to try our luck again at fishing. We had to get fish or starve.

Professor Hayden says in his famous reports on that section that no trout were ever caught below those falls. But it was not a case of what had or had not been done. The larder had been reduced to salt and tea and we just must catch a trout or go hungry. There was already a feeling of having missed several meals, and just plain salt did not sound appetizing. Once down at the water's edge the lines were thrown repeatedly and all known charms were used to tempt the wary tribe, and at last Pard gave a glad shout and landed a two pound trout. It was surely a special Providence; at least it was so considered, and we hurried up to camp loading ourselves with every stick of driftwood or rotten burnable stuff that could be found on the way.

There were no signs below of the return of the wanderer, and when we had again scaled that five hundred feet and saw no evidence of his coming, my heart ached for the courageous little wife who would not weaken in her belief that "William" was all right and would soon come.

The trout was browning over the tiny fire, and the tea was just ready when horses and riders were silhouetted against the sky on a distant cliff rapidly approaching. After a moment of breathless anxiety and keen survey the glad cry of recognition burst from every throat. Here came our gallant knight back to his lady love, bringing two horses and food, and with him came the same Robert Vaughn who had wakened our midnight slumbers to share the stage at Sun River. How glad we were that we had not been petulant or rude on that night when he wanted a warmer corner than the outside seat with the stage driver. He had taken his team out of the work, and at once gave the succor which Mr. Todd solicited.

Mr. Todd had walked forty miles since he had left us, not knowing where he was, but trying to follow a general guidance of the distant mountains. At night during the snow-storm he did not dare to stop. Daylight revealed how he walked round and round in a circle which was traced in the snow, but daylight had also set him right again and he trudged wearily on until he reached the Sun River ranch, where after a hasty meal they hurried to our relief. They also brought bread and bacon which was hastily added to our fish and tea, and made us a banquet that every one will remember to the end of time.

Mr. Vaughn is another example of western energy and per-

10

severance. He went to Sun River only eight years previous to this story with nothing he could call his own but his determination to win. From an employee he soon became the employer, then came his own herds of cattle and fine horses, until the world's abundance was his. To-day he is living in the city of Great Falls, near his earlier home—the city built almost upon the site of our adventures; the city of railroads and factories and smelters, the city of fine homes and horseless carriages; a city ablaze with electric lights and trams, and all the modern frills for comfort and happiness and thrift for its tens of thousands of inhabitants. It is like sleeping the sleep of old Rip Van Winkle and waking to find a new world, while old faces and old places have passed away.

J. J. Hill and his associates, in later years, located 6,000 acres of land in that locality, on which has been built the city of Great Falls, such an important feeder of the Great Northern Railroad. The location is just below the mouth of Sun River, taking in the Black Eagle Falls, and the most delightful spot in Montana. Here, too, is the most beautiful part of the Sun River Valley, a great, wide bottomland stretching off to the northwest. The valley of the Missouri partakes here of the same character, while the bad land banks disappear entirely from view. The charms of this place were noted by Lewis and Clark, the first explorers, and in the history of their travels they dwelt at length upon the beauty of the scene.

The joys of motherhood have often been envied as fond parents watched the budding and maturing intellects of their children and noted their development into men and women of honor and refinement, but it is no small compensation to help make towns and cities spring from earth in answer to the demands of an army conquering a wilderness as it follows the trail of the pioneer.

We made a short trip out to Kelly's where our benefactor left us, and the party divided to take up respective duties. Mr. and Mrs. Todd returned to Benton by stage, leaving the wagon to be drawn in by the first freighter who would take it. Our horses were not found until the following spring. The ropes with which they were tied were new ones resulting in the knots not being secure. The horses probably had worked themselves loose, and had roamed at will all winter, and were found rolling fat in the spring with a short rope still around the neck of one of them.

CHAPTER XIII

THROUGH IDAHO, SODA SPRINGS, BLACKFOOT, AND CHALLIS

"They talk about a woman's sphere as though it had a limit;
There 's not a place in earth or heaven,
There 's not a task to mankind given,
There 's not a blessing or a woe,
There 's not a whispered yes or no,
There 's not a life or birth,
There 's not a feather's weight of worth—
    Without a woman in it."

Colonel Linsley's baptism

WHEN we returned from the long trip in Montana the winter was spent in Omaha, then after nearly two months in Denver we started for the wild rugged hills of Idaho. We traversed the Union Pacific road to Ogden, thence by the Utah and Northern to Oneida, where we connected with the tri-weekly stage for the famous Soda Springs of Idaho, located forty miles to the northeast of Oneida on the line of the then prospective branch of the Union Pacific from Granger to Portland. The ride along the Port Neuf River was a succession of happy surprises in waterfalls and cascades, in mountain curiosities and forest shades.

At the springs we were the guests of the gallant Captain Codman and wife, who had chosen Soda Springs as their summer home in preference to all others of the world which their years of foreign and home travel had encircled. Captain Codman was an old sea captain whose family for generations past had been among the Four Hundred of Boston. They spent many years abroad, but found no place that afforded them as free a plane to lead their own lives as at Soda Springs.

The huge mountains of mineral deposits with their unique colorings were ever a source of interesting study for lovers of nature's mysteries.   There were more than a hundred springs in the locality and the most popular was the Hooper Spring.   The opening was five feet in diameter and the superabundance of gas kept the water in a wild commotion.   Poor little dead birds that had tried to drink from the spring were found in large numbers.

A child that fell in the water was snatched out before it was scarcely wet, yet it strangled beyond help, and the little one was laid away for its long rest.   An incredulous man tried to drink from it and was dragged away, just in time to save him.   But to drink the sparkling natural champagne from a glass was to enjoy a delicious and healthful beverage.   Our only disappointment was in the absence of all hot springs, as the warmest water would not exceed seventy degrees Fahrenheit.

There were many apertures in the ground which emitted strong fumes of ammonia.   The wily captain was full of his jokes on Pard whom he seemed to look upon as a tenderfoot. Once he insisted that Pard dismount and inhale the fumes from an opening in the ground, which were especially pleasant.   He told Pard to take in a good, deep breath, which he did at nearly the cost of his life.   He was instantly overcome by strong ammonia fumes and fell forward into the hole.   The captain saw his mistake and made a lightning jump, grabbed Pard by the feet, and pulled him out.   It was an experience that even the joke-loving captain said he would never repeat.

Returning to Oneida we learned that the people of the only hotel had gone away on an excursion and the house was locked up tight.   A glimpse or two in a couple of restaurants had decided us to leave Oneida supperless, when we spied the hotel picnickers coming home.   It required more than silver-tongued oratory to persuade them to prepare a meal for us, and in addition to other inducements the tired, crying baby was handed over to me to soothe and care for.   He opened his big blue eyes in astonishment when a stranger took him from his mother's breast, but the change seemed to please him, and his little smile clung to his features when I had cuddled him to sleep.

From Oneida we went by special engine and caboose over the unballasted track to Blackfoot from where we were to cross southern Idaho by stage.   That night in Blackfoot was a terror.

As soon as the town sprung into existence it became evident that the cowboys of that locality considered it their special property and they took possession of the town too frequently for the peace of mind of other people.

On this particular night we had but just arrived when a fusillade of shots and yells filled the air, as if a band of Indians had turned loose to destroy all the town. No one knew what might happen when such a mêlée was once begun, and at such times it was generally the innocent who suffered. They began by first riding into a saloon and shooting the lights out; then ran their ponies like the wind up and down the streets firing at every light they could see, regardless of what they might hit. They

Danielson's double-end store

rode their ponies right into stores and saloons, yelling like maniacs, and no one dared to check them lest he would get the next bullet. It was more than an hour before the sheriff and a posse of men got out and chased them for miles out on the highroads, but they did not capture the fleet-footed cowboys, who had left two men shot to death and a cyclonic wreckage that would be hard to describe.

Our old pioneer friend, T. T. Danielson, who was postmaster and one of the leading merchants of Blackfoot, was so familiar with cowboy ways, and so considerate of their comfort, that he constructed a double-ended building with wide doors at both ends, so that the boys could ride right through, and do away with the confusion and wreckage naturally resulting from a band of bucking bronchos turning around in the middle of a country store. The song of the cowboy does not half express his characteristics.

THE COWBOY

"I 'm a Buzzard from the barrens, on a tear;
        Hear me toot!
I 'm a lifter of the flowing locks of hair;
        Hear me toot!
I 'm a Racker from the Rockies,
And of all the town the talk is,
He 's a pirate of the Pamoas,
        On the shoot.'

" Sometimes I strike an unprotected town,
        Paint it red,
Choke the sheriff, turn the marshal upside down
        On his head,
Call for drinks for all the party,
And if chinned by any smarty,
        Pay in lead.

"I 'm a coyote of the sunset, 'Prairie Dude,'
        Hear my zip!
In the company of gentlemen I 'm rude
        With my lip.
Down in front!   Remove that nigger,
Or I 'll perforate his figure!
I 'm a fly, I 'm a fighter,
        I 'm a flip!"

Old Fort Hall, a few miles from Blackfoot, is one of the most thrillingly historical landmarks of Idaho, or even of the Northwest. It is on the old Oregon trail and it was the "Mecca" of overland travellers, an oasis for many a weary and worn pioneer.   Fort Hall was at the forks of the trail, one branch leading south across Bear River, and the other on to Oregon.

The fort was built of adobe brick and it was a strong fortress against Indian attacks.   Its location was on a point of land between Spring Creek and Snake River, which formed protection from Indians on two sides.   There is but little left of it now but its crumbling walls and tall chimney to tell of its seventy years of usefulness in days of war or peace, storm or sunshine.   What a history it might unfold of perilous journeys, of hopes and fears, of rescues, of massacres, and of courageous travellers bound for the new Eldorado of the great Northwest. The Bannock Indians were frequently on the war path and made one's life uncertain in that section even as late as 1880.   It was the Bannocks that had made our trip so perilous in 1878 on that first journey to Helena when we just slipped through between their guns.

One of the first Indians who visited Fort Hall for barter was called "Old Ocean" who in 1880 was said to be 114 years old; he with two companions traded six fine beaver furs for two tin cups and a pocket knife. Then feeling that they had cheated the white men they hurried away for fear of losing the cups and knife if they remained longer. He said it was a good many years before he learned who had been cheated, but the possession of that knife had made him one of the richest and most

Old Fort Hall near Blackfoot

envied men of his tribe. I tried to make him understand that he was not cheated if each side in the trade got just what he wanted, but he only wrinkled up his face in a way that was half smile and half frown and pulled himself down into his tightly drawn blanket as a hint that he would say no more.

It had consumed a week of time to visit the Soda Springs and be ready to leave Blackfoot by the Toponce and Myers stage line headed for the rich mining region of the Salmon River and Yankee Fork country.

The first forty miles west was through a sage-brush desert with not a drop of water the entire distance except what was hauled by teams from Snake River. The dust was insufferable, enveloping the stage in such clouds of ashy earth that we could not see the wheels of the coach and it spread over us like waves of the sea.

The "half-way" station was called "Root Hog" because of its filthy condition. It was only half way of the first day's drive. It was a hut where dwelt a dog and a man who cared for the stage teams. The dog was noted for being a remarkable snake killer, and the man for the filth he lived in.

We arrived at midnight at Lost River Junction—which was another dividing of the ways—one road going north to Challis and Bonanza, and one going southwest to Wood River, Camas Prairie, and Boise City. There were no accommodations whatever for passengers, and the winter time schedule was on, compelling night stops, whether there was any place to sleep or not.

A native entertainer in the sign language

Those who take chances in new countries undergo hardships that would be unendurable at times were it not for the vein of ludicrousness that runs through the experiences. The camping out and picking up first lessons in harnessing a mule, or a vain endeavor to throw the diamond hitch, are matters that may add a wrinkle of care at the time, only to be laughed away in after years. Time mellows many hardships and leaves sunny memories of even very strenuous pioneer days.

So now, when Pard alighted from the stage, shook off the first coat of dirt, and politely asked where we were to go for a bed and rest, he was met by the rebuff, "Well, great God, man, you 've got the whole territory of Idaho spread out before you. Ain't that enough?" There was not a bed within twenty miles of the place, and there was no choice but to stay in the coach by the haystack with the mercury below the freezing point, or to take an allotted space on the floor of the one-roomed building used as post-office, store, and living-room of the agent. The store was clean and warm and was the more inviting of the two situations.

I was the only woman, but there were twenty-six men, all looking for a place for a few hours' rest; yet almost with one voice every man demanded that I should have his blankets, insisting that he did not need (?) them, and instantly putting them in a pile down by the stove. We earnestly thanked them and declined more than necessary for our use. Our blankets were spread next to the stove (as the place of honor and comfort), and when all were ready to sleep the anxious merchant built a roaring fire. There was but one small window in the room and that was closed, but there was an aperture under the door wide enough to let in a whole winter. It was a strange night and I wondered what the good folks at home would think if they could have had a glimpse of our surroundings. It was a long night, too, and day had not yet come when some one began quietly to renew the fire. Groping about the floor in the dark for some kindling the fire builder got hold of my foot and it scared him nearly out of his senses, for those were days when men died for less cause than that. His apologies were profuse and sincere, and although we have made several trips through his place since, he always alluded to the incident as his "narrow escape."

It seemed, however, that something that was unexpected must always happen there at Lost River. Several houses were erected there soon after our first trip, and the merchant had a home and family of his own, separate from the store, where a few weary travellers were better cared for.

On a later trip in summer when we were stopping there his baby was left alone cooing on the floor, with an outer door open. The mother wondered what was pleasing the baby so much and keeping him so still. She peeped in to see, and her blood nearly froze in her veins when she saw the child encircled by a great rattlesnake, and baby having great fun squeezing it. The fatal strike, however, came quickly, and all efforts to save the child's life were useless, and the dear baby was dead in a few hours.

Snakes and mosquitoes were so numerous that life was a burden during the summer months. One very hot night there the mosquitoes were so bad that sleep was out of the question. We were exhausted by heat and dusty travel, and the winged insects made a night of such physical discomfort that even a flood of tears could not relieve. One could not be outdoors in the dark for fear of stepping on a rattler, and inside was the constant hum of insects ready to attack any exposed part of the anatomy, while the mercury nearly evaporated at the top of the thermometer.

We made five round trips over that line, but the winter trip and the store floor were heaven compared with summer trips. The road through to Challis covered 160 miles from Blackfoot, requiring at best thirty-six hours' travel, through an uninteresting country, until near Round Valley, in which the town of Challis is located. A rugged range of bluffs skirted the valley and a small creek ran babbling along their base.

This little town of five hundred people was the base of supplies for the various mining districts including Yankee Fork, Bay Horse, Beardsley, Salmon River, and several other camps.

On our first trip into Challis the only hotel in the place was a small seven-log, dirt-roof house of three rooms—one used as a dining-room, another for a sleeping apartment, and the kitchen was in the third room, a kind of slab shed. The stage arrived late in the evening with nearly a score of tired passengers all wanting a bed, but as Pard was the only man who had his wife with him he was at once assigned to one of the only two rough pine bunks in the sleeping-room.

Just as soon as supper was over and the men had picked out their places in various corners of the office room to sleep, or had gone to some livelier quarters of the town, a second stage load came in with several ladies, and how to arrange matters then was a problem not easily solved. Husbands refused to leave their wives, and wives refused to let their husbands go elsewhere for shelter. We could not keep the only room to ourselves with an extra bunk in it if the room was only ten by twelve feet, when so many were needing a share of it. Alexander Toponce's name was signed on our stage transportation and we could not do less than give him and his wife the vacant bunk for a night's lodging. The men of his party protested against Mr. Toponce and wife taking it and offered to play a game of Seven Up for the bed, for there were three men with their wives wanting a room, but Toponce refused to yield. It was suggested that the ladies take the room, but that did not meet with favor. The landlord came in and said he did not know what his own wife and children were going to do for a place to sleep, but the hour was late and something had to be done quickly.

Mr. Toponce said something about fourteen people for two beds and went out of the room leaving a trail of yellow words in a blue atmosphere and an impression that he was going to raise the roof or enlarge the room, but he only struck off to the stage stable and got all the grain sacks, saddle blankets, and lap robes around the place, and as many shake-downs were made in that little room as could be spread out. When every one was ready for bed and standing close to the spot he was to rest his weary bones on, the light was put out and all crawled into the blankets, taking off only such apparel as could be spared and tucking it under blankets to keep it from a general mix-up.

What a night that was! Four of the men were the boss snorers of Idaho, or any other "ho," and to crown all, the rain fell in torrents during the night and came through the dirt roof, bringing with it diluted mud and misery the whole night long. One party raised an umbrella, and another raised— well, the reader can guess it was not heaven; that would not be appropriate to express his feelings.

One forgot where he put his flask, and in reaching out to find it he passed his hand over the face of one of the ladies, who promptly gave a loud scream, and then followed profuse apologies by the thirsty owner of the hand. When morning came at last it sent a bright sun peeping in onto a most dismal scene. Mud was everywhere. The ladies' faces and gowns were spattered by the drippings through the mud roof. Some clothing was too wet to put on, and some people too mad to smile had they been clothed in the king's purple. It was indeed ludicrous in the extreme and sorely vexatious, but it was *pioneering*. Our bunk and clothing had been well protected, and we could but look with pitying eyes on those unfortunates in spite of the ludicrous side of the situation.

There was a little farming done in Round Valley. One Mr. Beerly had thirty acres from which he gathered 300,000 pounds of potatoes and sold them for five cents a pound. But the scarcity of water for irrigation made extensive farming almost out of the question. The Salmon River had ample supply, but it was so far below the general level that it would have to be flumed for many miles to bring it onto the surface around Challis.

A gentleman well known in the community started out a few days before our arrival with his dog, for a hunt of a few hours. Spying some game in the distance, he started on a run across a sage-brush flat, paying little attention to his footsteps, but throwing the bushes aside right and left with his hands, and hurrying on, for it was already dusk, when, without warning, he tripped and fell into a den on a mother bear and her cubs. She had dug a big hole under the spreading branches of the sage, where she deemed herself safe from intrusion.

Her instinct prompted preservation for herself and young, and before the poor victim could collect himself for action the monster had him in her cruel embrace. She broke both of his arms almost instantly, and was tearing him to pieces with the claws of her hind feet. At this juncture his dog appeared and began biting and plaguing the bear until she loosened her hold on the man and turned on the dog. The man, bleeding and almost helpless, crawled out of the den and found shelter under a neighboring sage-brush, but the dog and the bear continued their parley until the bear finally ran away with her babies.

The dog soon found his master's hiding place and commenced licking his wounds and face as his only way of expressing his realization of what had happened. With the aid of his teeth and a stick the wounded man attached a piece of his bloody garments to his faithful dog's collar and instructed him to go back to town for help.

The poor brute looked wistfully at his master as if he did not want to leave him, but a second command sent him running off at full speed. When the dog reached the village he ran through the street with such a dreadful howl that every one turned to look at him, and some men who knew the animal loosened the bloody rag from his collar. As soon as this was done, the sagacious dog wheeled around and started back to his master as fast as he could go, followed by men on horseback, and they found the man more dead than alive. The wounded man's condition was critical, but it was thought he would recover.

Col. N. E. Linsley, now of Spokane, Washington, and the

Hon. Peter Groat, who was then Immigration Agent of the Northern Pacific Railroad, were interested in the Ramshorn

"He tripped and fell into a den on a mother bear and her cubs"

mine near Challis. Mr. Groat was a man widely known in the West and familiarly called "Uncle Peter" by the majority of his friends and acquaintances.

Uncle Peter and Colonel Linsley "kept house" together in a little log cabin and one day there came an invitation to dine with them. It was in the year 1878, after the new hotel was built and run by Mr. and Mrs. James Burns, who are both dead and can never read these lines and learn how glad we were for a change in diet.

It was amusing to see these two capitalists aiding their chef in preparing dinner for their guests, and no housewife ever felt more anxious than they did. However, when one would think of a good story or joke on some associate which must be told at once, he would come from the preparatory corner waving a big wooden spoon, with which he had been mixing the salad, or perchance a huge fork or hunter's knife would be swung around for emphasis as the story and work went on.

The colonel is ever an encyclopedia of wood lore, and he could find the rarest plants of the woods, and tell many extraordinary tales of the forest and the language of nature. He is still one of the most genial companions in camp life that one could find in many leagues of travel. It has often been a matter of regret that the menu of that memorable day was not saved

The Burns house of Challis, Idaho

for it was an excellent dinner, with such jovial companionship that thoughts of it have ever been a joy and a solace in hours of reminiscence.

The colonel spent one night at the Burns House where he had a room on the ground floor. A fellow upstairs had come in too full of spirits to be steady, and he knocked over his wash-stand on the rather open floor. The poor colonel got a rousing good baptism through the cloth ceiling before he reached for his umbrella and raised it over himself in bed; then he began calling for the descendant of the Scotch bard, who kept the hotel, to learn what was the matter upstairs.

Mrs. Burns was a character not forgotten by the patrons of her house; she loved a social cup and made herself a conspicuous figure of the hostelry of Challis. She never knocked on entering any one's room, nor curbed her queries about any one's affairs. How she did love her toddy! bless her departed soul! Any one who ever visited the Burns House could tell a spirited tale of the mistress of the house and her tricks to increase the earnings of the bar.

The Beardsley mine was located on an eminence overlooking the Bay Horse village. It was owned and worked by the Beardsley brothers, formerly of Canada, who were gentlemen of high standing. They had a neat little cabin nestling under the broad sheltering branches of high pine trees, some of which were six and seven feet in circumference. While superintending the building of the chimney of the cabin Robert Beardsley found a smooth slab of slate which he carried in for the top of a stand, the frame having been standing several days waiting for a proper covering. As soon as he took it in the house it was noticed that on one side of the slab was a highly colored landscape of the forest rock variety. In the foreground were large pine trees, with a valley, mountains, and forest in the distance. The foliage and coloring would do an artist credit, for it was almost perfect in detail, and over the whole was the roseate glow of a setting sun. They had already refused five hundred dollars for the slab.

The mineral value was not alone the attraction of the mine, but it afforded fine specimens of ruby, native and wire silver, and some of the finest crystallized carbonates of lead that any mine ever produced. These crystals were found in pockets along the vein and were like threads of frost work delicately interlaced in patterns of rarest beauty. Some of the copper stains and deposits were of strange richness in a clear light green, with a surface like the nap of heavy velvet. The whole made the vein one of beauty and renown, from which specimens could be sold in the East for fabulous sums.

CHAPTER XIV

A LARK ON YANKEE FORK AND A SENSATIONAL RETURN TO SALT LAKE

"Merry it is in the good greenwood,
When the mavis and merle are singing,
When the deer sweeps by, and the hounds are in cry,
And the hunter's horn is ringing."

TOPONCE and Myers built the stage road to Bonanza from Challis, a distance of only thirty-five miles, at a cost of $30,000, but never did a road wind more picturesquely among the foothills, or afford finer views from lofty summits. Swinging around curves, overlooking precipitous depths and gliding through ravines with just a narrow strip of blue sky above, crossing high points, and then losing one's self in labyrinths of forestry, combined to make the most interesting day's drive that a lover of scenery could hope to find.

The road was full of freight teams carrying heavy loads of supplies for the Yankee Fork and other mines. Ten and twelve horses to a wagon stretched themselves out in long, muscular tension to pull the load up the steep grades with harness creaking and feet slipping on stones as the drivers trudged along beside them or rode the off-wheeler, and sent forth volleys of oaths with every crack of the whip while mumbling a jargon known only to themselves and their much abused teams. In fact it is said that the horses become so used to the oaths hurled at them that they would not travel without them.

Bonanza is encircled with heavily timbered mountains, the ground is gently rolling, and the Yankee Fork Creek dashes

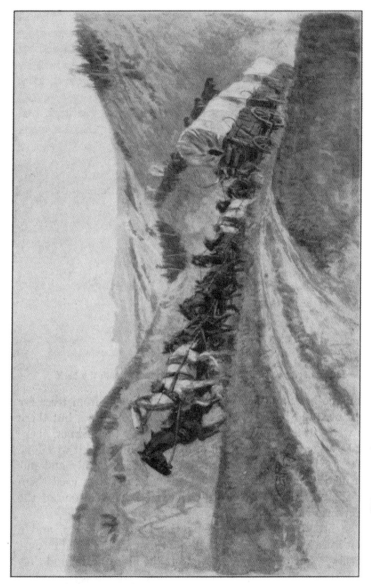

"Ten or twelve horses to a wagon stretching themselves out in long muscular tension"

11

through the town merrily laughing at every obstacle that tends
to check its course. There were only about two hundred and
twenty-five houses in the town, and there are not many more at
this writing, nearly thirty years later, but the people were fully
conscious of the beauty of their mountain eyrie, and in cutting
down the trees they left enough to keep their town most picturesque and to spare a double drive with a triple row of trees
for their principal street.

Just in the outskirts were many trees where the bark had
been very carefully and regularly stripped off. Indians often

Indians scrape the juicy nutriment from underneath the bark

cut off the bark and scrape the juicy nutriment from trees for
sustenance, and it will keep one alive for many days, but these
trees were cut so regularly and so ingeniously that I knew there
must be other cause than want of food, and I learned it was done
by the earliest settlers who cut out the strips evenly and put
them under heavy weights to flatten and cure, then used them
for shingles, and the curiously covered cabins were one of the
attractions of the town.

The little hotel was kept by the Dodge brothers, and a
quaint little house it was, too, with its thin partitions and meagre
furnishings, but they gave their guests the best of care, and they
were exceedingly hospitable and solicitous. It was a great place
for men to congregate, down on the shady side of the street in front
of the hotel just under our windows, and their voices floated up

into the room much more than they knew, and one could not help hearing much of the talk not intended for publication.

The first trip out from Bonanza was on foot to the Chas. Dickens mine, a mile and a half from town, where the pure gold stood out on the vein like dew on the grass in Eastern summer time. The morning was cool and bright, and as we rose above the town in our steady climbing, we now and then would lean upon our staves and look back upon the busy village and the distant snow-clad hills while waiting for our breath to catch up.

We were cordially received by Mr. Bill Norton, the principal owner of the mine, and a warm fire and a hot dinner were soon proffered as substantial evidence of his hospitality. Mr. Norton was a Michigan man and was the original discoverer of the mine in July, 1875. Inside of thirty days he pounded out $11,500 in gold with a hand mortar. In one night he pounded out $1130. He would take rock from the surface day times and pound it up at night. The following three months two of his men took out ore and shipped it to Salt Lake City, from which they realized $15,000, and that after paying as high as $100 a ton to packers to take it to Salmon City, thence $40 for teamsters to Corinne. Both gold and silver crop out in all purity. One nugget of white quartz about the size of a dozen walnuts was literally filled with gold, and its estimated value was $125. In 1876 Mr. Norton went to Corinne on the Central Pacific Railway all alone with 280 pounds of gold. An old-fashioned arastra ground up the ore, but it was not able to save all the precious metals, and the tailings were valued at $80 per ton. In five months, in 1879, it ground out $40,000. The arastra was located at the foot of the hill and presided over by the genial Johnnie Rohrer. He gallantly showed the workings of the simple little Spanish arastra and how it yielded its large quantities of gold and silver bullion from its one little pan and settler.

Bill Norton was the oracle and savant of the camp, a man of most generous nature and kind to every one but himself, as often his handsome earnings from the little hand mortar were laid upon a gaming table and lost even more quickly than made. He refused to sell the mine because it was his bank where he could always go and get money without having any red ink side to his account. When he died in a Salt Lake hospital a few years later he was mourned by every one who knew him, for in spite of his unkindness to himself he had a multitude of friends.

Every camp has its eccentric character and Bonanza had several, chief among whom was one known as Laughing Brookie, a cognomen earned by his genial laughter, which surmounted all obstacles or troubles and made him famous in many sections on the frontier. The laugh was like the braying of the long-eared quadrupeds; it was long, deep, and loud. He was known all through California, where he once had been a very rich man. A good story follows him of the last sumptuous banquet which he gave his friends of the Sierras. News had reached him of the loss of his entire fortune, which he had staked on some venture, and keeping his secret, he immediately gave orders for a dinner eclipsing anything he had ever given. He invited as many as could be accommodated; many choice viands were brought from distant cities for the occasion, and champagne flowed like water.

The evening was a memorable one for every friend within the radius of the town and many regretted the limit of their capacity and mourned when the feast was done. The next morning the landlord presented his bill, which showed that no expense had been spared to make the banquet the success of his life, but he was horrified to learn that Brookie had not a dollar in the world to pay for anything. The accommodating host was in a towering rage, and wanted to know why he had not been told of that before the banquet. Then Brookie straightened up and let out his peculiar laugh which rang through the rafters and was rounded out by the reply: "Why, I thought it would make you feel bad enough to know it this morning." Brookie's good nature finally won favor again and the host told him to take a light wagon and a team and go and catch fish for the house. The man with the laugh jumped at the offer, and was soon ready and off to fulfil the mission. He was gone just seven years, when one day he walked into the same hotel and strolling up to the desk where the same manager still presided, he said: "Say, pard, hee haw, hee haw, say, hee haw, I never had a bite so I 've brought the team home, hee haw." However many tears there may have been in his heart, his life was a song and he always carried the music with him.

The Custer mine presented a marked contrast to others, not only in its location and general properties, but also in its manage-

ment. It was situated a mile and half from Bonanza and just
above the little settlement of Custer. The ledge of ore was
largely on the surface of the mountain just as the ore lay on the
surface of the later Granby mine of British Columbia. It was so
easily worked that two men could take out ore enough to keep
the twenty stamp mill running day and night. While there was

"Dodge Brothers gave their guests the best of care"

no doubt that the mine was excessively rich, the owners were
said to be skimming the cream.

We wanted to ride in the tramway basket that carried the
ore from the mine to the mill, but the receptacle would hold but
a hundred pounds, and I could not reduce myself to that weight
and was denied the aerial flight down the mountainside, and
perhaps saved a dumping into the creek or an ore bin.

A good story which Bishop Tuttle liked to tell on himself
happened between Challis and Bonanza. The good bishop was

driving along on one of his rounds when he met a Methodist preacher newly arrived in that section, and whom the bishop addressed by saying: "Well, my friend, how is it that you can drive two horses and I have only one?" "Well," replied the stranger, "you are probably a one horse preacher," and without knowing that he was addressing the famous bishop he drove on.

We were indebted to the gallant Major Hyndman, the leading attorney of Bonanza, and to his associate, Hon. E. M. Wilson, for a day of rare experiences in mountain climbing and exploring, which has ever been one of the green spots in days of dusty travel. It consisted of a trip to the Montana mine on Mt. Estes. The party was well mounted and the horses, full of the ginger of the fresh mountain air, were more used to hard climbing than they were to flying skirts. But a little coaxing soon made them tractable and we galloped off.

The Montana mine was six miles northward from Bonanza, near the summit of Mount Estes. The ride thither was delightful for one who enjoys the zigzag mountain climbing, first along the Jordan Creek a couple of miles, where it was laughable to see the horses clinging to the little trail not much wider than their feet, and where a slip would have immersed us in the Jordan waters far below. The air was full of song from our own throats and those of happy birds that filled the wooded hills. We seemed almost in the depths of heaven itself, with the deep blue vault arched so near us that it appeared to be within our grasp. There never can be a bluer sky than that which glorifies the Idaho mountains.

Up Jordan Creek over a little narrow trail near the edge of the ravine, so near that I kept watching the feet of Pard's horse to see how near my own horse would have to go to the edge, for a horse can travel exceedingly well on a six inch trail; up and down we went, crossing and recrossing the swift little creek until with a right about we began climbing straight up the mountainside. Up a little farther and the jagged crown of the Saw Tooth range rose in the distance with all the glory of its lights and shades, its pillows of snow and its forests of pines, its lakelets and streams.

Messrs. Hooper, Franklin, and Cameron, the three gallant knights of this famous mine, made our sojourn among them one of joy. John Chinaman, who had the kitchen in charge, put his wits to work and brought forth a dinner that surprised us by its excellence and variety and the thoughtfulness of the providers.

It was a day appointed for a meeting of the owners of the mine, and we had the pleasure of meeting them and seeing them together. Captain Hooper brought out a supply of jackets and hats in which we robed ourselves and prepared to descend into the mine. It had not seemed possible that a mine way up on a mountain peak could be a wet one; one would think from the cone shaped contour of Mt. Estes that it would be as dry as a bone when the summer sun had melted the snow, but instead of that its interior walls seemed to generate water and it was a difficult matter to keep the mine dry enough to work at all.

It was quite a climb up to the mines from the cabins, but the day was perfect for mountaineering, and it was not long before we stood at the winze looking into the cavernous depths of the treasure house. But Mr. Hooper begged us not to look down for fear we might lose our courage and not make the descent.

There was considerable water in the shaft, caused by the melting snows, and when we were clothed in the rubber coats and hats and gum boots provided for the exploration, we made a picture that was grotesque and humorous, if not artistic.

That day the winze was not running, and the only way down to the lower levels was to climb hand over hand down the hundred and fifty-five feet on a ladder that was very much broken and had an occasional rung missing. One end of a rope was tied around my body and the other end was tied around Superintendent Hooper, who was the strongest man in the party and followed down after me, so if I missed my footing or lost my head I would not be hurled to the bottom of the shaft. A loose knotted rope also hung from each level down the side of the ladder to be used in case of accident. All kinds of encouraging words were echoing down the long dark passage, but in spite of them, the one thought of "What fools we mortals be" seemed uppermost in my mind. We were praised for courage but felt that those who remained at the top were the only ones with a grain of sense. The last six feet down in that great black hole were minus the ladder and we had to "shin a rope" and when our feet touched the solid earth again how I did wish they were on the earth above instead of on the earth beneath. We were given picks to loosen whatever specimens we wanted, and there

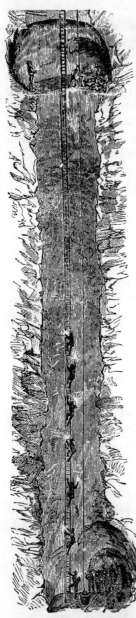

" Going down one hundred
and fifty-five feet into
the Montana mine "

were some rather inexperienced blows given to the valuable ore body, but some choice bits sparkling with gold now lie in our cabinet as reminders of that day's experience.

I was thankful for every fraction of my five feet five and three quarters when I had to go up the rope to get out of that hole, and the old broken winged ladder was not to be maligned. The upward climb was far more laborious than the descent had been, and it was a sensation of joy not to be expressed in paltry words when we had our feet on top of the ground and could breathe in the air of the pines in the sunlight again. No other woman had ever been down in that mine, and I am sure my own ambition was amply gratified by the experience. The first-class ore of this mine had thus far averaged about $4000 per ton, and there were then six tons of it on the dump awaiting shipment.

After a thorough investigation of the mine we climbed to the summit of the mountain for a view of the snowy ranges on the outskirts of that vast monumental park, of which Mt. Estes seemed to be the centre, with here and there a river, a forest, a valley, hill, or plain at our feet; above us was the bright flag which the mining company always kept floating there, and the clear August sky. Skirting our pinnacle far beyond were the ragged, pointed peaks of the Saw Tooth, Salmon, and Wood River ranges, rising in all majesty and grandeur, with their burdens of snow, forests, and precious minerals.

On the way back to the cabins we stopped on the slope for some trials of snow shoeing. We were quite surprised at the success of our first effort, and it seemed wondrous easy, but at the second trial some one suggested that we go in the path made by the first trip. It was a bit of wickedness which did not penetrate our slow wits until all that was visible of us was our heads peeping from under the beautiful snow. We went down the trail with such rapidity that we were not conscious of jumping the trail until completely buried in the ravine, and I opened my eyes on the rescuers digging us out. They worked with an earnestness that showed their fear that I might be seriously hurt, and it was now my turn to get even by keeping my eyes closed and just allowing myself to be dug out and lifted out upon a blanket; then I opened my eyes and complimented their strength and carefulness.

At the bottom of the shaft

The party was made up of people who have left their mark on pages of history. Captain Hooper was a handsome man in the prime of life, a lover of the mountains and of mining, and a genial generous host. Major Hyndman was the author of "*A History of a Cavalry Company.*" It was of Company A, 11th Pennsylvania Regiment, and the book gave its experiences in the Civil War. The Major was also an important figure in the history of the development of Idaho, not only in Yankee Fork and Salmon District, but over in the Vienna country and on down southward along Wood River to Ketchum, until a sudden death ended his work.

E. M. Wilson was a prominent mining man of the Wood River country, and a society favorite, and in later years became a member of the Idaho legislature, and still later mayor and banker of Fairhaven, Washington, where he married and lives, a young man still, who loves to talk over and enjoy again the pioneer days.

Mr. Cameron was mourning his life away for the sweetheart of earlier days and he was sure she mourned for him because she had never married, and he wanted a woman's idea of what he should do, and it was not long after that when we received the cards of his wedding.

After a few days in Bonanza my liege lord and two companions left for the Saw Tooth range and the Wood River country 150 miles southward on horseback.   I was left among new-found friends, with a good horse and saddle, and they thought I was also left with the conviction that the trip would be too hard for me. But who can boast of 10,000 miles by stage and half as many miles on horseback through the fastnesses and over the towering pinnacles of the Rocky Mountains and Coast Ranges without feeling chagrined at being stood at bay before so trifling a trip.

The mountain streams were swollen to the high water mark, and there was no trail or safe fording of the waters that must be crossed, so after much persuasion there was a feeble consent given to remain behind, which was later much regretted by both Pard and myself.

Mr. Norton, the godfather and oracle of the camp, had said it would not do to send a woman over that rugged Saw Tooth range with such swollen streams and an untried horse, and his word became the law.   Several most delightful weeks were then spent among Bonanza's hospitable people.   We climbed the summits of the mountains and carved names on the trees; we sang, we strolled through wooded trails, and told stories around the camp fires; we sketched the finest views, and penetrated the nearby canyons; we tried snow shoes again, but with no better success than at the first effort.

We watched the loading of pack trains with no little amusement.   Each little jack was blindfolded until his pack of three hundred pounds was made fast to his saddle with that wonderful diamond hitch in the ropes, the secret of successful transportation over the mountains and down the steep and narrow trails throughout all countries.   But no amusement could fill the vacancy made by the separation from Pard and I grew restless at delay.

When Major Hyndman went over the range with Pard he left

the key to his office that we might enjoy his library and a quiet
place for writing.   In describing the office, a quotation from a
letter to my mother could hardly be improved: "So here I
am this afternoon seated at the popular attorney's desk and
trying to borrow some of his dignity, as Nell Gwynn did in days
of old when she assumed the stolen wig and gown of the hard-
hearted Judge and played his rôle.   The table on which I am
writing is made simply of plain pine boards, some of Major
Hyndman's own carpenter work.   The floor is also of plain,
rough boards; there is a cupboard where he keeps his secrets,
and perhaps some spirits are in there too; a few pictures adorn
the walls, and give tone to the crude surroundings.   There is

Copyright by Detroit Photo Co.

" We watched the loading of pack trains with no little amusement "

also man's inseparable companion, a mirror (I wonder what he
would say to that) which hangs on the wall close by the window
where the light is best.   But the chief charm of the room is the
library, which is indeed an extensive one to find in such a secluded spot.   There is a world of interesting reading matter not
bearing upon the law, which accounts for his own versatility
and the composition which I found on the table, for it was no
less than his own book of memoirs of the Civil War which he
had left for me with his autograph.   I should not forget to
mention the spade in one corner of the room; a sack of ore, a
saddle, a box of old clothes, a few odorous pipes lying about in
artistic confusion, and a well worn broom.   Can you imagine the
completed picture?"

When Mr. Clawson and Major Hyndman returned from

Wood River, Pard went on to Boise City, and for my entertainment a party was made up for a fishing trip to be out two or three days, but the first day in camp two of the horses got away, Mr. Clawson's and mine. With his philosophical turn of mind he looked upon the incident as a huge joke, but when two days were spent in fruitless hunt for the straying animals the pleasure of fishing was lost, and the homeward trip was not jubilant. The gentlemen of the party took a turn about in riding and walking, on the ride and tie system. One man would ride a mile or two, then tie the horse, and start along on foot. The horse would then rest until the pedestrian caught up, then he would ride past No. 2 for a mile or so and tie again; that was kept up for about fifteen or twenty miles.

Mr. Clawson related how some one had stolen his revolver while crossing the range with Pard. They had stopped at a cabin where conditions pointed to the occupants being of the bandit order, and they kept pretty close watch of their horses and other belongings during the stay, and when they mounted they clapped their hands on the holsters to draw the weapons and be ready for trouble, but one revolver was gone, and, alas! it was my own pet which I had loaned him for the trip, and which I always carried with me but never had occasion to use. But it always gave me a sense of security to have the means of defence close at hand.

It was delightful sojourning among the hills, taking long rides through the valleys and picnicking in the groves. The whole village seemed to be turned into an entertainment committee. Mrs. Cal. Clawson took me to her own home and did a great deal for my pleasure, but the more I thought about the long and uncertain trip on which Pard had ventured, it seemed that I must get back to the railroad where I could more quickly get into communication with him and I started out for Salt Lake alone. At Challis I met Mr. C. A. Carrier, who was then city ticket agent of the Union Pacific Company at Omaha. He was horrified to think that I should make that trip out to Blackfoot alone, and endeavored to have me change my mind and wait until Pard came for me. Mr. Carrier had just arrived on a business trip, and said if he ever got over that road alive he would never cross that desert again until he could cross it in a Pullman car, and he kept his word.

The friends were numerous who watched the stage roll out of Bonanza and Challis and the words of cheer and solicitude worked wonders in driving away unpleasant features of the trip. Upon reaching the station of Big Butte, where I was obliged to stay for the night, things looked pretty blue for any place to rest. The house was crowded to overflowing, and no one was feeling very comfortable either. There was a nervousness

Saw Tooth Mountain bandit cabin where my revolver was stolen

among the people there that I could not account for. Big Butte station was one of the unavoidable places along that great desert highway, where freighters, and people driving private teams had to stay over night, as well as the tourist or traveller by stage. On this occasion the United States Marshal, E. S. Chase, was there with his wife, whom I had met several times. It seemed wondrously good to see some familiar faces in such a place, and to feel the protection of one having such authority. The marshal was driving his own team across the country on a business trip and had stopped there for the night.

Every available space was already taken and Mr. Chase insisted on surrendering his place and having me share the only private room with Mrs. Chase, insisting also "that the room was quite safe now." "Quite safe," I queried, "why, Colonel, what do you mean by that?" Then he explained that a big rattlesnake had just been found in the room and a dog that was good at catching them had been shut in the room to get the reptile. The excitement had been intense and the fight between the two had been a lively one, while the noise had been like a couple of wild animals entrapped there. When all was still the door was cautiously opened and the snake was found lying dead in the middle of the floor, and the furniture looked as if a Nebraska cyclone had demolished it. There was a state of wreckage not easily restored. The dog rushed out of doors and disappeared as it always did after being bitten by a snake, but it would return in a few days. Where the dog would go on such occasions no one ever knew, but probably to some mud hole far away, where he could cure himself. It gave me the "delirious tremblins" to think of sleeping in the house at all, but the chance of an encounter with one of the strikers was after all much less in the house than outside of it. If I had to live in a place like that I would not be satisfied with one dog who had such a snake-killing reputation, but I would have a dozen of them, and keep my pockets full of sweets so they would always be around me ready for business.

The next morning the marshal attended to my seat on the coach and located me on top with the driver, and his kindness at that time has never been forgotten, but in other ways it was a night to forget if possible. One could but feel sympathy for the woman whose lot had been cast in such a place. For it is the women who suffer most in pioneer life. The poor, hard-working woman at Big Butte was but one of many on our vast frontier who toiled without rest. My heart ached for them, and a word or two of sympathy would bring the tears to their eyes. Their husbands were not always cruel, only as they were cruelly thoughtless in heaping work upon them and giving them no rest, no help, no recreation, but keeping up the constant grind of cooking, cleaning, and making beds for all kinds of people who pass at all hours.

In all the thousands of miles of stage travel which our pioneering covered, there was none more uncomfortable and disagreeable than through the desert lands and lava beds of southern Idaho, which was still marked on the school maps as unexplored country.   The alkali in the soil poured into the nostrils and throat with every breath; it made the skin sore and rough, the eyes sore, and even irritated the disposition.   There was no escaping the pall of dust that enveloped the stage-coach during the long, hot summer, and penetrated every fold of clothing.

"The fight between the two had been a lively one"

When one emerged from the inner depths of the dust laden coach to waken his dormant muscles by a few moments' rest at a station, he might drop in the road and not be seen because of the unity of color of himself and the mother-earth.   His movements alone identified him as a living creature.

When passing through the gamut of idle spectators who block the passages when the stage empties itself at its destination, one feels as if he had just rolled from the brake beam of a freight car and owned no claim to respectability except his desire to hide, without being recognized.   Even in later years when I cross that section of country in a Pullman car I want to sleep and forget such trials of the old stage days.

CHAPTER XV

OMAHA IN THE SEVENTIES

FOR the winter of '79 we settled down to a quiet orderly life in Omaha. We chose the top of Farnham Street hill for a location, and when the foundation of a house on the corner of Eighteenth Street was being laid we set a snare to secure the house as soon as it was finished.

The spot was then far from the busy strife of the commercial centre of the town, and the views from its unimpeded heights were a charm not easy to find about an otherwise level country. No one dreamed of such an invasion of commerce that a magnificent court-house would some day grace one of those corners and great business blocks would crowd out the most desirable home centre of the city. No one thought the Omaha *Bee* would swarm from its little old home to a ten-story hive on the hilltop at Eighteenth Street, but Father Time is a wonderful worker in an ambitious city and transformations are wrought which no one can foretell. Those pretty little homes that once graced that proud eminence now exist only in "a composite picture" in the mind's eye hanging in mid-air forty feet above the present street. The dear old hill melted away under the pick and shovel to its present level and Omaha was deprived of the most beautiful residence quarter of the city.

The Grand Central Hotel was destroyed by fire and for many months the old Metropolitan Hotel, kept by Ira Wilson on lower Douglas Street, and the little Withnell House, managed by the Kitchen brothers, were the only hotels worth mentioning. The Metropolitan was an old ramble shack from which we were glad to emerge into our first home, and we went about the settlement with all the ardor of love's first nest.

Pard had such a big chest of notes to work up into readable

form that it appeared a lifetime task, and Mr. Kimball, General Manager of the Union Pacific, was in need of his information almost every hour at Union Pacific headquarters. I was eager to be anchored in a home, and the combination worked well toward a season of home life for us.

Omaha was not attractive for climatic reasons, if it was for others. The terrific sandstorms were a terror to a housewife, its bottomless streets were a menace to commerce in the wet season, and in the sultry season the thunder-storms were of such violence that the lightning was like fiery-headed demons coming out of earth and sky, flashing into every window, while pounding on every door and roof the thunder chased in a maddening din from which there was no escape.

The Missouri River valley is ever noted for its wild storms which follow the stream and play such havoc along its lands. They even drove the river from its bed, and not infrequently turned it out of the State. At one time during that winter the wind blew so hard for forty-eight hours that a special policeman patrolled every block in town to watch for fires, and women were not allowed on the streets at all.

In looking over letters sent to friends in those days, or during our visits to Omaha, there is scarcely one of them that does not give record of some awful storm. At one time not less than 500 feet of track was not only washed out in Council Bluffs, and ties and rails carried into neighboring fields, but the road bed was under four and five feet of water. The bridge across an arm of the river at Council Bluffs was carried out and we walked on the top of freight cars to a temporary ferry boat to cross to Omaha. It was not unusual for water to be several feet deep in some of the streets near the river.

The Missouri River made history in Nebraska faster than any other factor. Since the settlement of that State it has lost more towns in its adjustment to the river and to civilization than any other State in the Union. Some of the towns were wiped out by the river suddenly changing its bed, or by gradually pilfering the land until a town had to be abandoned.

When the Union Pacific Railroad was built the town of Decatur was selected as headquarters for the company and the location for the Missouri bridge,—but before the work was under way so many town lots had been swallowed by the river that the company changed its location to Florence, and then Omaha. Most of Decatur is now in the river bed.

For a time Florence had more population than Omaha, of which it was a formidable rival. It was on the Mormon route to Utah and was the western point of the heaviest immigration. It was the Union Pacific's change to Omaha that depleted the population from 5000 to a deserted village. Many towns were wiped out because of change of county seats, and many more were abandoned because railroads decided to take other routes than the old stage trail.

The first Territorial legislature met in 1855 at Archer, the county seat of Richardson County. The earliest settlers there

"When Pard went to the Rocky Mountains he had to cross the Missouri at Omaha on a ferryboat"

were mostly intermarried with squaws who raised large families. Later, when the Government put into effect the reservation method of caring for the Indians, it set aside a domain in Richardson County and Archer was left on a reservation. Its army post was abandoned, the State buildings left unoccupied, railroads passed it by, and soon its white population moved to other localities.

A large number of the lost towns of Nebraska were located along the great overland routes. The old Mormon trail followed the Platte River's windings. There was the California trail, the line blazed by the miners who took part in the Pike's Peak gold rush, and the trails followed by the freighters and pony express riders. All of these converged at Fort Kearney, midway across the State; beyond that was the hostile Indian country, and safety lay in travelling in numbers. When the Union Pacific Railroad came through it killed freighting on the plains, practically every one of the trail towns disappeared within a few months except Fort Kearney, and even that had dropped the Fort and became just plain Kearney, but it is a town to be proud of just the same.

When Pard went to the Rocky Mountains in 1870 he had to cross the Missouri at Omaha on a ferry boat and Omaha was just getting fairly well on the map, while Denver had only 4900 people. Our beautiful Spokane and Tacoma were not even started, Seattle was only a lumber camp, and Minneapolis yet to be built. Pretty much everything was wilderness north and south of the single railroad across the continent where there are now eight trans-continental roads, and the vast growth and commercial interests of eight newly constituted States.

There was no street paving, and the soil around about Omaha is of that adobe nature that when wet will hold all that any one can give it, whether it is a foot, a rubber, or a wagon wheel. I was convinced that there was greater affinity between molecules of Omaha mud than any other known substance. There were but few crosswalks and a novice in navigation in that river town could get into trouble in a hurry. One of my own experiences was a ludicrous one. It had rained furiously for two or three hours, but the sun followed with a clear sky. I did not yet know the mud was such a mortal enemy to pedestrians, and I sallied happily out, quite smartly dressed, and was halted at the very first crossing. The first thing I knew I was standing as firmly rooted to the spot as if I had grown there. I wiggled and wriggled and twisted until one foot was loose, only to find the other one in the mud twice as deep. I pulled my feet from my rubbers and hoped to get back on to firm ground, but alas! I was hopelessly stranded until kind Providence sent a strong deliverer to pry me out. It looked to me as if I covered the most of the five foot sidewalk, for the mud would not drop off my boots, but simply multiplied itself with my every effort to escape until it was cut off. I went home tired out, warm, and ruffled, but I had learned my lesson. I, perhaps, ought to have known better for I had often watched from our windows at the Grand Central Hotel the struggles of horses and vehicles to get through the principal city streets where they were frequently held for hours in the adobe clutch.

There were no water works in the town except a few private tanks where water was pumped up from wells. There was a great deal of talk about water works that winter, but they did not know how to utilize that Missouri River, with its twenty per cent. of mud, and there was no other available source. There

General Fremont, the great pathfinder, and his wife

must be more water, or better water, in Phillipsburg, Montana, for we received a paper from there saying the people were living on water and *Strahorn's Resources*, the title they gave Pard's latest booklet on Montana.

The crows were so thick in Omaha that the ground would often be black with them, and their incessant caw-caw was a torture to the nerves. When a flock of them would light upon a roof their claws would rattle like hailstones, and one often wished them to emigrate to other lands, and wondered what they found so attractive in that locality. You could not stone them for there were no stones in or around Omaha.   In fact, Nebraska is wonderfully free from stones everywhere.   A country doctor is never afraid of striking a rock as he drives to his patient in the black hours of the night, but there are times when he may drop into a mud-hole from which he may have to swim out.

One of the gayest times that Omaha ever had was when ex-President Grant was there in '79.   There was a big parade, with many bands, and a reception in the old customs house where everybody held him by the hand for one brief second. After our turn we got off in a corner with General Crook and some of his lieutenants to watch the crowd.

Only a few weeks before we had come from Cheyenne on the same train with General Fremont, and General Crook had met him at the train to pay all possible deference to the aging pathfinder of western territories.   We did not ourselves realize at that time what an important factor he was in the settlement of this great western land, but in subsequent travels we found his early monuments marking important places and epochs that are now enclosed in our nation's history, and his name as hon-

General and Mrs. George A. Crook

ored as that of Lewis and Clark, who did so much for the development of Oregon and Washington.   General Crook was loud in the praises of the pathfinder.

There was an interesting episode in the lives of General and Mrs. Crook that has never been given much publicity but it was important to them.   It was during the War of the Rebellion that the general first met his wife who was then a southern belle and a devoted adherent to the Southern cause.   The young officer fell in love at first sight and made bold advances into the enemies' lines to see the fair maid.   The beautiful Southern inamorata did not so readily yield to cupid's dart and she deliberately planned a ball at her father's house to which several of the Northern officers were invited and assured of protection. They were no sooner in the midst of the gaities of the evening, however, than the house was surrounded by Confederate soldiers and the officers of Uncle Sam were made prisoners of war. It was not until she looked into her young lover's eyes as he was being taken away that she realized the enormity of her beguiling. She knew in that moment that she loved the man whom she had betrayed and was sending to Libby Prison. From that moment she began doing penance and she did not desist in her efforts to undo her work until she had made him free again. They were married at the close of the war and lived happy ever after but she never enjoyed having that affair referred to.

Omaha was not without its quota of newspapers, but the leaders then were the Omaha *Republican* and the Omaha *Bee*, the latter with that aggressive and progressive Rosewater as its owner and business manager. The *Republican* was managed by C. E. Yost, who was not only a capable and efficient man, and is now the general manager of the Nebraska Telephone Company, but at that time Mr. and Mrs. Yost were the handsomest couple in Omaha. Their beauty was not confined to their forms and features, but their general lives were in keeping and they were loved and admired for their personal qualifications. The *Republican* was sold a few years later to S. P. Rounds, the Public Printer of Washington, D. C.

The Union Pacific headquarters were on the corner of Farnham and Ninth streets; they employed fewer men for all departments of the work than they now have in the Auditing Department alone. Yet Mr. C. S. Stebbins, who is now assistant to the auditor is about the only one left there of the force whom we knew so well. In the year '79 Thomas L. Kimball was made General Passenger and Ticket Agent of the Kansas Pacific Company, as it had become a part of the Union Pacific system, and the advertising for the newly acquired branch was added to Pard's department. Mr. Kimball was soon thereafter made General Manager of the whole system and he was sincerely loved by all those who were under him, yet he was a man demanding the duties of his employees to be well and accurately done. He was our good patron saint who not only opened up the opportunities for a life of greater usefulness, but he smoothed many a rough road by his kindly approbation of the work being done.

Pard had two able assistants in his office work, in correspondence, compiling time-tables and doing local work, who have so risen in the lime-light of affairs that they must have well-nigh

Thomas L. Kimball

forgotten that long stormy winter, were it not for the heart ties that the association cemented. They also became members of our home circle, and left an indelible impression of their worth. One, Mr. T. W. Blackburn, who had long been in the newspaper field, and was ably fitted for an assistant in literary work, has since then become one of the legal lights of Omaha. The other was the Hon. Chas. S. Gleed, of Kansas City, one of the most widely known and highly successful men in the affairs of the State of his adoption. His rattling cane was ever a welcome sound, for it betokened the coming of a ray of sunlight and cheery companionship wherever he entered. His life had not been a happy one and it was still full of sorrows and unsolved problems that he must work out to successful issue. Coming home from his busy office day he would hide himself in his room with his old Stradivarius, and weird and plaintive melodies would float through the house for hours while he scarcely knew what he was doing. Down on the broad of his back, with the room as dark as midnight, he drew the bow across the strings in melancholy pleadings until his mind found peace again, then with a lively reel, or a gay patrol to tell of his return to mental equilibrium he would appear all smiles and joyousness, as if he had not a care in the world. Early in life he had learned to hide his own unrest in his work for the happiness of others, and he had learned the lesson to a degree that few people achieve. There was a brief sketch of him in *Scribner's Magazine* in 1905 that should be read by every young man of the day who thinks his own lot is a hard one, for in its pages he would learn what earnest and persistent endeavor can accomplish under most adverse circumstances.

The restlessness of the springtime took forceful possession of our household. Pard was pining for his beloved Colorado and to flee from the desk work which was undermining his health. Mr. Blackburn had been so imbued with the connubial bliss in our family that he wanted to follow the example and take unto himself a wife.

Mr. Gleed and Pard had been laid up with mumps for several weeks and I myself was anxious to get Pard out into the hills. Mr. Gleed, therefore, took charge of the Kansas City office, and thus took his first steps in becoming a director and the foremost legal light of the Atchison, Topeka, and Santa Fé Railway. Mr. Blackburn bought our household effects and took possession of our home with his June day bride, and Pard was allowed to transfer the Literary Department work to Denver. Thus the three tillicums separated, each to build for himself as no man knew. Each one flapped his wings and plumed himself for new and more arduous work, yet with wider fields for conquest.

It was a joy, indeed, to flee from the hot bed of the smothering Missouri valley to the cool, sweet air of Denver, and as soon as Pard's office was well established in the new stone Union

Pacific depot building there we departed for the mountains and began the most strenuous year of our travels.

Mr. George Ady was the General Agent of the Union Pacific at Denver, and his assistant was none other than the now noted author, Francis Lynde. No one for a moment thought that gay Lothario would ever evolve into an author and a minister, and be the head of a household with six to call him father. It would have been the doublet of Jekyl and Hyde not to be thought of. No one would have believed in the sleeping talent lying under the gay exterior of the young secretary.

Even when we saw him standing in clerical gown in the little chapel at the foot of Lookout Mountain, in Chattanooga, the thought kept welling up within us: "What hath God wrought in this man?" Up in his "eagle nest" home hanging over the mountainside he had his little brood most happily housed, and around his grounds a high stone wall which he had himself built as an exercise and rest from long hours at his desk. His study was also his own handiwork, built of stone in a secluded corner of his shaded grounds, so that the attractions of scenery or company, or other disturbing or distracting elements might be shut out from view while he wove the web of romance for his many admiring friends.

CHAPTER XVI

IN THE ROCKIES AGAIN. COLORADO SPRINGS, MANITOU,
PIKE'S PEAK, ETC.

SUMMERTIME of 1880 was a season when railroads were being so rapidly constructed in Colorado that they seemed born of magic. One of the best equipped railroads in the State was the "Denver and Rio Grande" leading south to Alamosa, Canyon City, and on to Leadville. The road had two terminals on the southern border of the State: one branching eastward from Cucharas to Elmoro, one west over La Veta Pass to Garland.

The road was narrow gauge because it was believed then that the narrow gauge track was the only safe and feasible one for cliff climbing. It is only by expensive experience that the richest blessings fall, and this tentative method disclosed the fact that there are no impossibilities in railroad building, and the standard gauge now creeps along in its serpentine trail as safely as any, and it has crowded out the trail of lesser dimensions that was first hailed with such joy. The ride from Denver to Colorado Springs was like a picture book wherein every mile turned a new leaf disclosing greater beauties of nature.

Colorado even in the early '80's had a perfect system of irrigation, rendering every summer's crop a success and enveloping its watered slopes in robes of perpetual green. The long swards were topped by crowns of lofty pines that gave the landscape an appearance of some grand park.

The previous winter snows had been so light that old Pike's Peak was now for once without her snow bonnet, and she shook her dark tresses with coaxing coquetry to lure tourists to her

pinnacle to view the daily performances of the sun in its settings
of scarlet and gold.

There was no easy way to the summit of Pike's Peak, but a
long weary stumbling ride on horseback, and on foot for the last
part of the way, to be caught in storms without shelter and
to endure fatigue, bruises, and exposure that modern tourists
know not of.   But it was something to accomplish, wonderful to
see, and when done something to be thankful for.   But what is
there worth having that one does not have to strive for?

The old Cliff House at Manitou, surrounded by towering
battlements of stone, was the favorite resort for summer guests,

Top of Pike's Peak

and the two Concord coaches from the trains at Colorado
Springs six miles away were fairly well loaded with human freight
that came to enjoy the most famous scenic resort then known,
and the steam cars did not make their first run into Manitou
until about the middle of July of that summer of '80.

In front of the Cliff House a constantly playing fountain made
music with the flowing waters, and just on beyond, through a
shady lane, were the iron, sulphur, and soda springs.   The drives
through the Garden of the Gods were unsullied by man's con-
nivances, and every mile gave its impress of the mightiness of
God's work.   Monument Park, the famous Ute Pass, and the
Mesa Drive were all trips of interest, but there were two other

excursions that exceeded them all in grandeur and startling revelations.

One of these was up the Cheyenne Canyon, and the other was through Williams' Canyon and cave. Williams' Canyon is formed of walls of limestone of most wonderful formations in all stages of decomposition. There is very little verdure either on the top or sides and only a few scrubby pines broke the rugged rocky face of the narrow defile.

A quarter of a mile in the canyon from Manitou stands a lime kiln that was slowly utilizing the massive structures around it. The owner of this fiery furnace had a history. He had served in armies of three different nations; spent three years in Asia, two years in India, several seasons in the diamond fields of Africa, a few months in South America, and was master of many languages. He was not only doing a prosperous business with his lime kiln, but he also was the trusty guide through the Williams' Canyon mammoth cave, which was a gold mine to him.

The cave was half a mile up the canyon. To reach the entrance one must first mount a flight of steps, and then with steady head and firm grasping of projecting stones scale along the slippery trail that was too narrow for more than one to pass at a time, and where a little slip might send one rolling down with loose gravel and sand for two hundred feet. The hole that formed the doorway was six feet high, and two feet and a half wide. At first there was a gradual incline of about ten feet, at the bottom of which the guide provided us with little miners' lamps. It fairly chills one to think of the deep, dark holes that were on either side. The first part of the cave was fifteen feet wide, and the widest place in it would not exceed thirty feet, while the narrowest would just admit the body sideways; the height and depth seemed without end. Often we were obliged to ascend or descend a stairway of a dozen steps, and at one place we went down forty-five steps.

A formation called the Chimney Hole was raised some six feet from the walk; it was pyramidal in form and at its base it was ten feet across. It was hollowed out so that the sides were only about five inches in thickness, and as it appeared at the top the hole was not more than two feet in diameter. Its height was incalculable. We could not even see what held it suspended in its position. At another place a narrow shelf projected over a deep chasm which seemed to have no bottom. Just above this narrow shelf the wall bulged out so that in crossing over one was forced to bend his body forward and gaze into the blackness of the abyss. I hesitated and was the last to cross, but to remain behind with the bats and goblins seemed worse than to venture on. I can never forget my sensations as I

Hagerman Pass, Colo., 11,500 feet above sea level

edged my way along with my heart in my throat thumping so that it choked me and I wished for home and mother; but a glance at Pard with his smile of assurance gave me new courage, and I knew by his deathlike grip of my hand that if I went down my fingers would remain with him as mementoes of the exploit. I would have given all my possessions except my dear old Pard to have been afforded some other way of getting back than to re-cross that shelving rock. Thoughts of that black, bottomless pit underneath it give me the shivers to this day.

The Auger Hole was so named because of its literal resemblance to a hole made with an auger. It was perfectly round, some thirty inches in diameter, and seventy-five feet long. Some fifteen feet from the entrance of the Auger Hole there were two caves opening at right angles. We had to get down and crawl

Cheyenne Falls

like a worm through the Auger Hole for that fifteen feet to where the cave opened out again, and had the distance been the whole length of the Auger Hole I would be there yet, for I reached my limit of muscular propulsion in the fifteen feet that brought us to the first exit.

Our little glimmers cast fantastic and cadaverous shadows all about us, and our fancies ran wildly over the possibility of being swallowed by some yawning abyss or crushed beneath relentless walls of stone. We had not gone more than half a mile beyond the Auger Hole before the cave was so wet that we turned back, and never did God's sunshine seem so dear to me as when we emerged from that exploration.

We were indebted to Mr. George Palmer of Colorado Springs for some very pretty stalactites. To have his name among the immortals he lay face downward upon the earth and taking his dim light wormed himself inch by inch under a massive boulder to reach another part of the cave and obtain the valuable specimens. He was quite exhausted on his return and declared the trip came nearer making him immortal than he thought the venture at first promised.

Cheyenne Canyon's beauty and grandeur lie in its high walls and Seven Falls. When in nearly a mile from the entrance of the canyon we could see three of the falls at one time and forming a perfect half circle around them rose the mighty walls four hundred feet, as perpendicular as the most critical masonry could form them.

We were not satisfied with seeing three falls, for we had travelled far to see seven. So we wheezed and puffed and climbed a thousand feet above the stream, and from our dizzy height saw a panorama never to be forgotten. Far below each cascade fell into its rock-worn bed and forced its way over the edge and on to the precipice beyond. Away over the foothills we saw hundreds of miles of the bright prairie lands, and on the other hand rose peaks that had won the upward race over the one that formed our resting place. To scale these heights and view these lowlands, and see what God hath wrought in this wonderland of the Rockies is to hold one spellbound with awe, wonder, admiration, and adoration, and to thank God for sight and understanding and for the privilege of being there.

CHAPTER XVII

NEW MEXICO, SANTE FÉ, AND THE PUEBLOS

FROM Colorado Springs we went south to the Denver and Rio Grande terminal at Trinidad, thence by stage six miles back to Elmoro, to connect with the Atchison, Topeka, and Santa Fé road for Santa Fé City in New Mexico. At Elmoro the Santa Fé road crossed the Rio Grande Railway, but it allowed no passengers to get on or off because of the Santa Fé enmity toward the Rio Grande Company. At Trinidad Pard and I were given the bridal chamber, and the other four of our party were in a distant part of the house. They had no locks on their doors and barricaded them with the furniture of the room and had a good night's rest, but with us it was different. Our door was locked all right but too many intruders were already inside, and small as they were they made a night of misery for us. Trinidad then had about 4000 inhabitants.

Twelve miles south there was a long steady climb up the Raton Mountains, to the famous Raton Tunnel, some 2500 feet long. The arched walls vibrated with the motion of the iron horse, but their rocky hands were too firmly clasped to yield to even such a power and we merged into daylight from the tunnel's black chamber, and wound down the serpentine road to the valley below with a grade of two hundred feet to the mile, the heaviest grade on any main line American railroad at that time.

At Las Vegas, N. M., the famous hot springs were some miles from the town. Nature had done her share toward making the springs famous. There were twenty of them boiling up along the hillside, and the little park of seventy-five acres was completely environed by low mountains that were green from base to summit.

A small river crossed on one side of the park, and on its bank stood a three-story hotel with porticoes running the entire length of each story. Across the river and connected with an artistic bridge and broad walk was the mammoth bathhouse.

Santa Fé in 1879

This also was of stone and two hundred feet long. The temperature of the springs was from 100 to 140 degrees; the water was clear and strongly sulphuric, while the analysis was similar to the Arkansas hot springs.

Midday was very warm, but the nights were cold and flies were unknown. An amusing feature of the place was the squaws and Mexican women doing laundry work at two of the springs reserved especially for them. They used broad, smooth stones for their washboards, and after dipping and rubbing awhile they suspended the clothing in the hot springs to boil or soak, and it came out as pure and white as the driven snow.

At Santa Fé I really begrudged the time to sleep or eat, there was so much to see and study in the glorified silvery haired city. "Santa Fé" means "holy faith" and the many spires of

Catholic churches pointing toward heaven, together with the early establishment of that holy faith doubtless gave the city its name. The town is 7000 feet above sea-level, with pleasant summers and mild winters, but it often has electrical disturbance of its atmosphere that will interrupt telegraph lines for several hours at a time.

How old the place is will probably never be known, as it was the home of the Aztecs for many years before Christopher Columbus sighted America, and it is still disputing its right with

North Pueblo near Santa Fé

St. Augustine in Florida for the honor of being the oldest town in the United States. It was a populous place when the Spaniards entered it in 1542.

The oldest house known was built by Coronado in 1540. It was but twelve feet in height, but built in two stories of adobe brick. It was sixty feet long and fifteen feet wide; it was occupied by five Mexican families, and it looked as if good for another century or two.

In the adjoining yard was the famous San Miguel Church. Its tower had long since fallen to the ground, and the adobe was crumbling. Upon entering the church we saw a beam overhead bearing the inscription that the church was rebuilt in 1810. It was first built in 1582, but the original roof was burned off by the Indians. The walls are the same to-day as they were three hundred years ago, and two of the paintings that adorn the walls were brought from Spain, and were said to be at least a hundred years older than the church.

The front yard and the ground of the interior of the old church were filled with graves of unknown dead, and thus it was with all the old churches there. Brother Baldwin took great care in showing the building and the college near by, from the tower of which we had a fine view of Santa Fé.

The town was built around a plaza in the true Spanish style; its houses were mostly one-story adobes, and the streets were so narrow that a horse and buggy standing crosswise would entirely obstruct the passage. The plaza is what we in the East would call a public square.

In the centre of this playground a marble monument had been erected in honor of our brave soldiers who had fallen by the hand of the savage red men. Nearby the old government palace, built in 1581, was fast losing its antique appearance because of much

View of Pueblo from the south

remodelling inside and adding of verandas outside, but the walls were unchanged.

Ground space was no object to these people when they wanted to build. A model Mexican or Spanish house was of adobe and one story high, with one or more placitas or inner courts. All the rooms opened into the placita and nearly all opened on the street as well. The walls were from two to four feet thick, and the roof was made of tiles whose spouts projected two feet or more from the building to carry off the water when it rained. Our hotel had three placitas, the largest having an area of a quarter of an acre. The house was so cool that one would not dream how hot the sun was outside.

The women, except the Americans, still wore shawls about their heads, and held them close over the lower part of the face, and the men wore serapes held in much the same way as the Indian blanket. When these people went to market they carried their meat home with them slung over their shoulders or in a basket without a cover, so the flies and bugs had many a feast as they followed the carriers.

The ceilings were never plastered, but had simply plain, unfinished beams. There were no seats in the Catholic churches, and the congregation squatted on the floor. At any hour of the day devout Catholics could be found at worship or confession.

The bishop's garden was also one of the attractive features of the town. He had fruits of all kinds belonging to the temperate zone, and his artificial ponds had thousands of fish. The new stone cathedral after ten years of steady work was slowly assuming shape, and the Sisters' Hospital of brick was just completed.

Santa Fé was the queerest, quaintest place that one could imagine, with its narrow cowpath streets and its people so quaintly dressed. Its plaza was full of spreading cottonwood trees that made a densely shaded retreat for midday idlers, and at all times of day and night the seats were filled and the ground covered with lazy Spanish and Mexican gossips and drones, who listened to the daily concert of the military band. The blocks of the city had no regular dimensions, and varied from two or three rods to a quarter of a mile in length, as convenience dictated.

The Exchange Hotel, kept by Mrs. S. P. Davis, was a model of neatness and comfort, and never were we more modestly comfortable than under her roof. The rooms were large, airy, and clean, and the public parlor had many dainty womanly touches that made one think of home. The upright piano, with its abundance of classical sheet music, afforded opportunities for a most delightful evening. The quaint building occupied a whole block; its adobe walls were only one story high and the string of doors opening on the narrow verandas of its different sides made it look more like openings in a beehive with its inmates going in and out. Every guest had his own front door, and also a door opening into the inner court, and every room contained two single beds.

A suburban trip of interest was to the Taos pueblo, an old Aztec village then occupied by descendants of the old Aztec race and Pueblo Indians. Pueblo means people in the Spanish acceptance of the term, but it is often applied to the buildings in which the strange race dwells.

Without doubt the most picturesque inland town in the South-

The Sacred Grove of Pueblo de las Taos

west is this old pueblo of Taos, in northern New Mexico, thirty miles east of the Denver and Rio Grande narrow gauge road from Santa Fé toward Durango. In the days of the Santa Fé trail, Taos was one of the important points between Kansas and the coast, but with the advent of the railroads through the southern routes in the early '80's its importance waned.

The first English newspaper established west of the Missouri River was published at Taos. Here Kit Carson lived for many years, and is now buried, his house in the main part of the town being occupied of late years as a newspaper office.

Taos has long been noted as a rendezvous for artists and

writers who found unmarred the long-sought local color of the Southwest.   Frederic Remington studied at Taos, and other artists whose works are well known are Sauerwein (recently deceased), Couse, Phillips, Sharp, Rollins, Burbank, and Groll. The first four mentioned have owned or now own homes in Taos.   Here the old communal life of the Pueblo Indians, the Spanish customs of the native Mexicans, and the pioneer American home life have been blended in one community for half a century.

At the old Aztec pueblo the buildings were made of adobe brick, which is composed of mud and straw pressed into bricks and dried in the sun.   The Taos pueblo is two stories high and built around a plaza with the openings facing inward.   The outer wall formed the high exterior of the square of the plaza.

These queer people have no doors or windows on the ground floor except the one entrance to the inner square around which the extended adobe wall is built.   They climb up to the second story on a ladder in the court, and pull the ladder up after them.   Many of the apartments were very clean and neat, and again they were the embodiment of filth.   They were rather an industrious people, and while the men worked in the field outside, the women made pottery.   They made all kinds of hideous shapes, and their clay birds, children, men, and gods were most unmercifully distorted in their attempts to copy nature.

The natives were always peaceable, as were their predecessors.   Their ploughs were made of sticks and they walked in front of their teams instead of behind when ploughing.   Their ovens on top of the second story were made of the same material as their buildings.   It seemed impossible for them to get clothing enough on to cover their nakedness; their black hair was cut even with the eyebrows in front and hung down long in the back.

The lower part of the houses were generally used for storing their provisions, and in olden times for storing ammunition when there was need for defence from enemies.   They ground their own corn on a flint slab with long granite bars, and the movement was like rubbing clothes on a washboard.   They kept the meal brushed together with an old hairbrush which had active service in the two capacities.

No one knows how long these buildings have stood.   They were there three hundred years ago, and perhaps three hundred years before that. Some of the walls were crumbling down, but for the most part they seemed good for ages to come. The hours spent there were full of interest, and we were well rewarded for our trouble.

On the way home we spread our lunch under the roots of a mammoth cottonwood tree, on the bank of a stream where the waters had washed away the soil, and the gnarled roots were intertwined and stood out in bold relief, making a canopy of shade as if in anticipation of such a party as ours.

The burros or Mexican donkeys were about the size of an American colt six months old. The Indians and Mexicans drive them to town loaded with wood or timber, which is tied to the little patient animals with ropes. It is said that when grass

San Juan plow and car

gives out they live on pebbles and tin cans.

The Mexican jewelry was a great novelty and it was from their patterns that Americans have adopted and learned the filagree work. There was one bracelet on exhibition that was sixty years old in 1880. It required twelve months to make it. It was of massive gold, made with vines, berries, and leaves, with over four thousand precious stones, the largest one not much larger than a pin head. It was valued at $5000, although it was not for sale at any price.

Twenty miles from Santa Fé is the only turquoise mine of which our noble country boasts. It was first worked by the Aztecs, and many stone implements with which they used to work out the matrix have been found in the rifts. The mine had not been worked for many years until leased by Eastern capitalists, and as a piece of perfect turquoise the size of a nickel is worth over a thousand dollars it is quite a comfortable mine to own.

A good story of the troubles of an American to grapple with the Spanish language was published at the time we were in Santa Fé in the Albuquerque (N. M.), *Democrat*, and ran as follows:

"A few days since a stranger from the unconverted wilds

San Juan Dago and his burro

of the East, where tenderfeet attain their highest state of sensitiveness, came out to Albuquerque, New Mexico, to visit a friend. While walking along Railroad Avenue, he said to his friend: 'There goes a man I met up at La Junta' giving the J its natural pronunciation. 'You mean La Hunta' the friend replied 'That is a Spanish name, and in that language the J takes the sound of H.' 'Is that so? Well I must try to catch on to that.'

"Then after strolling along a short distance farther he asked: 'Where are those James Springs of which I see so much in the papers?' 'You should call them Haymes Springs; they are over in the mountains about sixty miles.'

"'Darn the language—it breaks me all up. That's a pretty nice house over there—that Armijo House, isn't it?' and again he gave the j its proper pronunciation. 'You mean the Armiho House; yes, it's a good one too.'

"'Damsicha way of abusing the English alphabet. I reckon, then, that must be Haffa Bros.'s store down the street there?' 'No, that is not a Spanish name, I think it is French. However, it is pronounced as spelled.' 'Well, how in Santa Fé is a fellow goin' to tell what's Spanish and what is n't? Why could n't they spell their language accordin' to the original plans?' 'Oh, you 'll soon catch on. You will find it safest to give the Spanish pronunciation to nearly everything here.'

Pottery of the San Juan Indians

"An hour later they sat down at the table of the San Felipe Hotel, and, after scanning the bill of fare, the stranger said to the waiter: 'You may bring me a nice, huicy piece of roast beef, some pig's howl with caper sauce, some fricasseed hack-rabbit, some pork with apple helly, some boiled potatoes with the hackets on—unskun, you know—some tarts with currant ja—I mean currant ham, and, ah some——'

"At this point the waiter swooned and the guests in the room let out a roar of laughter that gave the chandeliers the chills and fever. This made the stranger mad, but his friends got hold of him and took him from the room, and as he went through the door he remarked: 'I kin take a hoke, but, it makes me mad to be played for a greeny.'"

We call our native country Fatherland and our language Mother Tongue, but a foreigner will find just such absurdities in the English language. An acquaintance who was struggling with its obstacles said to us: "When I discovered that if I was quick I was fast, if I stood firm I was fast, if I spent too freely I was fast, and that not to eat was to fast, I was discouraged; but when I came across the sentence, 'The first one won one guinea prize,' I was tempted to give up English and learn some other language." And who could blame him?

CHAPTER XVIII

MIDDLE PARK. A THRILLING SIX-HORSE RUNAWAY

 FTER a few days' rest in the quiet shades of Estes Park, following the trip through New Mexico, Pard thought it was necessary for him to go over the mountain range to Middle Park on horseback for the purpose of noting the timber and other resources, and to study the water-courses. I whispered to him, to hunt and fish on the way, and he did not deny the soft impeachment, but the smile that flitted over his face would make one think he already had a trout on his line.

Mrs. W. B. Waters, one of my sisters from Chicago, had been persuaded to enjoy some of the Colorado scenery with us for a month or two, and while Pard crossed the range from Estes Park under the trusty guidance of Hank Farrar, sister and I preferred the roundabout route by rail and stage. There were no good horses for the trip over the range for us, and as we would have to use the cross-saddle, for which we were not prepared, we could only watch them ride away without us. A rendezvous had been planned in Middle Park, and the first stage out carried us down to Longmont, whence we went by rail to Denver and Georgetown, then by stage again for seventy miles to the point of convergence.

The morning we left Georgetown was bright and clear, and the six-horse coach came up to the Barton House for its eleven waiting passengers with a clanking of harness and rattling of wheels that betokened a dashing ride. Five grown people and four children made the unpromising load for the inside, and a sick man with a ten-year-old boy with the driver.

The driver was cracking his whip and spurring the horses to the usual parade within the town limits, when a man suddenly ran from a cabin where he had been sitting in his shirt sleeves in the doorway reading a newspaper. He threw up his hands in an excited manner as he ran toward us, and stopped the stage, begging the driver to wait just five minutes for him as he *must* take that coach. The "major-domo" on the box grumbled a reluctant consent and told the man to hustle himself for that "stage could n't wait long for nobody, specially some feller that 'ud read 'stead o' puttin' on his clothes"; and he continued to mumble on in a disgruntled way until the man was aboard and the wheels turned again.

We could see him put on his vest, tuck a few things in a small bag, grab his coat, and start out, slamming the door behind him, without giving it further attention, and donning his coat as he ran. We could not understand why he was not ready if it was so important for him to take that morning's stage. He climbed into the coach all out of breath, puffing like an engine, but with a look of satisfaction that quite reconciled the other passengers to the delay. He bore the euphonious name of George Washington Giggy, as we afterward learned, and his home was in Boulder, Colorado. He had a large stock-ranch near Middle Park and had promised to ride a horse up to the ranch for some man in Georgetown, a valuable animal that could not be trusted to an unknown personage.

He was not inclined to be talkative at first, but when he gained his composure he seemed to feel that some explanation was due, and after a slight smile had played over his countenance a few minutes he said he had not the slightest intention of taking that stage until he heard it coming up the street; then a feeling came over him so strong that he *must* take it that it was like a power not his own that impelled him to demand the stage to wait for him. Now that he was on his way he wondered what he did it for and what the owner of the horse would think of him.

Among the other passengers was a woman with four little girls and a nursemaid, and we were no sooner whirling along the curves of the mountains in the swinging coach than three of the four children began to be seasick, and they continued to be ill all the day long. We were unfortunate enough to be on the inside, having surrendered the outside seat to the man who was ill,

"Quick as a thought he was pulling his great stalwart figure from out
the coach"

and then to have those three children seasick made our condition rather deplorable.

The first fourteen miles was a steady ascent along as grand a mountain road as one could imagine. From below, the road, high on the mountainside, looked like a mere scratch on the rocks.

There was a post-office at the entrance to Middle Park kept by a Mr. Ostrander, and with the long shadows of a dying sun creeping down the mountainside, we drew up in front of this important distributing point. The nursegirl got out with the children, that they might get a few minutes of exercise while the mail was being changed.

The driver well knew that he had a pair of runaway bronchos in the lead of his six-in-hand, but he carelessly wound the lines around the brake without leaving any one to watch the restless animals, and went to the back boot to readjust the mail and to add a new sack. The untamed roadsters soon felt the lack of a restraining hand and made a wild dash for liberty. The driver rushed for the lines and perhaps could have succeeded in getting hold of them had he not tripped and fallen, and thus left us at the mercy of six wild horses.

The invalid on the box was too ill to even get the lines in his hand and the young boy who was travelling with him was so frightened that in an attempt to jump off he lost his balance and at the outset we saw the poor lad falling doubled up between the wheels, and we knew the stage ran over him.

There was a stretch of more than a mile of corduroy road ahead of us with its rough pole ends sticking out to the ditch on either side and if we upset we must be dragged along on those wicked logs to our doom. Mr. Giggy clasped his hands as if in an attitude of prayer, and his face betokened a look of the most abject terror; he was facing me and I will never forget my horror in the thought that he had gone mad. Suddenly his face lighted, he looked out and saw the lines still wound around the brake and said, "Oh, if I can only get hold of those lines!" and as quick as a thought he was pulling his great stalwart figure from out the coach and with superhuman strength he grasped anything that would hold him until he had climbed to the front boot, where he did get possession of the lines. He gave a glad shout to us that he had made it, and though he knew he could not stop the mad race of the horses who had the bits in their teeth, he could guide them until their strength was spent and perhaps keep the stage from going over.   He pulled on them with all his might as he pressed the brake to check their speed.   We could hear the bark of his breath in his strenuous work, and knew that

" Crossing its pure, swift waters half a dozen times "

every bit of his strength was being exerted to prevent a direful catastrophe.

Sister and I had all we could do to keep the frantic mother from leaping from the coach, as she called loudly for her children and she became so insane with fear that we had to hold her by main force as we were buffeted about like feathers in a storm.

Mr. Giggy did guide the horses safely over the entire length of that corduroy road, but when the smooth roadbed was reached they took a fresh plunge; fortunately they were too nearly winded to keep it up, and turning them into a wire fence he brought them to a sudden halt.   When he had rested himself a moment he turned the horses around and drove them back to the post-office.   The driver was following on the way, having.

started out on foot after the stage, and when Mr. Giggy again took his seat inside, still trembling from his exertion, we all said it was no longer a mystery what power had impelled him to come on that stage, for it was a special dispensation of Providence that he should be there to save our lives.

The poor boy was not killed but he was badly hurt and we had to leave him there with the man who was himself too ill and weak with fright to continue his journey even had the boy not been hurt. The rest of us continued on our way with nothing worse than the loss of some of the color glands of our hair and the equilibrium of our nerves, but we were glad when the day ended, landing us, about eight o'clock, at what was called the Middle Park Hotel at Hot Sulphur Springs.

A plunge in the hot springs baths refreshed our physical powers and washed away some remembrance of trouble. There were more than twenty hot springs that boiled up and united their waters in one common stream that rolled over a ledge of rock into a natural basin made by the falling water wearing out a great bowl in the huge rock, three or more feet in depth, twenty feet wide, and thirty feet in length. Over this had been built a stone house enclosing the swimming bath. The temperature was 120 degrees Fahrenheit, and one needed to play around the edge a while before making a final plunge. This had been a favorite resort of the Ute Indians for centuries and they came even yet to an annual pow-wow. The springs were discovered by a party of prospectors sent out by Wm. N. Byers, of Denver, on Christmas, 1859. While little of the precious metal was found, the discovery of these springs would prove more valuable than a gold mine if they could be made more accessible.

Settlers were coming in steadily and there were some fifty buildings at the springs. The Grand River and its tributaries abounded in fine trout, and just over the foothills close by there were plenty of elk and other wild game.

Our merry huntsmen came in over the range from Estes Park next morning, bearing some saddles of venison and some sensational experiences, but not so serious as ours had been. Pard declared he would never let me get away from him again for fear I would not be so bravely rescued as I had been on this occasion. And truly enough he has saved my life on several occasions since then.

We soon began to explore the park and enjoy its pleasures. Mounted on good horses we followed Grand River up the valley for twenty-four miles crossing its pure, swift waters half a dozen times, together with several of its tributaries.   Ever and anon the mighty current seemed determined to punish its intruders by taking us all bodily down its treacherous channel.   But at the end of the twenty-four miles Grand Lake appeared before us as a

Grand Lake, Middle Park, Colo.

beautiful sheet of water five hundred feet higher than the springs, and almost encircling its dark mirror-like depths were the wooded peaks rising two and three thousand feet, and sending continuous contributions to this unfathomable body of waters.   The main tributary was a large stream that tore its way down a narrow gorge for many miles, often making leaps of over a hundred feet, dashing its volume of water into the whitest spray, and quickly regathering its force for another and grander leap; thus on and on, one grand leap after another until, with a final roar of satisfaction, it poured its uneasy mass into the depths that know no end, for a line has not yet been found long enough to reach a resting place at the bottom of Grand Lake.

We found an old leaky boat moored on the beach and rowed ourselves across the lake; there we rested on a huge boulder in the spray of the last waterfall and climbed far above and explored to our satisfaction the mysterious windings of the stream. So long as our eyes were lifted up our minds were full of the beautiful and sublime, but when our gaze was allowed to fall upon our own feet, what a contrast! We acted like a bevy of peacocks and tried to hide the unsightly appendages, for dangling over the side of that boulder on which we were resting were three pairs of boots that had waded above their tops in mud and mire, through brooks and through briars, over dead and fallen timber. Unconsciously, and yet with wondrous lazy motion, they turned themselves in the sun and courted its warm rays, but to no purpose, for the home stretch had to be made over the same muddy road. Gradually each pair was withdrawn and put in motion and when the boat's mooring was reached every foot was so laden with mud that it was dropped into the boat like a sack of ore.

The lake was some two miles and a half long by one and a half wide. The wind had risen and the white caps and splash of the oars made a rippling accompaniment to our jests that hid any uneasiness or discomfort that white caps and leaky boats are bound to produce.

We had invitations to a dance for that evening, and although we would have been content to hide in our tent unseen there was no escape from donning our best clothes and presenting ourselves at the party. Mrs. Shaeffer prepared us a wondrously wholesome supper, and when we were ready to join the gay dancers we were so rested and refreshed that we were quickly converted to the gayety of the hour.

The cabin wherein the party was held had but one room, which served for all purposes of family life. How quaint it all was! One could imagine his spirit had flown back to the ancestral days of the Pilgrim landing. The low wide door, with heavy wooden hinges and its old-fashioned latch, opened into a room about thirty feet square. Opposite the door a huge fire was glowing and crackling cheerily against a bull pine back-log, and off in a corner was the old homemade dish cupboard, holding also the stores of provisions. Opposite that useful case a rude table was pushed up against the wall to make more room for the expected guests. The one low window had but a single sash, and for seats there were rude benches, boxes, two or three old chairs, and some of the guests were even sitting on the floor.

The mantel was graced by shining tea and coffee pots, broken pitchers of wild flowers, ancient candlesticks with tallow dips, a dilapidated timepiece, and a few extra table dishes. At least twenty good, honest country people were sitting around the room, and as many attitudes almost instantly caught the eye. From grandfather down to the baby in arms they were listening to the strains of "Dan Tucker," "The Fisherman's Hornpipe," and other familiar airs; and now and then the pure soprano of a young girl, the rich bass of the lad chimed together with the cracked yet sweet voices of the aged, and even the cooing babe joined in the old home songs, familiar to every one, and everything rang with the contagious mirth.

Old Father Shaeffer, who was nearing his ninetieth year, came in for his share of the pleasure, his white hair and beard shone like a silver wreath around his happy old face, and he was a welcome guest. Twenty years had passed since he moved into the Park, and he said in his tremulous way: "When I die—if I ever do die—I want to die right here. Why, I tell you, when God made the world he had all his best stuff yet on hand and he lumped it off in a heap right here in Middle Park." Money would not hire him to spend one week outside the Park, and during the Indian troubles the year before his sons had to take him by main force to a place of safety. He was a favorite with both old and young, and few people at his age command such love from every one.

Later a bright fire blazed in front of our tent, in itself an invitation to the needed rest we were anxious to get, and lying half awake and half asleep, with the light flickering through the open tent fly, and the great full moon showing its silvery pathway across the wonderful lake, we thought how happy these people were in their simple lives, living so close to nature, and to nature's God. The Bohemian element of my own nature made me wonder if, after all, the thirst and greed for knowledge and civilization and more sordid things are worth the price we pay.

In the morning a large, beautiful horse, the pride of the camp, was placed at my disposal while we remained. What a joy it was to be in boots and spurs on such a magnificent animal.   He arched his neck and pranced about as if he realized the compliments that were showered upon him.   His training was perfect, and he was guided by gently dropping the rein on his neck on the opposite side from which he was to go.   Always used

"The branches rubbed me out of my saddle"

to guiding an animal by the bit I did not trust myself so much as I did the horse, but Pard and I galloped off scarcely realizing that I was not in a cozy rocking-chair.

The test came, however, when, suddenly changing our course where a tree stood in the forks of the road, I gave my pretty bay a tap on the wrong side of the neck, so that he went dutifully up to it, instead of going away from the tree; the branches rubbed me out of my saddle, throwing me backwards to the ground.   When

I returned to consciousness I called for my horse, which was quietly grazing near by. He was not at all excited and came at my call, sniffing his regrets as best he could, but after all he seemed to have a look of disgust in his eye such as I have seen hunting dogs have when a shot failed to bring down the game.

As soon as possible I was reseated in the saddle, but being slightly hurt we curtailed the ride. I was too proud to own the cause of our speedy return, and put it entirely upon the grounds of generosity toward some one else who might want to ride. After being secretly bathed and sponged with spirits and hot water, and taking a dose of life-giving bitters, I was permitted to remain quiet the rest of the day.

Three sides of Middle Park are walled in by the snowy range, the fourth side allowing the waters to pass off toward the western slope. The surface is broken with hills and peaks that render it picturesque in the extreme, with its many streams winding among the depressions. The hills are so high that only a small portion of the Park is visible from any given point unless from such an eminence as Mt. Bross, which stands close by the springs.

One is amply repaid by a trip to the summit of that mountain, for the Park lies like a greensward at its feet, while beyond the snow gives rainbow reflections that mingle with the green trees and grass, and the silver waters shine as far away as the eye can see.

Semi-precious stones are found all over the Park in immense deposits. There are hundreds of acres of agates, jasper, and opal, and a whole mountain of chalcedony and endless quantities of petrified wood. Some rich deposits of silver ore had also been found on the range toward North Park.

It was a joy to us that our exploits were not all for the home-seeker, the investor, or the scrambler for wealth, but that we could also reach such places where future villages would find all the charms of nature, and be imbued and awed by the marvellous works of One supreme over all. We felt like calling from the mountain tops to the whole world to come and see the stupendous scenery of the great and glorious Rockies.

It was a matter of regret that we could not linger at places which pleased us so much, yet we never moved on but that we found new wonders to hold us enchanted again.

As Pard's work was done the time came to say good-bye to

Middle Park, with all its towering peaks, its bottomless waters and its Bohemian life, but the glorious life-giving atmosphere was a blessing common to all the Rockies, and breathing in its life-giving ozone we wended our way back to the steel rails again to seek other unwritten lands.

CHAPTER XIX

IN August, 1880, we visited the Gunnison country which was then opening up to the world a new mining field of great promise. The direct route was by the South Park Railroad to South Arkansas station near Poncha Springs, where the Barlow and Sanderson stage line met the train Monday morning and carried passengers sixty-five miles in time for supper at Gunnison City, if good luck and fair roads favored them.

To our utter dismay there were to be seventeen passengers, eleven of whom occupied the three seats inside the coach, and the remaining six climbed on the roof; then there was the usual amount of mail, baggage, and express. We averaged 500 pounds on a seat inside, and there was no computing the weight ouside. I had the heartless assurance offered me if the roof gave in that a man weighing 250 pounds was sitting just over my head. As we rolled out of Poncha our day of trouble began. The motion of the coach soon made two of the passengers very ill. There was no help for them, but they made plenty of discomfort for the rest of us. I was riding backward on the front seat and a man and woman on the respective ends of the seat facing me had their heads out of the window incessantly to dispose of the last week's ration, and there was but little cessation the whole day long.

The steep places between Poncha and Gunnison were all on the left side, and strange as it seemed the road slanted that way down the mountainside, and to make matters still worse our coach thoroughbrace was sprung in favor of the ravines.

We had not gone many miles when one of the hind wheels struck a boulder and came so near upsetting us that two men lost their balance on the top and slid down into the green depths of the canyon.   One escaped unhurt and turned to help the other who had sprained or broken his ankle.   The poor fellow had to be carried up and the passengers of the coach changed about so as to put the injured man inside.   The men above had no sooner climbed to their places again than every one was handing down his bottle of "cure all" and a row of bottles hung in festoons around the upper part of the doors and windows of the stage. But it was once when brandy lost its magic power, and when we met the down stage our suffering passenger was sent back to Poncha.

It was not long before the driver ran too close to the mountain-side, when there was a steep pitch and again we were saved from destruction by one of the heaviest men grabbing a well-rooted sapling and holding it fast until the wheels dropped to a level again.

A little farther on we locked wheels with a freight wagon and turned the wagon over, spilling its contents to an accompaniment of profuse bad language of the freighter, and we delayed long enough for our passengers to help the man gather his load again.   This is not just the place, although it may be the time, to repeat what the freighter's remarks were about the accident, but we hastened away without writing them down.

The day wore on in a series of mishaps and delays and it was four o'clock in the afternoon before we reached the dinner station.   One of the passengers had a good supply of raisins, which he handed out most liberally.   We had never before realized how good raisins are.   The six o'clock breakfast had become a dream and dinner seemed a myth not to be materialized. The raisin man, whose name I am sorry to forget, said that he never travelled in the mountains without raisins as he found they were food and drink when everything else was gone.   It was a bit of knowledge that we never forgot, and found useful on many a hard trip when we could not eat the food that was placed before us, for we never travelled by stage after that that we did not carry a goodly supply of that succulent fruit.

At four o'clock, however, a good dinner was on the table, after our belated coach rolled up to the stage station door, and a lot of hungry people were doing it justice, when a hungry yellowjacket crawled up my wrist and presented his sword to me in such wondrously wicked way that it drained a liberal supply of blue ancestral blood.

With fear and trembling at what might yet befall us before the day was over we clambered again to our seats in the stage. The driver was in a hurry to get his load settled and be off, and he slammed the heavy stage door on a man's hand. The passenger had hold of the casing and was looking the opposite way when the accident happened, and he gave a yell of agony as he pulled in the bleeding, mangled mass that was sickening to see. We delayed at least another half hour that the bruised member might be comfortably cared for.

The driver lost his feeling of haste and was exceedingly tender in his care of the wounded hand. He explained his anxiety and hurry by saying there were two dangerous spots ahead of us and he wanted to get past them before dark, and if he told us to lean a certain way as we drove along the bad places we must do it quickly, and try to keep the stage from upsetting. One old pioneer remarked, "I am no tenderfoot, but an old mountaineer, used to danger and exposure, but this trip beats all, and my thoughts have been with home and God all day." One of the women, though perhaps used to better surroundings, had less exalted thoughts than the sturdy frontiersman, for she did nothing but scold, scold, and fret, fret, from first to last.

About six o'clock the sick woman, Pard, and I changed our seats to the outside. Pard sat above and behind me, and I sat between the invalid and the driver. Once we came near being hurled top down into the Gunnison River. It was a wondrously bad place. The embankment was a straight up and down cut of six feet or more, and the water of Gunnison River was running deep and swift against that shore. A quick cry of "to the right" from the driver made everybody lean that way, while he himself stood out on the brake block and we passed in safety and thanksgiving.

After that escape a hush seemed to fall upon the whole party with the solemnity of the night itself, and darkness closed the day and veiled other dangers from view. The quiet was finally broken by another warning from the driver, and we all leaned to the north, but our time had come, and in spite of all efforts we went over rattle-ty-bang-smash-crash, coach, bodies, baggage, mail, treasure box, and tools, in a heap and all in the dark. The first that I realized was that Pard was pulling me head first under some brush to get me away from the stage for fear the horses would drag it over me. The horses made a lunge forward but men were at their heads in an instant; the driver had jumped with the lines in his hands and the stage was not dragged far.

"Are you hurt" went the rounds with lightning speed, and the door of the coach was hurriedly opened to see who was hurt inside. Such a heterogeneous mass is never found anywhere but at just such a time and place. Heads, satchels, feet, baskets, limbs, bodies, and bags were so mixed up that it was very uncertain which to take hold of to the best advantage, so they were taken out in the order that they presented themselves. The coach lay on its side and the passengers had to be taken out of the door which was then on the top; it was pitch dark and the lamps of the stage were used to throw a glimmer of light on that internal mixture so difficult to extricate.

When every one was out we found no one seriously hurt, but all were bruised more or less. The woman next to me kept telling that I fell on her and hurt her, as if it were a fault of mine if I did. I finally assured her that I had not chosen the spot to fall on and I was sure her bones had broken one or more of my ribs. All the baggage in the front boot, including the treasure box, mail sacks, and case of tools, showered themselves over us in a very liberal manner. I did not feel at all slighted for want of attention in the way of bumps and bangs, but I would have taken them all cheerfully if the shrew had only bitten her tongue, but even that pleasure was denied us, and it wagged on worse than before, until we wished she would just get too sick to talk. It was a heartless wish, but with everything going wrong in a way that none could help it was the duty of every one to keep himself or herself from adding to the discomforts of others.

Pard had been ready for two hours to slide off if we did go over, and he landed on his feet, with only a strain of the muscles and a bruised ankle. Sage-brush fires were finally lighted to aid in finding and reloading various belongings and when the stage started on again most of the men walked the remaining miles to Gunnison.

"We went over with baggage, mail, treasure box, and tools"

We did not attach any blame to the driver, for he did the best that could have been done. But we did blame the owners of that toll road for our day of misery. I am not given to fault-finding without reason, for accidents will occur sometimes in spite of every caution. But in the 3000 miles of stage travel that we had had up to that time we never spent such an unhappy day, when every moment was in anticipation of disaster, or filled with the woes of others. Nothing would have tempted us to return that route to Poncha unless on horseback or afoot. Fortunately, however, we hoped to reach the railroad again by swinging around a circle to Alamosa.

When we drove up to the Gunnison Hotel at the witching hour of midnight I gave a quick searching glance at the house to make sure that it would stand until morn-

Gunnison disturbers of the peace

ing, then hastened to the quiet of our own room for a few hours of rest. How thankful we were that we had arrived there without more serious mishaps. I held my Pard at arm's length and beheld with pardonable pride that he was neither lame, halt, nor blind, and I pinched myself to make sure I was all together.

The morning opened to our view the beautiful Gunnison valley, and the town which lies almost at the juncture of the Tomichi and Gunnison rivers. For miles in every direction the ground was as flat as a table, but on the outskirts the mountains suddenly rose and encircled the valley.

The only disturbers of the peace were one or two hundred burros that made the nights musical or "noisical" with their incessant braying when people wanted to sleep, and it was surprising how they aroused volleys of heavy exclamations that paper walls could not smother.

The valley was fertile and well watered, and camps for miles around afforded a most excellent market and good prices, and the citizens were sanguine of success and prosperity for their favored town. The first steam whistle in Gunnison valley sounded its shrill shriek the 2d day of August, 1880, and was echoed by over a hundred voices. The Gunnison country included not only Gunnison County, but all the country drained by the river of the same name and its tributaries. Gunnison City seemed destined to be a railroad centre and distributing point for miners' supplies and provisions as it was an important junction, from which many roads would emanate to the mountains, and south to the San Juan region.

Gunnison County was capable of supporting a larger population than was then in the entire State of Colorado, and its area was more than the States of Massachusetts and Rhode Island combined. As yet the ranchmen devoted their time and attention mostly to raising hay, which was by far the most profitable of agricultural employments. By proper care in irrigation many have raised from one hundred to five hundred tons of hay that brought them from sixty to one hundred dollars per ton. The town site of Gunnison City as then laid out included about a thousand acres and offered inducements and opportunities for many branches of industry. Several sawmills were already in operation, and they dotted the country everywhere, and still there was a demand for more; the timber was plenty and of large growth. The pioneer newspaper, the *Gunnison Review*, was first issued on May 15th, edited by one Colonel Hale, and, the first copy was sold at auction for $100 to Gen. George A. Stone. There were three weekly papers in 1880 giving the local and mining news. Thus far the country promised well, and from reliable information gained there our trips to the mining camps and coal fields resulted in aiding the development of the mineral wealth then hidden in its treasure vaults.

There were three stage lines running from Gunnison to Ruby Camp, a distance of thirty miles; also stage lines to

Crested Butte, Lake City, and other towns and camps, and when we had gathered in all the knowledge we could absorb in Gunnison we wended our way on toward Irwin and Ruby Camp.

A sharp turn

CHAPTER XX

ROUGHING IT IN RUBY CAMP

WHEN leaving Gunnison the ride up along Ohio Creek was as smooth as a floor. For twenty miles or more the land was taken up for hay, and the little frontier homes, though miles apart dotted the wayside and offered hospitality to many a weary traveller. We selected the home of Mr. Edward Teachout, twelve miles from Gunnison City, as a place to rest quietly for a few days before making any further researches in the mining belt around the Ruby Camp. There were times when bodies and brains reached the limit of usage and endurance and this was one of those times. I must say, however, that Pard never stopped. Here, as elsewhere, during a temporary halt, he was up and out on a horse or afoot examining mines or forests, farming lands, or whatever the country had to show. His appetite for facts was insatiable and his energy and endurance in going after them passed my understanding.

Mrs. Teachout was a cultivated woman, and no doubt was a reigning belle in her younger days as she still retained much of her maiden beauty. Miss Fairchilds, a niece and guest from California, made a charming companion, and together we roamed the hills and fields and gathered flowers and grasses, watched the cutting and stacking of the hay, and withal enjoyed a week of quiet outdoor life that was an elixir for our regeneration. A young lady with such rare accomplishments as Miss Fairchilds possessed was a prize in that part of the country and she was truly appreciated. Such a woman on the frontier in the '70's and early '80's was like an angel from heaven.

Away on the left between Teachout ranch and the camp of Irwin was the grand Castle Rock, the most worthy of the name of many that bear the same title in the Rockies. Its peaks are many and pointed, and but for its immensity would be declared a very castle indeed. A little farther on was King's ranch, which became so noted for its comforts and discomforts the previous winter. Many people found a cold winter's night closing around them as they neared this place, and rather than risk farther progress in the stormclad hills would apply there for lodging. To every applicant would be given a royal affirmative, and as fast as he would fall asleep his blankets would be stealthily taken off and given to the next comer at one dollar per; as long as anyone came the blankets would continue to be purloined and passed along. The men would be so sound asleep that they would not know the blanket had been pulled away from them until awakened by the cold. No one ever failed to find a good fire burning to make up for the absence of the coverings, but with mercury at the freezing point or lower they cried for blankets when they were paying a dollar apiece for a bed. When some one would lose his temper over the treatment, Mr. King would finally tell him there was no promise to furnish blankets with the bed, and it became quite a saying throughout the camp for anything that was lacking to be "as scarce as King's blankets." But King and his partner kept the boys all good natured by sometimes giving up their own beds and blankets and sitting up to keep the fire blazing.

We had the top seats engaged for the drive from King's Station but a big coarse drummer, disregarding the efforts of Pard and the stage agent to put me there and notwithstanding their polite explanation that I was ill, brutally responded, "It serves her right; a woman has no business travelling in this country," and roughly forced his way to the seat. A crowd was gathering, Pard was furious, but I managed to get him inside. At the first station the drummer crawled down to stretch himself and Pard, remarking that he would now proceed to take that seat, and I should follow when the trouble was over, quickly mounted the box.   The ruffian came on the run, cursing at every jump, and started to pull Pard to the ground.   But he ran his face against the cold steel of a six shooter and was advised that a creature so devoid of every attribute of a gentleman would surely get his deserts if he persisted.   He muttered dire vengeance while I was being elevated to the coveted perch, but the belligerents finished the journey on the same inside seat like two turtle doves.   Years afterward the man recognized me in a distant State, brazenly introducing himself as the party who had so narrowly escaped being shot by my husband in the Gunnison country.   Advising him that I was annoyed at his effrontery and did n't care to renew the acquaintance he turned muttering half to himself, "Well, by thunder! you 're most as nervy as the old man."

We found Ruby Camp a stirring and wide-awake place, 10,300 feet above sea-level.   The only hotel or lodging house was graced by the inviting title of Ruby Home, so we were hardly prepared for the rude quarters that we found within. There was no register, and the proprietor ushered us

The beautiful Gunnison Valley

through the office, up a narrow flight of stairs, to a room without a number, as were all the others.   The room was about nine feet square, and contained a slat bedstead, covered with a thin straw tick, but no mattress.

In another corner was a pine stand without toilet conveniences of any kind.   Glancing around the room I saw half a dozen pairs of eyes scanning us in a most exasperating manner, and the voices belonging to the eyes seemed to be talking in my very ears.   The house had no semblance of a "home" inside or out; it was simply a pile of boards nailed up in the shape of a house with only plain, rough board partitions that had shrunken apart so far that there was absolutely no privacy in the room. Lifting my eyes from the hypnotic gaze of those already peering at us through the openings we saw that even those rough boards between the rooms were raised but a few inches above our heads.

Pard dispatched himself to get a hammer and tacks and came back bringing also a pail of water and a tin basin. He had asked the man in charge of the combination barroom and office where I could go to wash off the heavy dust and had been told I could go "over there" indicating with his thumb turned backward that I could go to the same place where a dozen or more miners were "washing up" for supper in a small hole in the wall under the stairs. Pard declined the suggestion to make my toilet in that spot and immediately got busy hunting some facilities for our room. He had to buy the basin and pail, but the man did give him a little ten or twelve inch towel. But we always carried our own towels and soap.

What newspapers we could find, together with wraps and wearing apparel not in use, were tacked on the walls to cover the openings into other rooms and shut out the inspection of inquisitive neighbors. On one side was a doctor's office, on the other was a couple belonging to a variety troupe, and more of the same kind were across the hall, and in fact the house was pretty full of hard characters of a class which frequent mining camps.

The rain descended in torrents all the afternoon and confined us indoors; the roof leaked and everybody had to skirmish about and care for his belongings and hunt a dry corner. There was a sunny spot in it all for us as Pard came up bringing an old college friend who had become interested in a mine there and who related his tenderfoot experiences in a most amusing way. It was not only amusing to us, but the chuckles that came from the other side of partitions revealed the presence of others who were also entertained.

What a rude anchorage that was. Never before or since have we been in a mining camp with rougher and more unsightly environs than in the camps of Irwin and Ruby. The stumps were not yet cleared away and the virgin soil was bottomless, not a board to walk on anywhere, not a place in the great woods where one could have an hour alone. Everywhere the prospector was digging for gold and the "yellow fever" was as contagious as that of the Sunny South, and often as fatal in its financial results.

As night came on bands began to play, and the most popular dance hall was the one towards which our only window opened.

The sounds from the Bacchanalian hall floated through the room until the small hours of the night were well on and we were at a point akin to suicide. From our room we could see the stars through the roof, the trees and the beautiful scenery through the side walls, and by looking in another direction could watch the changes of fortunes at the gambling tables, and the beautiful glide of the undulating, delicious waltz.

Irwin was the supply town for some three thousand people, and fully that many got their mail at that post-office. Mr. Soule, the postmaster, appointed the January previous when the camp first opened up, had made many solicitations that Pard write up the mines and the country's prospects for the Union Pacific's advertising publications.

"**The house had no semblance of a home inside or out**"

Mr. Soule's hopes for the camp were so sure that he had remained there all winter with his cabin sixteen feet under snow, with a stairway of snow and ice leading up to daylight. A prospector coming up the mountain on snowshoes one day suddenly saw a man appear before him in a way we used to read about in fairy stories. The stranger inquired the way to Irwin, and when told that he was above the town he wanted to know how far back he would have to go to reach the post-office. Mr. Soule told him that he would not have to go back far, but about sixteen feet under, and bade the stranger follow him and they disappeared in the hole in the snow. Mr. Soule spent most of his time making snowshoes which he sold at $8 per pair, and in the spring he put the money into town lots, which he bought at $10 apiece.   In the summer following the same lots were selling at from $1000 to $8000 each. He also whittled out 168 boxes for the post-office with his penknife, and a large case of pigeon holes for the general delivery. The scales for the post-office were composed of two tin plates suspended by wires from an old broom, and the cross-bar on which they balanced was simply a small knife-blade, while the weights were bits of metal. The mail was delivered that summer through a hole in the window to the outside, because the office was too small to admit the crowd, and it was an interesting sight to look across the street when the miners came in at night, and see the masses waiting for news of home and friends.

The primitive candle was the only illuminator, for coal oil was a dollar and a half a gallon, making it too much of a luxury for common use.   Every drink over the bar cost the imbiber twenty-five cents in money, to say nothing of the days of life it curtailed.   No cigar was sold for less than the proverbial two bits, and the till of the tobacco vender was always full.

They told the story of a tobacco famine that spring when the supply had run out, and the wholesale order had been long overdue.   Such a miserable set of men I suppose is seldom seen. An eye-witness told me that a man walking along the street would put his hands in every pocket from one to three times in going the length of a block, besides asking every man he met for "a chew."   The request would be answered with an agonizing look indicating that he was "dying for a chew" himself, and without a word and only a woebegone shake of the head he would pass on.

In all mining camps men bunch together and cook for themselves, either taking a turn about or having one of their number do it all, and then share equally in whatever the others can find in prospecting.   They would live that way for five or six dollars a week, but otherwise it was from twelve to fifteen dollars a week and upward according to distance from base of supplies.

There were seventy-five business buildings in Irwin, but they were built on the same helter-skelter plan as the hotel; they made a cover for the merchandise and that answered the purpose for the time.

The mines, of course, were the all-absorbing attractions, and they were indeed rich and tempting to the poor man as well as to the capitalist. A majority of the mines of Colorado, it is estimated, are named after women and children. The earnest affection which so many mining men feel for their families, the desperate efforts which they make to attain wealth, often sacrificing the present for the uncertain future, is well typified in the names given to their properties. It may be well imagined that when a man names his mine the Emma, that Emma is his wife's or his sweetheart's name and that he is fighting the world for Emma's dear sake. Many a miner has sat over his campfire on a bleak night, while his heart was filled with thoughts of his wife and children. The sunny hopes and the dark fears which cluster about the names of mines are many. When a man names a claim "The Only Hope" or "The Bottom Dollar," there is doubtless more pathos than humor in the association which suggests it, although the title usually calls a smile to the lips of the uninitiated. The names were probably suggestive to those who risked their little all with small prospect of return.

The most famous mine in Ruby Camp, however, was the Forest Queen, 250 feet above Irwin and overlooking the town from the head of Coal Creek. The surface cropping was at places a thousand feet long and from seventy-five to a hundred feet wide, while at the beginning the pay streak was three and a half feet, and in places had widened to eight feet. The returns received of one carload of ore was 619 ounces of silver to the ton.

There were several kinds of silver formations in other mines there as well as the Forest Queen. The ruby silver, so rare in other parts of Colorado, ran plentifully through these mines and the ore was a rich ruby hue in spots. The brittle silver had more the appearance of lead and was scattered through the ruby ore and in some of the richer specimens they were bound together by the dainty fibres of wire silver. Any one of these varieties were largely pure silver. This mine had paid upwards of $200 net per foot for every foot sunk. The owners were such well-known men as Col. D. C. Dodge, of the D. &. R. G. Railway, George M. Pullman, of palace-car fame, Gen. J. W. Palmer, president of the D. &. R. G. Railway, and R. W. Woodbury, proprietor of the Denver *Daily Times*.

While waiting for Pard to come out of a prospect hole that he was investigating, I was entertained by Supt. S. R. T. Lindley of the Goodenough Mining Co., who evidently thought I was the greenest kind of a pilgrim, as he related to me the following incident:

Spectre Monument

"I crossed the country from Missouri to California in '49. I started with five wagons and eight oxen to each wagon, plenty of provisions and $3500 in money. I had to fight Indians and Mormons all the way across the plains and they finally stole nearly all my stock and grub, and so I burned all my wagons but one. When I reached South Pass in Wyoming I had been living on mule meat for nine days and was about starved. There I found a man just ready to eat his dinner, and I saw before him a plate of well-cooked beans. They looked mighty good to me and I began by offering him $5 for his plate of beans, then on to $50, $100, $200, $500, but still he refused to share with me, so I drew my roll of bills from my belt, and slapping down two $500 bills on the table before him I gathered the beans from him and left. I tell you, Mrs. S., those were hard days to travel, but the Mormons gave me more trouble than the Indians did, by far."

I expressed my sympathy and thanks as well as I could and preserve proper decorum, for my risibles were fast gaining the mastery, and I made my escape. I came back to our fantastically draped room and swung the window back on its hinges to the wall to catch a glimpse of my face in the little mirror and see if I did look so verdant as to believe such a story, and then sat down to ponder over it. His animals were all *oxen*, but just the same he lived on mule meat nine days; he paid out $500 bills long before they were issued by our government, and fought more

Mormons than Indians four years previous to the first Mormon outbreak, as it was not until '53 that they gave any trouble to overland travellers.

On the bank of Brennan Lake above the town there stood the fine residence of Richard Irwin, a noted mountaineer, after whom the camp was named. In spite of the altitude of Irwin the mountains rise around it in emerald heights over a thousand feet, and rich forests extend almost to the tops that will make the buzz of the saw resound for many years.

One of the largest feathers in the cap of the Centennial State was the finding of large beds of anthracite coal. Three miles from Irwin, down Anthracite Creek, were 1000 acres of anthracite coal cropping out all over the surface. A tunnel had been run in fifty feet and the vein found to be seven and eight feet thick, with the indications that it would run from fifty to a hundred feet, and the largest vein in Pennsylvania is only thirty feet thick. Coal exposed here for ages was as bright and solid as it could be.

Eight miles east of Irwin was Crested Butte, connected with the former and also directly with Gunnison City by stage. In all probability it expected to be the terminus of the railroad, as the road bed could run at a water grade over the range into the limits of the town by any one of the four passes—Cottonwood, Alpine, Monarch, or Marshall. It was not so near the rich mining district, but it was a thousand feet lower, and would be the home of the miners and the officials of mines and railways. There were openings into the valley from all directions, and it was the natural home and supply town for the surrounding camps.

As might be guessed from the above showing of a possible great railway centre, my first venture in real estate in a mining camp was at Crested Butte. Then after my paying taxes on the lots for several years the Denver and Rio Grande pushed into the town and occupied the ground until it thought it had a better right to the property than I had. The company surely had possession and I was miles away, and they still have it. I am no longer paying taxes on it, although they never bought it.

Eight miles farther east was the little camp of Gothic, with its Sylvanite mine. Masses of ore weighing from one hundred to five hundred pounds literally studded with ruby, native and wire silver, were taken from the mine almost daily. Ingots of nearly pure silver, weighing from half a pound to a pound and a half had also been taken out. Two sacks of ore at the mine, weighing eighty-five pounds each, contained $800 worth of silver each, and twelve tons then ready for shipment would average $3500 per ton. The mine produced some of the most beautiful cabinet specimens of any in the State.

These were developments which it was believed would astonish the mining world and attract more attention during 1881 than residents could imagine. The Gunnison country was no longer a wilderness "out of the world" of which capital need be timid for stage lines ran to and through nearly all districts.

In later years when our steam train rolled gaily along through Gunnison en route to Salt Lake we were indulging in memories of our stage experiences through there and commenting on the luxurious comforts of our Pullman car when, without warning, an engine came at rapid speed after us and plunged into our car, tearing off the rear platform and doing much injury to our train. My first thought was that the train was attacked by bandits for we came to such a quick halt. I had just retired and, though stunned from the concussion, I felt the sensation that I had been shot in the head and expected to find my hand bathed in my own blood when I took it from my head, but it was dry. The window was not broken and yet there was such a scampering and running through the aisle that my worst fears, aside from being shot, seemed confirmed and I began looking out for Pard, who had been standing in the passage way. He had been thrown down with others and made a toboggan slide to the other end of the car, but was not badly hurt, although he came up rubbing various bruised places, and told me a wild engine had struck us and bounded right back, not coming on again to see what the damage was.

Arriving in Salt Lake our car was found to be split almost from end to end, and it was considered a marvellous escape that it did not fall apart on the winding precipices of Black Canyon.

FROM Ruby Camp back to Gunnison, thence to Lake City, our only travelling companions in the stage were another man and his wife, who were exceedingly anxious to reach their destination. The road was in a distressful condition. The anticipation of a railroad and a hurry to make money had left the road full of chuckholes and perilous places. The poor little woman began to be very ill and never did man's eyes glow with more loving solicitude

Ready for the trail

than did the distressed husband's. We hurried the driver with all possible speed to the next station where we left the young wife a happy mother of a new born babe.

We spent several days in Lake City entertained at the home of Col. Henry C. Olney, who was then editor of the *Lake City Herald*. Pard and Mr. Olney made trips to Silverton and Ouray looking up statistics and conditions for new railroads. A fine pair of twin babies had come to make the Olney home an Elysium of joy, and now that they are grown to manhood and womanhood they are filling all the promises of their tender years. They are now married and rearing families of their own in the glorious state of Washington. Colonel Olney had left a position on the *Rocky Mountain News* to try his fortune in the new

Gunnison gold fields where towns rise and fall in a night with the news of richer prospects farther on. When news comes of a rich strike and the local lodes are disappointing, then the hammers and saws get into active service, tents come down, goods are loaded, horses are brought in, harnessed and saddled, busy wives gather the children and belongings, and a hamper of food, and by the time day comes again the sun shines on only a few stragglers who hope to subsist and perhaps profit on the pickings of the deserted camp. It is a sad but oft-repeated struggle for the one who can not resist the charm of possibility, the hope of much for little, calculating not on the actual percentage of successful ones, and believing the next victory may be his. The hunger for gold in a mine is a disease more contagious than measles, and once in the blood it is seldom, if ever, eradicated.

From Lake City to Wagon Wheel Gap was one of those never-to-be-forgotten trips that were occasionally sandwiched into our unusual experiences. According to expectation, we were bundled

Hunting on skees.

into the coach at the unseasonable hour of half past five A.M. Leaving Lake City we were soon jolting along up Slum Gullion Gulch over the corduroy road, bumpety bump, bump. The driver was a cross, surly old fellow who had a good word for no one.

When Pard engaged our seats at the stage office he was told some of the peculiarities of the driver for that day, and among other things he was said to be a confirmed "woman hater," and that the outside seat with him might not be pleasant for me. Pard insisted that I should have it as there were five or six men booked for the inside, making the choice, if there was any, in favor of sharing the driver's seat. In spite of his frowns and cursing the horses as he drove up for us, I determined to try his society and keep in the fresh air.

The six white horses were full of ginger until they came to the steady pull up the mountain, and then the heartless fellow laid on the lash. He did not want a woman outside, and he determined to sicken me of my bargain and make me glad to go under cover. He drove like fury over that twenty miles of corduroy road, and more than two thirds of the time I balanced between heaven and earth, clinging to the straps and iron bar at the end of the seat with a tenacity of a life and death effort. He would venture within a hair's breadth of going off the bridges and turn out to the very edge of a precipice, as well as doing other stunts that led me to believe the man was crazy as well as queer. I knew he was trying to make me scream with fright, which I as stubbornly refused to do.

Beyond a long swinging curve was a down grade of a mile, and with a yell and a flourish of his whip the driver urged his horses to a dead run. The six passengers on the inside had to hang on for dear life, and every half minute the lumbering stage seemed bound to go over the cliff. I could hear the men on the inside being thrown about like bags of sand, and the epithets that emerged from there proved to me they were glad a woman was not there to check their wrath against our jehu. That he kept going and did not give them a chance to get out was all that saved him from a thrashing. Once, after a very close call for a tipover, the driver growled that it was lucky that we did not hit a rock that time, or we would have been food for the bears.

At last he became wearied of his efforts to make me demonstrate my fear, and ventured the remark, "Well, I guess you've been on a stage before, for you don't seem to scare very easy." I was boiling with indignation and fear but I swallowed hard again and managed to tell him that I had been on a stage *once* before, but I did not have a grizzly bear for a driver, so I was really enjoying a new and novel experience. He actually grinned, showed a fine row of teeth, and gave a big grunt, much as the beast he had been likened to. My answer to him had been just what he needed and it mellowed him surprisingly. He had, of course, expected tears and remonstrances, but this straight shot at his armor weakened him, and where he had only given a jerky monosyllabic "yes" or "no" to questions heretofore, he became exceedingly loquacious and told me many interesting tales of the locality, as only a stage driver can.   But I was only too glad to reach the dinner station at an altitude of 10,780 feet above sea-level, and the end of many hundred thousand feet, as it had seemed to me, of corduroy road.   It was a bouncing ride such

Gate of Ladore, Colorado River.

as I would not want to repeat, and if he kept up his habit of trying to scare people he doubtless met the fate he deserved.

The man who handled the ribbons after dinner was not only a saner man, but a gentleman, although his language had degenerated to the vernacular of his later associates—a man who had been prominent in Eastern railroad affairs, but through adverse fortune was now buried on this wild stretch of road, hidden from all his old associates, who knew not his whereabouts. But he was a great, goodnatured whip who used to know "Tommy Kimball" (meaning Thomas L. Kimball, General Manager of the Union Pacific Railway Co.) down in Pennsylvania. "We used to do railroadin' together down there," he said, "but he has kept at it and done well, and I went off into Old Mexico and went to drivin' stage and have kept at it now nigh on to twenty-six years. Tom was allers a mighty good fellar, and if he ever comes out here broke and wantin' a job, he can just have my sit, sure as you're born."

He also added, for our benefit, that the driver we had that forenoon "was a cuss that was n't worth livin'." He heard him bragging round the barn about how he tried to scare a woman all the way up the gulch, and added that "a lot of our drivers 'll scare a d——d sight quicker than she would and she just had a good time, 'peared like. Leastwise she never said she was a bit scared and did n't yell a once." Then he went on to tell other things about our morning driver that showed it was not always a woman whom he vented his venom on. "He tried to skeer a man to death here a spell back, and he generally does scare folks pretty bad.

"He came out to take his run one morning and looking over the passengers selected a small, pale-faced man, and invited him to climb up beside him. While the pale-faced man was mounting to the front boot the driver whispered to the rest of his passengers and said: 'I picked him out to skeer him to death, and I 'll bet I 'll do it.'

"When they struck that corduroy road—it 's mighty steep down one side you know, and that bridge over the creek ain't got no railin' on it—Jake just laid on the whip. When he run close to the edge of the precipice the pale-faced man coolly told him that he was only about four inches from the edge that time, and old Jake just kept on trying to do mean things, but the man never lost a puff of his cigar.

"Three or four miles farther on the driver tried his man with another curve. In his determination to make a close call of it one wheel ran off the edge of the precipice, and only a sudden effort of the horses saved the coach; the passengers inside were flung in a heap and frightened half to death.

"Finally Jake asked the fellar if he wanted to drive plumb over the precipice that was a thousand feet high, and he was pretty nigh knocked off his seat himself, when the fellar told him that he had come West to die, and it made no difference to him how quick he did it.   It just knocked the sand out o' Jake for once, and I ain't heard of his doin' nothin' of that kind since 'til to-day.

"I guess some woman must a done him 'long back and he

Copyright Detroit Photo Co.

Wagon Wheel Gap

feels sort o' spiteful against 'em all, but he had a lot o' good things to say 'bout the one he brought up to-day."   And with a chuckle he added, "O, Jake's all right, he ain't all bad, but he orto die."

We reached Wagon Wheel Gap, fifty-five miles southeast of Lake City, at three o'clock in the afternoon.   We found mine host McClelland of the Wagon Wheel hotel, with his carriage at the stage office ready to convey us to the Hot Springs Hotel, about a mile distant.   Here there is a hot sulphur spring, elliptical in shape, about ten by twenty feet across the top; it shoots up, not in little bubbles, but in columns, at a temperature of 114 degrees Fahrenheit; by the side of the main sulphur hot spring is a cold soda spring, so close that you can almost dip cold water with one hand, while dipping hot water with the other.

While the hotel was not large there were good accommodations for fifty guests. No hotel in Colorado set a better table than this little McClelland house. A billiard hall, croquet grounds, swings, a piano, and plenty of reading matter were afforded the seekers of health or pleasure, and neither Mr. nor Mrs. McClelland spared any pains in making their guests comfortable, happy, and contented.

Fishing and hunting were extraordinarily good. White-

A herd of antelope scenting danger

tailed deer, elk, wild-cats, mountain lions, antelope, jack-rabbits, mountain sheep, besides grouse, ducks, geese, and various other attractions for the sportsmen were plenty. The angler was enveloped in a halo of bliss as he readily landed the gamiest of mountain trout weighing from half a pound to four and five pounds. The best hunting and fishing was in September and October. The springs are only sixty-five miles from Alamosa, and the Sanderson Stage Company ran a morning and evening coach, making the time in ten hours.

Four Scotch scientists, after visiting all the American mineral springs, pronounced these of the greatest value they had found. Upward of three thousand people had been there that summer. There were large specimen beds of chalcedony crystals and petrified wood to be found within easy walking distance of the springs hotel, and other beautiful specimens of less value.

Wagon Wheel Gap was on the main stage line between

Alamosa and Lake City, and derived its name from the finding of a wagon wheel in a narrow gap through which the wagon road and the Rio Grande River pass.   The wheel is said to have been left there by General Fremont's party in 1853.

We spent a charming week at this delightful place.   The baths, the pleasing draughts, rides, walks, and merry talks made us exuberant in spirits and joyous in heart.   We left there with the fond hope that we might soon return, but we have never been back to renew the happy times we have cherished.

We left the Gap about eight o'clock one beautiful morning with every prospect of a pleasant day.   The sky was cloudless, and the stage passengers were especially agreeable.   But the clouds gathered, as clouds will, and before the day was half gone they had favored us with a bounteous supply of condensed vapor.   I am at a loss how to express the beauty of the rainbow that followed the storm and its strange effects.   It seemed to start from the middle of the road in advance of us, and arched over the hills in dazzling kaleidoscopic grandeur.   The nearer we approached it the brighter were the hues.   The childish story so often heard in younger days of the pot of gold that could be found where the rainbow kissed the ground came vividly to mind.   Nearer and nearer we advanced till the horses' ears were colored, then like a flash we were baptized in its radiance and it was left behind.

Twenty miles from the Gap, or about forty miles from Alamosa, and within ten miles of Del Norte we entered the famous San Luis valley, which is the most remarkable park in the West. It is supposed to be the bed of what was once an inland sea and there are many evidences of it throughout this section.

In the northern part it is broken and hilly with an altitude of over 8000 feet, but it gradually flattens out its entire length until it is as level as an Illinois prairie.   On the west are the snowy peaks of the San Juan range and on the east the white crest of the continental divide in the Sangre de Cristo range. Across the southern portion of the park is a low divide separating it from the Rio Grande valley.

Thus the park is a vast reservoir which receives the waters of hundreds of mountain streams, many of which are swollen into rivers of goodly size and form the group of San Luis lakes; but here the mystery of Great Salt Lake has its counterpart for this great basin has no visible outlet.   Unlike the Salt Lake valley, however, this one is fertile and rich, especially along the streams and foot of the mountains, all hardy cereals and vegetables grow to perfection. The foothills and minor valleys were covered with rich grass that afforded pasturage for thousands of cattle and sheep.

Entirely around the edge of the valley, as if affording the mountains a footstool, runs a smooth glasis resembling the sea beach as it looks at the junction of land and sea.

The immensity of the mountains of the great San Juan country is beyond compare. There are a hundred and twenty peaks in that small section of southwestern Colorado that are over 13,000 feet high, and the waters of the world seem to spring from these snowy beds in midair and come tumbling down the rugged stairways of the mountainsides.

Alamosa had been the terminus of the Denver and Rio Grande Railway, but the iron bands now reached seventy-five miles beyond to Garland, and the line was about to be put into operation. The railroad company erected machine shops and other improvements and business was

16

A San Juan trail

prosperous, and for that winter at least, Alamosa was *the* city of southwestern Colorado.

Next morning we boarded one of those little palace day coaches of the Rio Grande road at Alamosa, to journey north and west again to Leadville, and with a good comfortable fire crackling cheerily in one end of the car we settled down in the richly cushioned seats for the day. The Denver and Rio Grande Company declared it possible for a narrow gauge to run wheresoever the human mind willed. The curious windings of this road around Veta Pass should be seen by every tourist. He should take a position on the rear platform of the car in making the trip from Alamosa to the little town of Veta, the last stop before reaching the famous muleshoe. One is filled with admiration for the master brain that leads such work of art and science to perfect completion. At times the engine and rear car stood almost side by side, the wheels creaked and groaned as the curves were safely rounded, and the long steep ascent began. Zigzag, around and across, and before you can cease to wonder at the mighty task, you can look almost straight down 500 feet to the track you have just left. Suddenly another turn is quickly made, and on and up goes the brave little iron horse 2369 feet in fourteen miles. At the last abrupt turn or second muleshoe the road doubles on itself for two or three miles, and a well-beaten trail plainly indicated where many had jumped from the train and crossed over the mountain on foot to catch the

Copyright by Detroit Photo Co.

The Royal Gorge

cars again on the other side. The trains run around the pass very slowly, and that morning almost as quickly as our eyes discovered the trail our feet were upon it too. We strolled leisurely along and gathered our arms full of wild cypress, daisies, and blue-bells, and by a short cut reached the track half a mile below just in time to see our train swing around the curve two miles above, and at times it did seem as if the cars would jump right over the engine. The great black horse came down to us grunting and panting with self pride as if expecting a complimentary caress.

At Pueblo, 130 miles northeast of Alamosa, we had dinner, and changed cars for the Leadville division of the Rio Grande running through Canyon City, and within a few miles entered the Grand Canyon of the Arkansas. The canyon proper extends to the station called South Arkansas, sixty-three miles from the entrance near Canyon City. The hills were low at first, but gradually became rugged and wild until the mighty grandeur was appalling. Thousands of feet, almost perpendicular, the massive walls of stone formed the Royal Gorge and the walls grew nearer together until the road-bed was no longer resting on rocky buttresses, but on a suspension bridge swung out over the waters for the track to rest upon through the narrow passage.

The awful grandeur holds one entranced, while the insignificance of man seems forced upon the mind by the comparison, and the wonder is that we are ever worthy of such special care by our Heavenly Father. We beheld His mighty works on every hand in which man is the merest speck. One great beauty of this canyon is the rich, deep, and varied coloring of the rocks. The lichen in the crevices of the massive walls struggle for existence. The rose-tinted vines, and now and then a scrubby pine of rich green, form the whole scene into one vast panorama of beauty of which artists can give but a meagre expression.

We reached South Arkansas at half past six—in good time for supper. We had made the grand round from this point and consumed many weeks on the trip. Many passengers left the train here for Poncha Springs, or to try their fortunes in the famous Gunnison. This South Arkansas station had been our place of starting into the Gunnison country, in the late summer days, and now we were safely back again. Swinging around the

circle of mountain roads by stage and riding on the second highest railroad in the land, we had come to the welding of the
circle, then after another brief stop we tossed back our good-night
in a snowball from Colorado's miracle town of Leadville.

CHAPTER XXII

BUENA VISTA AND LEADVILLE

THE only place of importance between South Arkansas and Leadville was Buena Vista, which was so long the terminus of the South Park and Rio Grande railways. The town was at the junction of the Arkansas River and Cottonwood Creek, in a very pretty valley, surrounded by frowning mountains, dotted with tall cottonwood trees that afforded a shade seldom found in the mountain valleys. The principal attraction, outside of business advantages, was the Cottonwood hot springs, six miles west of the town. The water of these springs had proven an excellent specific for blood poisoning.

Buena Vista had its newspapers, its board of trade, and its banks, and was, in fact, a wide-awake, stirring little town. The South Park and Denver and Rio Grande Railroad companies had a bitter rivalry in their efforts to reach Leadville, but a compromise was finally made and a common track was used from Buena Vista to the city of gold and silver. A. G. Smith, heretofore mentioned, had been promoted from Alkali Station in Nebraska to the joint ticket agency here for the two roads.

Our party was delayed in Buena Vista by lost baggage and Pard returned to Pueblo, where he found the trunks all properly checked, but stored away in the baggage-room. The conversation between himself and the baggageman has never been made public.

While Pard was on the baggage hunt the rest of our party were domiciled with Mr. Smith's mother. She was a dear old soul and has been kind as a mother to me since I first met her in Omaha in 1879. She was then making her first trip West to her boy, who was station agent in that little God-forsaken station of Alkali in Nebraska.   The station is now called Antelope and has acquired some little excuse to live; but Alkali then was all its name implied, with the section house, depot with a few living-rooms attached, and sage-brush full of tree rattlesnakes that coiled in shiny gray rings, in glistening harmony with the sheer white of the poison earth and pearl gray sage trees, and that was all there was to Alkali.

Fresh from a good home in Pittsburg to such desolation

To Leadville in its early days

would destroy the heart and life of almost any woman but a mother or a bride. She has earned her dear little vine-covered cottage in southern California and as she nears her ninety years she is full of activity, wit, and humor, and with the same expansive love and generosity for her associates that was so prominent in her younger days.

The ride from Buena Vista to Leadville, where the rails were being rapidly pushed on to the land of promise, was one to be remembered. The stage was loaded to the limit with all kinds of humanity; some seemed to be fairly clinging on by their eyebrows and there was much scuffling on the outside, even fighting for something to cling to, that they might be speeded on to the goal.

The famous camp of Leadville had already become a city of 30,000 people, though it was not yet two years old.   The old deserted camp of Oro, with its sudden bursting into the lime-light with 10,000 people in 1865, was all there was on the map to guide one to the location of the great new gold field.   Such an inflation into the realm of citydom was worthy of being called the eighth wonder of the world.

We went trundling into this metropolis on the top of a dingy stage-coach, dusty, begrimed, and weary, but were soon lost in the most conglomerate host of people that had ever assembled on American soil. We were glad to get through alive and without accident to the Clarendon Hotel.

Old California Gulch or Oro, with its bits of shining gold sluiced from the pans, was not thought of in the same breath with

Chestnut Street, Leadville, in boom times

this bustling younger sister town. Leadville was the magic word that drew thousands of people into the vortex of dissipation, vice, and plunder, and the few who would be honest had a struggle never dreamed of. The fabulous wealth of its hills was irresistible to those who were not immune to the chase of fortune in its sparkling vaults, and many other camps were entirely deserted and moved bodily to this great throbbing centre of gold seekers.

We were drawn into the maelstrom of humanity just to see what it was like and to visit some of the best mines. There was no need of Pard's services in writing up that section, which was already so widely known to the whole world, and railroads were pushing to the goal with all possible speed. But he did send some long descriptive letters to the New York *World* upon request.

The early part of the day, when the debauchees were sleeping and the miners were at work, one could get about the streets very comfortably and with a degree of safety as well, but the early afternoon brought out the musicians again, with harps, dulcimers, cornets, bugles, accordions, concertinas, sounding boards, brass bands, hurdy-gurdy and rattling bones, to say nothing of the gentler mandolin, violin, and other more alluring soft-stringed instruments, whose discords or melodies filled the air.   Then the sleeping populace awoke to a renewed carnival of vice and folly.   The miner's day came to an end and he joined in the avalanche of humanity swarming the streets.   At night the highways were illuminated to the glare of day, business houses were ablaze with light, and barrooms were never closed.   Millionaire and beggar, vagabond and priest, good and bad, saint and sinner, nudged one another's elbows in the swaying crowd and fought their way through with gentleness or strength, according to the bully that was in them.

The wealth poured in from the hills was poured out again upon the populace and every enterprise prospered for a time, from the bootblack and scrubwoman up through the category of vocations both good and bad.

It was from this pot pouri that H. A. W. Tabor came forth into the world of affairs.   His long, swarthy hair, flowing black mustache, and beady eyes, his broad slouch hat and loose hanging clothes, and a mouth full of tobacco and bad English made him a figure upon the streets of Leadville and Denver never to be effaced.   Mr. Tabor was but a small merchant when Leadville opened up to commerce, and for $17.50 he outfitted some prospectors for a third of what they should find; it took but a few days for them to open the great ore vein on Fryer Hill and Tabor burst from a wingless worm to a flying centaur almost in the wink of an eye.

Under his flowing locks lurked egotism and vanity as handmaids of his ignorance, yet it was said his flattering intrigues, backed by his shining gold, bartered and tricked his way into the gubernatorial chair and the United States Senate and made Colorado the laughing stock of our whole realm.   From the Nation's Capitol he flaunted his $500 silk nightshirts, while in Colorado his scandalous divorce proceedings excited the ire of respectability.   The wife who had shared his poverty and been

his helpmeet in adversity was not the one with whom he wanted
to share his fleeting riches, and the Colorado courts gave him
his way.

But he did some things to redeem himself in the public eye
in the building of the Tabor Block, the Tabor Grand Opera
House, and the Windsor Hotel in days when Denver needed such
institutions exceedingly.

Many stories were told on Mr. Tabor and one of the best
ones occurred on a railroad train en route east from Denver.
Several card sharks had been trying for several hours to

" Then the sleeping populace awoke to a renewed carnival of vice and folly "

engage him in a game of poker, and suspecting a snare he would
only play "seven up." At last one of the party exclaimed how
much he wished he was playing poker with the hand just dealt.
"Well," said Mr. Tabor, "if you will give me that queen on the
table we will make a jackpot of this deal." The burly Jew who
had proposed the change was more than delighted, and round
and round went the betting until every one in the car grew excited and watched the jackpot grow, and when at last the call
was made the excited Jew threw down his four kings and reached
for the pile of gold. Then Mr. Tabor cried, "Hold on, don't be
so sure my friend, that gold is mine," and he laid down four aces.
The Jew was dumbfounded, as he had staked his all on the sup-

position that Mr. Tabor held the four queens, and in an agonized voice cried out, "But mein Gott in Himmel, Mr. Tabor, vat has de kveen to do mit four azes?"

Mr. Tabor's life of wealth was like a whirlwind that spent itself in haste, leaving him penniless as before the Leadville boom, and though he could have written millions where the Puget Sound man wrote his thousands, yet he kissed his last coin as the other man did his twenty-dollar bill that was received a short time ago at the Dexter Horton Bank in Seattle, and across the face of which was written: "This is the end of a Klondyke find which netted one hundred thousand dollars; good-bye old bill, and tell the next fellow who gets you to beware of wine and women." That Mr. Tabor died without money and with but few friends is but the fate of thousands whose cyclonic lives shoot up like a rocket and are lost forever in the maelstrom of dissipation and excesses.

We sat in the hotel window and watched the masses of humanity moving along the streets. It was like a rolling sea of heads moving like a huge serpent along the great thoroughfares. Some were singing, some cursing, and some with stern, set faces, as if they had thrown their last dice and lost. Its gay debaucheries were from sun to sun, but from the setting to the rising, using the whole night, which was all too short for their loud revelries.

We were glad to slip into a carriage for a drive to Mt. Massive Soda Springs. The boulevard drive was a happy surprise and a great credit to the highest town in the world. The hotel at the springs was kept by a man who was his own housekeeper, and no woman could have found fault with the immaculate condition from his kitchen to his roof.

Desiring to return to Denver on the South Park route we had to first stage it for forty miles, via Mosquito Pass, then we boarded a beautiful new chair car, that was a delight to every one. The hospitable managers of the Clarendon Hotel had tendered us a fine basket lunch when we left them in the early morning, and once in the bright new car we lost no time in spreading out the delicacies. Everything was so agreeable in glistening newness about us that it gave an additional zest to our appetites. Among other things we had a can of chicken, which, with many flourishes of a great chef, Pard proceeded to open. But alack!

and alas! as soon as the blade penetrated the tin the chicken did the rest, and it flew all over that fine new car. Fortunately there were but few passengers aside from our own party, but it was difficult work to rid ourselves and the car of that terrible baptism.

Pard implored me to find a bottle of cologne for the other passengers while the good work went on. An old German, who was immensely agitated with the ludicrous side of the catastrophe, went out on the platform where he could give way to his

Pack train loaded for the mines

loud ha ha's as he rocked his body to and fro with laughter. Surely no one had an appetite for lunch that day, and everything was dumped out of the window, while Pard, to this day, will squirm at the mention of canned meats.

When in Leadville again some months later the mushroom growth was rapidly falling away. The large class of villains and bulldozers who flock to new camps were leaving for pastures new, and their places were filled with solid business men and capitalists who worked a radical change in business methods and society. The hasty rude cabins and business stands were being replaced by solid stone or brick business blocks, and the steady strides of real prosperity were visible in every direction. The pleasant homes indicated not decline, but a permanent and successful mercantile and mining centre.

The endless mineral wealth towered mountain high around the town. The nature of the mines differed largely from the Gunnison and San Juan, inasmuch as the latter were all fissure veins, while around Leadville the ore deposits were an immense flat bed of carbonates resembling the deep black or dark soil as seen so common in the Eastern States. These beds are sometimes a dozen miles long, and have been found over a hundred miles long and three or four miles wide, and often fifteen or more feet deep. The ore is covered with a stratum of porphyry rock, or iron and sand in thickness varying from thirty to one hundred and thirty feet. This covering is either stripped off or the ore tumbled out, and almost every ton of the dark soil taken out yields richly in silver and lead.

There was no reason why Leadville should be chronicled as an unhealthy city. The native purity of the atmosphere was unexcelled; to be sure its altitude was high (10,200 feet), and no person with pulmonary troubles should attempt to live there or in an altitude of over 6000 or 8000 feet at the highest, and then the patient should keep almost absolutely quiet until he is fully acclimated; nor should any one go suddenly from a low to a high altitude without putting on a full quota of winter clothing to guard against the evils of a sudden change. Owing to the sheltered position of the town, even midwinter affords less bleak and extreme cold days than Denver and many towns of the plains.

Six brass bands supplied the citizens with music and made the very hills resound with general good feeling. Leadville had reason to be proud of its military companies, its fire department, and its secret organizations, and they gave ostentatious displays nightly by marching behind bands of music.

Two years before Leadville was incorporated as a town of less than three hundred people. In September, 1880, it was the marvel of the generation with a population of 30,000. The total production of the Leadville mines for July, 1880, was $1,041,185.15; for August, $1,480,000.

In this young and giant-like city one saw a great deal of human nature, but there were too many crude democratic natures there, girdled with bullets and "heeled" to "pop his man," but even they were learning that Leadville could do better without them and that they must disappear.

The sidewalks were still crowded with a surging mass of people and the highway was full of carriages and conveyances of every kind, but law and order had won a coveted victory in a few months that was daily lessening the calendars of crime, and Leadville, the boom town, was already mellowing into a Leadville of justice and dignity.

CHAPTER XXIII

EARLY DAYS IN YELLOWSTONE

IN the fall of 1880 we made our first trip into Yellowstone Park, that land without a peer in the known world. With all the grandeur and marvellous wonders of Colorado fresh in our minds, we found the great Yellowstone land a fitting climax for the majestic and glorious works of our Creator.

The Utah and Northern Railroad had now reached Red Rock on the southern border of Montana, whence a rough stage ride of about one hundred miles took us to Virginia City, the real starting-point for the park and where arrangements were soon completed for entering the great geyserland.

The dear ones at home were in constant fear of our falling into the hands of Indians, or that we would starve or freeze, or a thousand other things that can arise in an anxious parent's heart. So before starting for the park they were told, on many pages, about our flannels, our leggings, our felt boots, mittens, scarfs, overcoats, ulsters, felt skirts, knit jackets, heavy woollen shawl, pillows, blankets, and aside from wearing apparel, told of many nice edibles that had been sent to us by new-found friends, remarking as I closed the letter: "There Pard, when Mother reads that letter there will not be one thing for her to worry about this time. She does n't know anything about the early storm season here, and I did not mention that!" But Pard's incredulous

remark that she would think of something proved quite true,
for when we received her answer, bless her heart, she rejoiced
that we were so well provided for, and "it seemed as if we could
live a good while on the provisions of our basket, but after
all *cold food* was not the proper kind for any one living such
strenuous lives as we were."

The Marshall and Goff Stage Company sent the first
public conveyance into the park, 120 miles distant, and we
were to be the first passengers. Many Virginia City citizens
begged us not to take the trip so late in the fall as early snow-
storms were too hazardous and too severe to allow the trip to be

A beautiful herd of elk

made safely. The story was several times told of the party of a
dozen or more who had been overtaken a year or two before, and
all had perished. But the plans had been carefully in progress
for some weeks, and with the hour at hand for the trip we could
not be persuaded to yield such a privilege; we would take our
chances and trust in God and good horses. With the best of
drivers in Mr. Marshall himself, and Pard and I as the only occupants of the stage, at just daylight on the morning of October
1, 1880, we heard the wheels go round, and soon we were whirling
merrily along the beautiful Madison valley.

We had a sumptuous breakfast in the tidy log cabin of Gilman
Sawtelle, who was a Yellowstone Park guide. Then on to the
top of Reynolds Pass from which point the "Three Tetons"
rose before us in all their grandeur, their glistening pinnacles

shone in the dying sunlight, while the first snows covered their rugged outline, and mellowed the jagged rocks of three of the mightiest peaks of the Rocky Mountains.

There were numberless herds of antelopes that eyed us curiously and galloped away; the streams were alive with mountain trout. Poor Pard was crazy for his rod and reel, and so, in the theme of Stanton,

> " He just fell a wishin'
> He was where the waters swish
> For if the Lord made fishin'
> Why—a feller orter fish."

But soon the island dotted waters of Henry's Lake claimed all attention with its deeply indented shores, and mountain guardians 3,000 feet high. The deep green of the pine trees in contrast with the autumnal foliage lent a rare charm to the five miles of waterway. Every little depression leading to the quiet lake carried its silvery rivulet bordered with willows and the brown and yellow grass made a strong contrast to the flaming sumac. The autumn panorama was a marvel of brilliancy that any lover of nature would rejoice to see. Here we were at the fountain head of the great Snake River which we later followed a thousand miles south and west to the Columbia and the Pacific Ocean.

The stage drew up to quite a pretentious building on the lake shore about half past eight in the evening. But enthusiasm weakened when a nearer view of the house revealed no doors or windows, but in their places strips of canvas flapping over the openings.

The ranch house belonged to the same historical Sawtelle who had given us such a good breakfast, but during the late Indian troubles he had abandoned this house before it was finished, and had cached his doors and windows for fear the house would be burned. He intended to return there and open a public house if travel increased, but it was a most forbidding place at that time. Not expecting company, the stockman, sheep-herder and two mail carriers who were camping in the house were somewhat surprised to see a woman emerge from the darkness into the glare (?) of the candle light.

The house was without furniture except a few cooking utensils, an old stove, a pine table, and some crude stools to sit on.

Mr. Marshall made himself busy trying to get supper from supplies that had been brought from his house in the Lower Geyser
Basin.   He said he was awfully glad I could eat beans, but it
was a case of mustard or beans, and the mustard was out, so
there was not much choice, although instead of a gun of Dame
Corbet to compel me to eat the unsightly beans there was a
mighty vigorous hunger that made me say the beans were good.

Pard and I gathered our blankets to go back to the stage to
fix a place to sleep, but Mr. Marshall insisted there was a nice
lot of hay upstairs where we could be more comfortable, and
handing us a candle, directed us to the stairway.   It was a rickety
passage, with the wind howling through every aperture and holding high carnival with every loose board in the house.   Once
upstairs the room to which we were sent seemed about forty
feet square.   The glim-
mering candle would light
only a corner of the great
black space, and a gust of
wind would blow out the
glim at intervals until the
place seemed full of spooks
and goblins.

Pard and I gazed at
each other when we could,
and when we could n't,
well, maybe I cried — I
don't quite remember.
He had persuaded me to
buy a very heavy pair of
shoes in Virginia City, because he had been told

The windowless house at Henry's Lake

the ground was so hot in some sections of the park that thin
soles were not at all safe to wear, and would soon be burned
through.   Then he had proceeded to hold them up to ridicule
all day, and I had finally wagered five dollars with him that
in spite of their looks I could get both of my feet into one
of his shoes, if I was from Chicago.   So there in the dim candle
light, with any number of sashless and paneless windows, with
the pallet of hay down in a dark corner, partly covered with
canvas, with the wind shrieking requiems for the dead and threats

for the living, and with the rafters full of bats, I called to him to bring me his shoe, and let me win my wager.

I put on his number seven and declared my foot was lost and lonesome in it, and he cried out, "Well, then, now put in the other one! put in the other one!" I began at once taking it off to put it on the other foot, when he cried out, "Oh, no, not that way, but both *at once*." But I revolted and said, "No, that was not in the bargain; I had not agreed to put both in at the same time." In deep chagrin he threw a five-dollar goldpiece at me, which was lost for half an hour in the hay before I could find it, while he gave a grunt or two that will be better not translated. And so we went on with our merrymaking, trying to forget our surroundings, and dispel thoughts of our discomfort, but it was a glad hour that saw us started again on our way with a new sun.

We fared better for breakfast than we had for supper, although it was served on a bare table with tin dishes. One of the mail carriers came back to the house to tell me there was not another woman within thirty-five miles of Henry's Lake. That reminded me of Col. Paul Vandervoort, an earlier writer on the marvellous charms of this section, who said that "lovely woman's sweet voice" had never floated across the surface of that placid lake, and we wondered whether the charm for him would now be broken because a woman's voice had floated thereon.

Henry's Lake is a magnificent duck-shooting resort, and with that and Goose Marsh so close together, where the mallards, redheads, teals, and canvas-backs flock by the million, there is joy unlimited for the hunter.

Leaving Henry's Lake our course was almost due east into the park; part of the drive was over a natural boulevard on a smooth plateau dotted with pines and elevated about thirty feet above the Madison River. At the end of this beautiful drive we reached the Riverside station, where one trail branched through the Madison Canyon, and the other climbed over hilltops to Lower Geyser Basin. The stage company had chosen the latter route, and from the summit we obtained a glorious view of the valley and surrounding ranges of mountains. It was not until darkness settled around us that we reached the Lower Geyser Basin, at the entrance of which stood the new and

unfinished little log house built by Mr. Marshall,—the first
and only semblance of a house in the park. It was with a
twinge of disappointment that we were obliged to retire without seeing a geyser, but needing rest we were soon tucked away
for the night and locked in slumber.

Next morning there was an early review of our surroundings;
the log house was far from being finished, and the part we occupied was partitioned off with a canvas wagon cover. The
second floor was
only partly laid,
and a window
or two was miss-
ing in the upper
part while the
unfilled chinks
between the logs

Lords of the Yellowstone

allowed the rigorous October breezes to fan us at will. At that
time the office and sitting-room and dining-room were one, and a
single stove did its best toward heating the whole house. It
was amid such cold discomfort during the season that followed
that Mrs. Marshall gave birth to the first white child born in the
park and the parents urgently requested me by letter to give
the child a name. Mr. Marshall said the first white woman to
completely tour the park should name the first white baby born
there.

In the frosty morning air the steam was rising from every
point of vision and the whole ground seemed to be on fire, for
boiling springs and geysers were almost without number. The
first point to visit was the cluster of springs two miles from the
hotel. The road was through fine meadowland and groves, and
beside a rippling stream that was fed only by the overflow of
the springs in question.

The first one reached was known as the Thirty Minute Geyser, as that is the interval of time between its eruptions. It was
getting ready to spout when we arrived and gurgled and groaned
and spouted a little; then after dying away to regather its force,
it dashed up in the air some twenty feet and sustained its height
for three minutes. There were other springs only a few feet
away that constantly boiled but did not spout. A quarter of a
mile from this cluster the Queen Laundry Geyser covered an

area of at least an acre and a half. The main basin of the Laundry was not over fifty feet across, but it flowed down in a series of pools nearly half a mile from its source and there became cool enough to bathe in, and to do laundry work, for which its waters were especially adapted. Around the boiling basin were various formations of a brittle nature from a pure white to a dark crimson, giving the whole rim a brilliant rainbow brightness.

The boiling pots close by had overflowed until they built around themselves huge walls some thirty feet high. The centre of the mound had an opening thirty feet in diameter and as round as a ring, with the water boiling and seething from a bottomless pit amid walls of fire. Nearly all the geysers and boiling springs in the park have funnel-shaped pyramidal craters or apertures, with curiously formed linings of their own deposits, while the waters are a dark blue and green, so clear that the walls and shelving sides could be seen as clearly at a depth of forty feet as near the surface.

These springs filled us with astonishment and we were inclined to be angry when told that we must not loiter for they were scarcely worth the trouble to see when so much grander ones were but a few miles away. Near one of the small laundry geysers sat a workman who had been haying in a meadow close by, and whose facial expression betokened deep trouble. After some questioning he said the boys told him that if he put his woollen shirt in the geyser when it was getting ready to spout that the cleansing waters would wash it perfectly clean while it whipped it in the air. He had followed their advice and twisting a piece of flannel about three inches square in his fingers, he said that was all he could find of his shirt when the waters got quiet, and he said he guessed it had gone down to H—— to be ironed, and he marched off declaring he would "lick them fellers" if they would not buy him a new shirt.

Leaving the Lower Basin by way of Prospect Point, on which some government buildings were to be located, we followed up the east bank of the west fork of the Firehole River with geysers all along until we reached the big springs or geyser lakes, where we crossed the river and drove up to a level with the water.

There were two large springs and one smaller. The first was on the river bank down almost at a level with the river. The boiling cauldron seemed to have cropped out of the earth from under the beautifully scalloped edges of dark overhanging walls; an obnoxious odor of sulphur filled the air and made the cold chills chase each other up and down my spine. The place was rightly named "Hell's Half Acre." As I looked into the black depths, when the breeze blew the fumes from us, the groaning of the waters was heard like evil spirits in dispute. It lacked only the fabulous Pluto with his mythical boat to row us to the entrance of Hades, and our illusion would have been complete.

Excelsior Geyser

The surface of the "Half Acre" measured two hundred and fifty feet in diameter, and on the side farthest from the river the deposits of the waters spread out over the boiling cauldron like a thin shelf for thirty feet and it looked as if the weight of a man might break it. Should it ever give way under his tread no human power could save the victim from a terrible death.

Forming a hundred good resolutions for the rest of our lives, we turned to the sister spring about half as large and circular in shape, only a few rods from the great spring. This is also a boiling chasm, but the waters are even with the surrounding mound of its deposit. For a long distance down the sloping sides were the rich deep colorings so common around all the springs, while the waters were so clear as to expose the mosslike incrustations that line the mystic sides to a fabulous depth. Around the edges we found petrified grasshoppers in abundance, also feathers in all stages of petrifaction. Formations of a peculiar sediment were in all shapes, such as little boats, boots, embroidered cushions, and other curious things; but when dried they lost their beauty and became too frail to handle. The larger spring had no period of eruption and it was not seen in its greatest glory until 1886 when visitors to the park who happened to be in the vicinity witnessed a rare spectacle, and it was named the Excelsior Geyser, because it is undoubtedly the most powerful geyser in the world. It suddenly broke out about three o'clock one Friday afternoon and continued to play for over twenty-four hours. The witnesses pronounce it the grandest and most awe-inspiring display ever beheld. The spoutings were heard several miles distant, while the earth in the immediate vicinity was violently shaken as if by an earthquake. The noise of escaping steam, and the internal rumbling were deafening. An immense body of water, accompanied by steam, was projected to an altitude of about three hundred feet, and the Firehole River, which is only a few rods distant, soon became a torrent of boiling water. The display was kept up, with gradually decreasing force, until the Excelsior went back to its normal state.

Between these two boiling lakes and a little farther back from the river there was a spring twenty-five feet in diameter, whose funnel-shaped basin was highly colored and marvellously beautiful, but its waters very cold. It was the only cold spring of the geyser class that we found in the park, but it was very disagreeable to the taste. All around these springs could be seen what were once large pine trees that had been gradually buried in this deposit of liquid silver, until only the tops were seen above the slowly growing mound.

Above the "Half Acre" we crossed back to the east side of the river, and found a spring boiling up through an old hollow stump. It stood close to the river, so that the waters washed it slightly on one side. The stump was three feet high, and the waters boiled constantly two feet above the top of it, directly through the heart of the stump, which was gradually becoming petrified.

Without waiting to examine the hundred or more geysers on our way, we continued up the river to the Riverside and Fan geysers, where we again forded the stream and continued on until we reached the Castle Geyser, where we pitched our camp.

The Castle seemed to be making a terrible fuss about something. Its crater looked more like a lighthouse than the ruins of a castle; it was indeed beautiful and majestic, rising some forty feet from the surrounding level, although the principal dome was only twenty feet above its own pedestal. The outside of this chimney resembled the surface of a cauliflower in its formation, only that each little bud or blossom was round and smooth like a pearl, and the whole was a clear, grayish white. It had quieted for a moment when we reached it, so assuming a courage we did not feel, we went close to it, and were measuring the distance and possibility of a climb to the top, when suddenly, with an angry growl, like

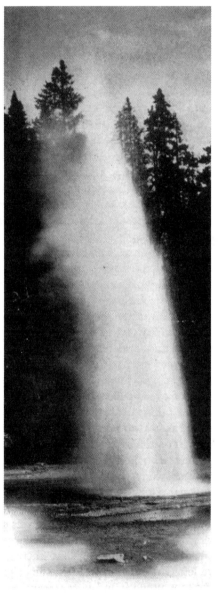

Courtesy Northern Pacific Railway Co.

" The river of water tore its way up through the bowels of the earth and dashed high in the air "

a cage of enraged lions, the river of water tore its way up through the bowels of the earth and dashed high in the air. I could not begin to guess the height, for, with a wild scream, we ran for life, much to the amusement of the rest of the party who were just approaching. We happened to be on the side from which the wind was blowing, and ultimately regained our position on the top to our great joy and advantage. The eruption continued for fully an hour; the column of water would shoot up from eighty to a hundred feet, and send sheets of steam far beyond that. The sunlight deflection brought out the most brilliant rainbows. The chimney wall was two feet in thickness at the top, and the orifice through which the boiling water was forced was two and a half by five feet in diameter. We afterwards heard the roaring and rumbling of this geyser fully a mile distant.

A few yards above the Castle was Old Faithful, so called because of its perfect regularity in spouting, for every hour it throws the spectator into ecstasies of delight. It is so regular in time of spouting that it has often been called the "Big Ben" of the park, after the famous old Westminster clock of London. One hundred and fifty feet it threw its column of water six feet in diameter, and held it unbroken sometimes for ten minutes, and never less than five minutes. Its mound had long, gradually sloping sides, terraced with a succession of ivory-lined reservoirs of every conceivable shape, that had been made and worn by the falling water. Many of these reservoirs had been converted into stationary card baskets; at least several names were written on the bottoms of these little receptacles by explorers and soldiers who had ventured there before us. Although written in pencil they could not be erased, the water having formed a transparent glaze over the lines that will preserve them forever.

We slept on the ground nearby without tents, glad with the joy of seeing such wondrous marvels of Nature, and yet upon our camp grounds to-day stands the largest log house in the world.

A peculiar thumping sound attracted us toward the river and we left Old Faithful to learn the origin of the noise. Every foot of the way we found new attractions, and petrifactions were all around us. Old socks which had been thrown in the water had been bleached to snowy whiteness, and were so brittle that a gentle pressure would break them in bits, and petrified wood was in all stages of transformation. At the river the opposite bank was a perpendicular wall some thirty feet high and seemingly of solid stone, but about four feet above the surface of the water was an opening in the rock about twenty inches square, as if cut by human hands. Through the opening the water poured with regular pulsations, and the roar inside the rock sounded like the machinery of a great Corliss engine.

We crossed the river just above this strange phenomenon by walking on an old tree that had fallen across to the other bank, and went down the river to what we afterwards decided was the Beehive, but there were so many formations similar that we could not at first determine. It looked like a defunct geyser mound shaped like an old conical beehive, and not more than five feet higher, but there was no steam arising from it. We were very tired and stopped there to rest awhile and watch for the next eruption from some quarter. Pard climbed up and sat himself down on the summit of the cone, while the rest were content to lean against it or sit at its base. We waited in vain for half an hour, then went up to the foot of the hill where some large geysers were showing signs of activity. But we afterward saw the same geyser that afforded Pard a resting place throw its waters 300 feet straight up toward the heaven. Pard gazed on what might have been his elevated position, then with his usual expression of "the great smash" he examined the ground around as if assuring himself that he was not standing on another geyser of like dangerous inclination.

When we stepped up to the edge of the Grand Geyser its waters suddenly disappeared like a thing of life that was frightened or angry at our approach. It had an aperture of thirty feet in diameter, and down its curiously shaped crater we could gaze and comment on its strange beauty, as well as its remarkable conduct. When the water all dropped down out of sight, I looked at Pard and then at the hole in the ground. He said it was evident that Mr. Grand did not receive calls at that hour and had gone out. We were wondering whether the water would come back, when there was a groaning and grumbling as if a conclave of witches was in session in the subterranean vault, then the water rushed up about half way and as suddenly dropped out again, and a shock from below shook the very earth; then without further warning the whole boiling volume of water, sufficient for an ordinary river, shot up fifty feet into the air. We jumped back from the crater and ran like wild deer, but we could not escape the baptism. Fortunately the water was thrown so high that it was sufficiently cool not to burn, but it was wet and so were we, thoroughly drenched. Out of its power we looked back and saw it gaining glory every instant, and finally lifting its column over two hundred feet, lashed into fury by

the escaping steam, and falling to the earth like a shower of diamonds, then rolling down the hillside its vast tribute to the river. We returned after this display to our horses and moved our camp for the night farther down the stream to a little point of timber between the Grotto and the Giant. Both of these latter named geysers showed signs of eruption, and while partaking of our supper the former seemed greatly agitated. We dipped the dishes in a hot spring close by and they were washed and wiped at the same time; then hiding the bread and bacon from Jack Frost we went over to the Grotto. The dome of this geyser was remarkable. Over the centre of the main opening an arch obstructed the direct passage of the water. The force with which the

Where Pard might have been

water had been thrown back on the sides of the cave had worn great holes through the walls, forming a half dozen or more orifices through which the water poured with great force.

Campfires were built on two sides of it, and looking at the blaze through one of these openings (which was large enough for a man to crawl through) it gave the appearance of a blaze of fire coming up the chimney, and the steam had such a weird unnatural appearance that one might expect almost anything to step out of the mazy shroud. The display lasted half an hour, and although that geyser had a record of spouting several times a day, that was the only eruption that we saw. We prepared several fires ready to light around the Giant, but it failed to favor us during our stay.

I will never forget how good the fried potatoes were that Mr. Marshall prepared for our supper that night, and we gave him credit for much forethought in regard to the mess box, but we learned later, at the expense of empty stomachs, that he only

" With only the stars for a canopy we lay in the midst of the greatest wonders of the world "

provided for one good meal, regardless of the time we expected to be out on any trip.

Just before we rolled ourselves in our blankets for the night a crackling noise was heard in the dead brush close by and we knew it meant some wild animal. An investigation failed to reveal the cause, but a little later the horses became restless and neighed and stamped in fear, and an uncanny feeling settled upon ourselves and our guide.

We had no tents, and with only the stars for a canopy we lay in the midst of the greatest wonders of the world—with a roar like many storms and battalions of artillery breaking the quiet air.

We hung our wet clothing around the campfire, and with the ground for a mattress and pine boughs for a pillow we passed the night in waiting, listening, and sleeping by turn, but withal we rested our tired limbs and made ready to endure the fatigues still ahead of us.   Mr. Marshall said he kept vigil until daylight, but the morning sun revealed fresh bear tracks around our camp as large as a man's hat.   Having no desire for a closer acquaintance, we did not hunt for bruin.

There are no snakes in Yellowstone Park, making the place an ideal one for camping, as it is much easier to avoid wild animals than the quiet creeping reptiles.

The morning after our return from the Upper Geyser Basin our party, including Mr. and Mrs. Marshall, of the Lower Basin, Pard, and myself, started for the Mammoth Hot Springs, a distance of forty miles, in a light wagon.   It was necessary to make it a two days' trip because of the numerous points of interest along the way, and also because of the horrible road. There are no adjectives in our language that can properly define the public highway that was cut through heavy timber over rolling ground, with the stumps left from two to twenty inches above ground, and instead of grading around a hill it went straight to the top on one side and straight down on the other; whereas a few hundred dollars, properly expended, would have made it one of the finest drives in the world.

We had to abandon the light wagon and returned for a new start on horseback, for it was impossible to get any conveyance over the stumpy road, so Mrs. Marshall then decided not to make the trip but remain at the Marshall cabin.   It was the only attempt at a road in the park, and what had been done with the Government funds was pretty hard to see.   The trails in the park, with one or two exceptions, were very difficult to follow and we often lost our way.   It was a trip in marked contrast to the beautiful roads and well-equipped stages and good hotels of to-day.

The day was one of nature's loveliest, while the air was clear, and just a little frosty; the eye could easily detect the location of a geyser or a boiling spring, by the rising steam.   We crossed Canyon Creek ten miles from the cabin.   It was a pretty little mountain stream, noted for its abundant supply of shellfish, which resemble somewhat the Eastern clam.   Half a mile from the creek were the Gibbon Falls, but a careful watch for the guideboard was necessary, for the falls are five hundred feet almost straight down the hill and hidden by the timber. It was a long hard climb over a dim trail, but we were well paid for the trouble when we saw the clear water pouring over the long, smooth, inclined slab, for these falls are not perpendicular.

A little farther on was a pretty little lake, swarming with feathered game, and before we ceased our comments on the lake we entered the Gibbon Canyon. The barren walls on one side rose two thousand feet above us, while on the other side the less pretentious pinnacles were clad in bright robes of varied coloring.

In this defile we heard again a puffing sound like the steady pulsations of some monstrous engine. A short curve in the road soon revealed the secret. An aperture in the perpendicular wall on our left some five feet in diameter was sending forth a volley of steam with a boom-boom-boom and it never ceased to beat with regular pulse like a pounding sea.

From here we found small geysers and hot springs all along the way through the canyon. Sometimes in the very edge of the river, again nearer by on the hillside, while two or three times where the road-bed was elevated a few feet, they would spurt out of the hillside below us as if indignant at our intrusion, and were threatening to tear the ground from under us. Huge boulders glutted the stream and afforded some queer studies. "The Twins" were a couple of massive rocks almost exactly alike, in the middle of the stream but a few feet apart.

At one of the fords of the river there was a monument of solid rock thirty feet high without a bit of soil upon its tall, well-rounded form, yet right on the summit, like the spire of a village church, stood a tall, solitary pine tree.

Leaving the canyon we entered Elk Park or Gibbon Basin, which was full of fine grass for the horses and plenty of good water, so we rode up to a little cluster of trees and pitched our camp for the night.

A blazing campfire was soon warming the air around us, pine boughs were brought in plenty for beds, and active preparations were in progress for supper when the shades of night began to gather about us. A tent was an unknown luxury with us in camping out on these trips, and the stars now twinkled at us through the treetops as if assuring their protection.

The squirrels skipped frantically among the trees chattering and scolding as if we were going to broil them for our supper. Even the butcher birds came hopping around for crumbs, and their little white, owlish faces and beadlike eyes glistened through the firelight and shone almost as bright as the stars themselves.

When supper was over we gathered around the fire that had been piled with pine knots, each began to think of hob-goblin stories of younger days, and then took a turn in spinning yarns; so by the time the embers began to die we were well prepared to see all the stumps and trees in motion and to fancy all kinds of sombre sounds; and no one seemed surprised when Pard declared the screeching of a wild goose in the distance to be the whistling of an elk.

When the morning came out on the hilltops we had breakfast and were on our way to the Paint Pots, a quarter of a mile from the road east of Elk Park. We groped our way along over broken and dead timber like a person in the dark, for there was no trail, in spite of the signboard that told us there was. The Paint Pots were like the boiling springs in their general outline, but instead of containing their clear ethereal waters they had a thick, pasty substance that bubbled and spurted like boiling mush. Their charm is in the different colorings. The first was white as alabaster, and it was said this substance had been used for plaster and paint with eminent success, but where I know not. The next one was a delicately tinted pink; then a deep red, and one still deeper in color, and more than that were a repetition of those mentioned. Around each of them, where the boiling paint had overflowed its curiously moulded bowl, the coloring included all the shadings of the rose, also both white and black, and in little nooks where only the steam could moisten the ground there grew the richest green moss that eyes ever beheld.

The pots differed in the size of their openings from a foot and a half to ten and twelve feet in diameter. When these paints were exposed to the air and cold they became as hard as granite, and when partly cooled they could be moulded like putty or stiff dough.

Several of these paint pots were on a side hill, and the overflow produced a kaleidoscopic coloring too beautiful to describe.

Returning to camp we found that another ten minutes' delay would have been disastrous for our party. We had left a fire burning believing it would soon die out; but instead it had crept up a log leading to our trappings and was lapping its fiery tongue around the mess box and having a merry dance with some gunny sacks close by our bedding then under the end of the pine bough canopy. How glad we were that nature had not held us longer in her famous art gallery can best be realized by a like experience. Order was hastily restored, our lesson learned that we must not leave fires burning, and soon we were trotting along to the Norris Plateau, or Norris Geyser Basin.

This plateau embraced twenty-five square miles and seemed to be not only the most elevated and largest, but may also have been the most important and doubtless the oldest geyser basin in the park. It certainly was the hottest and most dangerous for pedestrians. The first little joker we reached was the Minute Geyser, and with an orifice of only a few inches it spurted up some five feet every sixty seconds, and then died down and showed not a ripple on its placid surface until it spurted again on time without any warning. To the right of the Minute Geyser was the Mammoth Geyser, and well it deserves its name. When it is quiet one can go up to the crater and study its beaded chimney, and look down its long dark throat, and shudder. Its chimney was about four feet high, with an orifice two feet by three feet in diameter. Its voluminous outbursts have fairly disembowelled the mountain at whose base it stands for a distance of a hundred feet or more, and at least forty feet in width, while its greatest depth that can be seen does not exceed twenty feet.

While walking around in this excavation the ground began to shake beneath us like an earthquake, and we stood not upon the order of our going, but went at once toward other ground. We were none too soon in our going, for after a few groans and puffs of steam it threw such a volume of water as we had never yet seen; the water was lifted many feet above us, lashed into fury by an unseen force and hurled into its surrounding basin, where it ploughed like a giant river that had burst its bounds and for a short time flooded the lower part of the plateau.

When the road was again reached we were startled by a tumult of discordant sounds, and fitful paroxysms coming from

the side of the embankment.   The hole looked like the very
entrance to Hades, and the groans and hisses seemed the dia-
bolical laugh of Pluto and his imps giving the mythical degrees of
torture to his victims.   The blackness of night was upon every
rock, and through the dismal, darkened dive came only the
murky stream laden with the sickening fumes of sulphur from an
overheated cauldron.

"How great and wonderful are thy works, O God," had been
the constant cry of my soul, and yet there seemed no end to the
mysteries before us and on every side.

Provided with good heavy sticks to sound our way we were
about to step out on that part of the plateau which needs so
much care for safety, when a signboard attracted our attention.
It just gave the name of the plateau, but underneath some one
who had evidently tried Colonel Norris' favorite road with a
buggy, had added in pencil: "Government appropriations for
public improvements in the park in 1872, $35,000.   Surplus on
hand October 1, 1880, $34,500."

The rattling and tapping of the canes on the ground gave
warning of the soft or thin spots, and we were soon in the midst
of a sea of geysers.   The whole crust of many acres was formed
by the deposit of siliceous matter from the springs, and upon it
were many curious formations.   People have broken through
this crust and been very badly scalded.

One of the first geysers seemed to be wholly sulphurous and
the fumes were so strong that it would strangle us.   Around its
orifice were beautiful crystals of deep yellow sulphur so delicately
interlaced that even a breath of air would displace them, then
again there would be great chunks of sulphur, and from the
edges and jagged sides in the orifice, which was several feet in
diameter, hung a network of stalactitic beauties, while the water
looked as clear and pure as any other spring.

Another geyser spouted and drew our attention as if fearful
that we might pass it unnoticed.   Around it were little drifts
like newly fallen snow in large flakes.   It was so pure and white
that I tasted it and found it to be alum with the crystals still
moist with spray and soft as snow itself.

The ground was so hot all over this plateau that our boots
were badly burned and our feet uncomfortably warm.   Every
few steps there would be an escape valve with the steam whis-

tling up through a hole perhaps not more than an inch across. We were never in doubt when we were standing on one as to its force and temperature, nor did it take long to arrive at a conclusion.

The Alabaster Fountain was on an eminence near the side of the road, and its constant overflow had trimmed its pedestal in narrow terraces, and pure white as alabaster could be, and as solid as granite. It was about six by eight feet across the surface of the water, and there seemed no end to the distance that

Courtesy of Northern Pacific Ry. Co.

" Pure white as alabaster could be and as solid as granite."

we could see down the deep funnel. Not a speck of dust darkens its clearness, and its very purity seemed to defy the greatest vandal to touch it with a pencil or otherwise deface its glory.

A few miles beyond this great basin we passed the base of Obsidian Mountain, which is the divide of the Missouri and Yellowstone waters. The mountain looms up like a sheet of glass and its shiny surface gives many colors in the sunlight, including black, brown, yellow, and red, and every little splinter has the same glassy appearance as the mass.

The Mammoth Hot Springs of Gardner River were at last in sight, after a very long, hard pull over a mountain, where several times we felt riveted to the spot, unable to go another step from sheer exhaustion of both man and beast.

18

The gorge in which the Gardner Springs are located is over 1200 feet above the level of Gardner River. From the river up there are fourteen terraces, and the largest and hottest springs are near the top. The waters have rolled down and deposited their lime until they have built huge bowls or reservoirs one after another. The limestones which dip under the river extend under

Courtesy of Northern Pacific Ry. Co.

Gardner River Hot Springs

the hot springs, and are doubtless the source of lime noticed in the waters and deposits. One can walk almost anywhere on the terraces as they are secure and firm. There is so much lime that it gives the whole earth a white appearance, while the inside of these natural bathtubs seem to be porcelain lined and the water is a beautiful blue white. The outside crusting is rough and uneven with stalactites in profusion, which in some instances united with the stalagmites from the terrace below.

Each level or terrace has a large central spring, and the water bubbling over the delicately wrought rim of the basin flows down the declivity, forming hundreds of basins from a few inches to six and seven feet in diameter and often seven feet in depth.

The main terrace has a basin thirty by forty feet across, and the water is constantly boiling several inches above the surface; but a careful approach will permit one to peep into the reservoir and get a glimpse of the mossy vegetable matter that lines its sides in a rich light green that constantly waves with the ebullition of the water, and as the blue sky is reflected over all it lends an enchantment that no artist can duplicate.

Our attention was called to a monument some fifty feet high and twenty feet in diameter. No one was able to give any reason for its existence. The top was shaped like a cone and on the very summit was a funnel-shaped crater which would lead one to believe that it had once been an active geyser, but it bore the significant title of "Liberty Cap."

On the terrace just above Liberty Cap is a fountain known as the Devil's Thumb. I poked my head into one of the many large caverns which had once been boiling reservoirs, and inhaled the sickening fumes of Hades. I not only expected to see his Satanic Majesty's thumb, but his entire self as well, and could fancy he would drag me in and carry me down for his dinner.

There are incidents of travel that are more interesting to read about than to experience, and I am sure that a part of our trip to Yellowstone Lake and Canyon is a more agreeable memory than the living reality.

The sky was full of threatening clouds the morning that our little party started out with saddle and pack animals for the upper Yellowstone River. We followed the same old Indian trail that General Howard and his troops did two years before, and although there had not been a dollar spent on the road it was the only respectable trail in the whole park. For several miles we rode along the east fork of the Fire Hole River, and then began a slow but steady ascent of the Rockies' main range.

After starting on this climb we saw what seemed to be a flying centaur coming rapidly toward us, but it proved to be the wings of Colonel Norris' great coat flying in the wind as he rode madly down the trail. We had missed him at the Mammoth Springs, and now he insisted upon retracing his steps and making one of our party. He started ahead over a trail so plain that a child could not lose it, the only visible trail we had found, and every half mile he turned to assure us that we need not worry about getting lost, he would keep in the lead and there was no danger.   Colonel Norris was the Superintendent of the park.

There was but one mountain range to cross, and on the summit "Mary's Lake," with its rockbound shore lent great charm. Many sulphur springs and spouting geysers lined the way, and finally we cut off through the timber to the renowned Yellowstone Lake.   The lake is one hundred and twenty miles from

Jupiter Terrace of the Mammoth Hot Springs

the head of the Yellowstone River, and its peculiar position and topography as well as other natural features render it one of the most remarkable inland seas in the world.   Its shape is that of a hand with the four fingers and thumb, and it is situated in a vast depression that can be seen miles away.   Its western and northern shores are pebbly beaches like most large lakes.   It is thirty miles long and from ten to fifteen miles wide.   Around its edges are numerous hot springs near which one can stand and catch a fish from the main body of the lake, and without taking it from the hook throw his line into a boiling spring and cook his fish at once if he likes it that way.

Cold gray mountains lift their snowy heads and gaze with just admiration at their reflections in the vast wealth of blue below.   Numerous swan, geese, pelican, ducks, and even seagulls, were seen floating on the placid bosom of the lake, and flying around, while tracks of wild animals were too many for comfort.

The lake was dotted with pretty, heavily timbered islands, and Dr. Hayden's report says some of them are impossible to explore because of the dense growth of underbrush, and being dangerous from the number of bear, mountain lions, and other wild animals that inhabit them. The rare specimens found around the lake are worthy of mention. In one locality there are implement handles, knives and forks, cooking utensils, and many utensils of a clay slate, a substance formed by the action of the mineral water on the claylike soil.

There were also deposits of red sandstone boot soles as perfect as could be. Again there were shaving cups of other formations, which when split would form the cup and cover. A strange peculiarity is that none of these can be found by digging into the bank or beach; they are only on the surface, and though picked up every year they come again with the summer time. The fact that they belonged to the Aztec race, as some writers declare, cannot be true, or they would be found by digging. We broke camp early in the day and rode some twenty miles around the lake, then reluctantly started for the Yellowstone Falls twenty-five miles away. There was every indication of a storm, which at that season was not an agreeable anticipation, and this one broke about 3 P.M. We were peppered with hailstones until the horses became unmanageable. There was a call to dismount at Sulphur Mountain to rest our horses for a few moments and the word was scarcely given before every foot was out of its stirrup.

Sulphur Mountain was composed of yellow suphur and lava and there were a number of boiling sulphur springs around it, the principal one being shaped like an egg, and named "The Devil's Bath Tub" by a Helena party who thought the temperature about right for his Satanic Majesty's ablutions. At the base of the hill is a cavern down which we could see some fifty feet. The water in it comes through a subterranean passage from the mountain above, and is black and muddy and constantly lashing its sides. It was the most horrible, infernal looking thing that we had encountered. Darkness had settled when we reached the Yellowstone River and we hastened into camp. Pard had been commissioned to get an elk on a neighboring hill and Colonel Norris rode ahead to select the camp, while Mr. Marshall and I rode along more slowly until the colonel called us to the camp of his selection.

Instead of selecting a place under good trees, he had stopped in the middle of an opening on a side hill. The rain began to fall almost as soon as we were out of the saddles. Pard had come in without his elk, and everything betokened a dismal night.

Fishing at Yellowstone Lake

The beds were made at once and covered with canvas to keep them as dry as possible.

I longed for something good to be brought out of the mess chest, but it was the same old bread and bacon, and the same old excuse from Mr. Marshall, but a ride of thirty-five miles made us glad to get even that. After supper we stood around the fire to dry our clothing, but as fast as one side was dry another side was wetter than ever, and thus we kept whirling around as if on a pivot until we gave up and went to bed wet to the skin. We were lulled to sleep by the deep, sonorous voice of Colonel Norris who forgot to stop talking when he went to sleep, and he was still talking right along when we woke up at midnight. The rain changed to snow, and through the storm we saw the disconsolate face of Mr. Marshall, as he stood near the smouldering campfire muttering to himself as if he had become demented. Upon inquiring the cause of his trouble he said as soon as he saw the snow he went to look for the horses, and they were gone. "Gone ! ! !" we all exclaimed in unison and despair. The horses were gone and we were at the end of our rations with a big storm upon us. The many warnings not to go into the park so late went buzzing through our minds like bumblebees. The snow was several inches deep and falling faster every minute. Mr. Marshall had walked several miles but could find no trace of the animals. "And that was not the worst of it," he groaned, and while we held our breath for a worse calamity he continued, "I lost my pipe." Five miles from the falls and thirty miles from

" In camp near the Great Falls "

the base of supplies at Lower Basin, buried under the snow with little hope of getting out, no food, and the *pipe gone*, was indeed a deplorable condition.

Pard seldom lost his temper when things went wrong, but he was furious when he learned about the horses. He had earnestly pleaded with Mr. Marshall to tie the horses for fear of just such a calamity and now he declared that Marshall must get me out of there if he had to carry me every step on his back. The situation was too serious to be ludicrous at the time and every one was astir about camp. As soon as daylight came the men started in search of the horses. I was left all alone in the camp for several hours waiting with my rifle in hand, until after a hard and hurried chase the horses were overtaken and brought back. They had stopped to feed on the bank of a hot creek which we had much difficulty in making them cross when we came out, and they were then struggling between their dislike for the hot water and their desire for home on the other side of it. It was with loud hurrahs that I hailed their approach, and I am sure every heart beat with joy. We knew that we should hurry home as quickly as possible, but to be within five miles and not to see the falls was asking too much, and with the return of the horses we resolved at once to go on.

Superintendent Norris thought it was not best for me to go to the falls; the trip must be a hasty one, and the start home was not to be delayed longer than possible for fear of continued storm. The snow ceased falling soon after daylight, but the sun did not appear and there was every indication of more snow. Pard was reluctant to leave me, as he knew what disappointment lurked in my detention, but he was overruled, and with Mr. Norris he started off leaving me with Mr. Marshall, who was to have everything ready for the return to Fire Hole Basin on their return.

The more I meditated the more I felt that I could not give up seeing the canyon and falls. To endure what we had only to be balked by a paltry five or ten miles was more than I could stand. I called to Mr. Marshall to saddle my horse at once for I was going to the falls. He laughingly said "all right," but he went right on with his work and made no move toward the horse. I had to repeat the request the third time most emphatically, and added that I would start out on foot if he did not get my horse without more delay. He said I could not follow them for I would not know the way, but I reminded him of the freshly fallen snow, and that I could easily follow the trail. He was as vexed with my persistence as I was with his resistance, and he finally not only saddled my horse but his own, and rather sulkily remarked that if the bears carried off the whole outfit I would be to blame. When well on our way I persistently urged him to return to the camp and he finally did turn back, but waited and watched me until I turned out of sight.

Alone in the wild woods full of dangerous animals my blood began to cool, and I wondered what I should do if I met a big grizzly who would not give up the trail. The silence of that great forest was appalling and the newly fallen snow made cushions for the horse's feet as I sped noiselessly on. It was a gruesome hour, and to cheer myself I began to sing, and the echoing voice coming back from the treetops was mighty good. company.

The Falls and Grand Canyon of the Yellowstone

The five miles seemed to stretch out interminably. When about a mile from the falls other voices fell on my ear, and I drew rein to locate the sound, then gave a glad bound forward for it was Pard on his way back. Mr. Norris said any one might think that Pard and I had been separated for a month, so glad were we to see each other.

Pard could not restrain his joy that I had followed, and sending the superintendent on to the camp he at once wheeled about and went with me to the falls and canyon that I came so near missing. Up and down o'er hills and vales we dashed as fast as our horses would carry us until the upper falls were reached, where we dismounted and went up to the edge of the canyon to get a better view. These falls are visible from many points along the canyon, and the trail runs close to them and also by the river for several miles, giving the tourist many glimpses of grandeur. Above the upper falls the river is a series of sparkling cascades, when suddenly the stream narrows to thirty yards, and the booming cataract rushes over the steep ledge a hundred and twenty feet and rebounds in fleecy foam of great iridescence. The storm increased and the heavens grew darker every hour, but we pushed on.

Midway between the upper and lower falls are the famous crystal cascades of Cascade Creek, over which is a rustic bridge from which we watched the torrent pour its offering into the grand canyon and race its waters for the first leap over the brink. The cascade consists of a fall of five feet, followed by one of fifteen into a little grotto between two tall boulders which nearly form an arch at the top. A deep pool is formed at the base where the waters rest for an instant and are then forced to roll from the grotto over a slanting slab of one hundred and twenty-five feet to the Yellowstone below. The river widens to a hundred yards between the falls and flows with a gentle current. The bluffs converge again near the lower falls, the one on the west side bulging out as if to intercept the stream, but the waters held an opening a hundred feet wide, and with a wild roar they dashed over the verge three hundred and ninety-seven feet. The awful grandeur of the scene, the opening of the grandest canyon in the world at our feet, the raging storm and gathering snow, afforded a picture worth a world of trouble to obtain. The foaming, frothing spray lifted high above the verge of the

cataract and rose in a column of fleecy purity.   It was grand,
indeed.   We lay flat upon the ground and peered down, down,
down into the deep canyon, and in spite of the snow we could
catch glimpses of the fine coloring that decked the mountainsides.

Moran has been chided for his high coloring of this canyon,
but one glimpse of its rare, rich hues would convince the most
skeptical that exaggeration is impossible.   We longed to stay for
days and weeks and hear this great anthem of nature and study
its classical and noble accompaniment, but there was a stern
decree that we must return, and that without delay.

There was no hope for sight-seeing as we kept on our way
back to the Lower Geyser Basin.   My horse was always tired and
hungry.   I pegged away with my little whip to make her keep up,
but she did not mind it as much as she would a fly.   When there
were any streams or ditches to cross she would absolutely refuse
to wet her feet until the whole party would return and show her
the strength and power of a few lashes, then she would paw the
air while dancing on her hind feet, until seeing no avenue of
escape she would leap over the ditch.   Those were the only
times she ever exhibited any disposition to have any style about
her.

Without giving our horses or ourselves over half an hour to
rest at noon we rode on and on, up hill and down, through woods
and plains, fording the Fire Hole River again and again, until
at last the lights of Marshall camp were in sight.   The storm
had continued all day, turning again from snow to rain in the
valley, and O how tired I was when we rode up to the door.
Our forty mile ride was ended at seven o'clock, but it took three
men to get me off my horse, for I had stiffened into the saddle
until I was helpless.   We had ridden eighty-five miles in two
days, and one hundred and twenty-five miles in three days, and
I had been obliged to ride a man's saddle as the trails were so
dangerous that we were absolutely refused a horse for a side-
saddle.

The day after our return from the falls I was so lame that I
wanted to scream with pain, and tears rolled down my cheeks in
spite of my efforts to make fun of my decrepit condition.   There
was considerable raillery regarding my condition, but also much
sympathy expressed, and the others talked of their plans for the

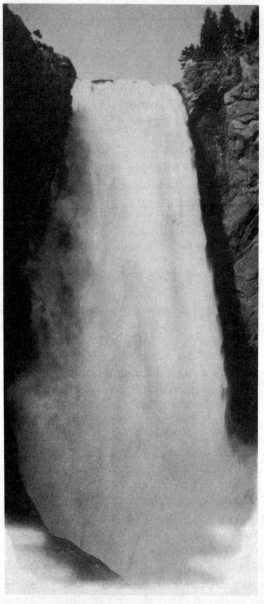

Great Falls of the Yellowstone three hundred and
ninety-seven feet high

day without including me, and they were not a little surprised when I ordered my horse saddled with the others. Their eyes opened with amazement; no one believed that I meant it but Mr. Marshall, —his experience of the day before made him know when I was in earnest, and I was not to be coaxed to remain in an easy chair and have them make a trip without me.

A platform was improvised nearly on a level with the horse's back, and with plenty of help and agony I managed to slide into the saddle. We rode twenty-five miles that day and I ate my lunch in the saddle for fear I could not get on the horse again if I got off.

Aside from visiting geysers and

springs, Mr. Marshall and Pard did some hunting on the way
home, and brought down a fine elk having seven pronged
antlers. It was a wild fight. When the elk was believed to be
about dead, Pard waited for the death struggle when suddenly
it jumped up and sprang at them. Elks are fearful fighters
and with their hoofs they strike and stamp without mercy.
There was little chance for Pard to escape, but fortunately
the elk's strength was shortlived. It was his final effort, and
he fell dead as he made the terrible leap.

It was a case of necessity to get game, for food was getting
low; we had had no meat for several days previous to getting the
elk, our time had come to leave the park, and every day made it
more perilous to remain. Superintendent Norris had assisted
us in making a fine collection of specimens, which we considered
invaluable, and had them carefully packed to ship home. The
elk head was shipped to Denver and mounted for Pard's office
in the Union Pacific depot.

There were as yet no laws against taking specimens from the
park or killing wild animals. Very few people had visited that
section; indeed I was the first white woman who made a complete
detour of the park, so that really the pick of the place was offered
us by Mr. Norris. He knew that it would be the best kind of
advertising for park tourists, and indeed it was.

The specimens were so valuable that when they were loaned
as a collection to a Denver exposition a special guard was placed
over them, but in an unwatched hour the major part of them were
stolen and never recovered. They would be of priceless value
indeed now when one dare not pick up even a pebble in the
park.

We left the park with the hope of spending a longer season
there at an early day as there were many places of interest that
we had to lightly pass, and perhaps many that we did not see at
all. There is not a section of the park that has not its peculiarities. Dr. Hayden estimated that there are ten thousand
boiling springs and spouting geysers in that strange region.

With beds on the hard ground and little over us but the
stars, with modest fare to work on, and blind trails to follow, the
trip through the park was in marked contrast to the elegant
coaching trip of the present day, where boulevards lead the
traveller to luxurious hotels at convenient intervals for his night

of rest.   But we had the compensation in the charms of nature which go with the wilderness and wonders in all their primal glory.

There was a wealth of jewels on the trees on the frosty morning of our departure, such as mortal man has seldom seen. The steam had settled on the trees and caught by the wintry night blast was held in crystalline spheres until the rising sun melted the rigid chain.   The shimmering motion of warmth and wind made the air resplendent with liquid diamonds and iridescent glory.

When full day came over the hills we cast a long admiring glance over the magnificent view and were borne reluctantly away to the Rodgers House in Virginia City where we roughly estimated that more than four hundred miles of travel in the park had been made on horseback.

CHAPTER XXIV

FROM Virginia City we staged it around a 500 mile circle, first taking in Bozeman, Fort Ellis, and other settlements to the eastward, then northwestward to Helena, southward through Butte to the Utah and Northern terminus at Dillon, from where we were to again enjoy a day's travel by rail to Blackfoot, which was still the jumping-off place for central Idaho. We found much improvement in such of the country as we had visited two years before. Even old Virginia City had put on some new life, and the valleys of the Gallatin, Madison, and Jefferson, those noble triple heads of the Missouri, were showing much activity as a result of the railway approach to their various settlements. We had now gone entirely around the beautiful heads of the Missouri on foot, horse back, or stage, and even down near the great forks mentioned found the waters so perfectly clear that we could hardly believe they could ever have such dirty faces in the prairie lands to the south.

Pard had a joyous surprise in Bozeman in a call from Captain "Teddy" Egan, commander of the "Egan Grays" under General Crook, during the Sioux war. These two companions in days of peril were like a couple of schoolgirls in their joy and clatter of tongues, telling how they and Major Luhn divided the last spoonful of beans and lived on horseflesh for many days; how the men had divided the night watch, that comrades might not sleep the sleep of death on the Yellowstone campaign when the mercury was down to thirty below zero every day for a month, with not a single tent for the 500 troops, and only two blankets to the man. How when Crazy Horse surrendered, Bob was the first man after General Crook to shake the warrior by the hand. These two were in General Crook's "mess," but there were seldom any luxuries that the rank and file did not have; officers and men shared alike in all things in General Crook's command.

They had one good laugh over a time when Pard had disobeyed orders and fired a gun. One day on the march, when rations were scarce, Pard, who was riding out of sight of the command, in a neighboring ravine, fired his gun when there were strict orders that no guns should be fired or fires lighted to betray the soldiers' presence to the Indians. The commanding officer demanded in thundering tones to be told who was disobeying orders and that the culprit be brought to him immediately. When the officer saw that it was Bob Strahorn he did not lessen the severity of his voice, but wanted to know why such strict orders had been disobeyed. "Well, General," said Bob, meekly, "I was so near some grouse that I could fairly smell a chicken pie and my hunger must be my excuse. I am ready for the penalty, whatever it may be." As the officer was also in the same "mess" with General Crook and Bob, he drew a little nearer to Bob and whispered that it would make a d——d sight of difference whether he got the grouse or not; then as he spied the fine pair of birds that Pard had kept concealed, he resumed his gruff and austere tone and said, "As this is your first offence you can go, sir, but don't let it happen again—never again, sir." And the mess ate the chicken pie.

Helena was rapidly improving, and the people were the same whole-souled, hospitable citizens as of yore. No one could feel like a stranger in their midst, when their hearts and homes offered such cordial welcome. The town was spreading out more over the valley, and its suburban districts afforded fine roads for pleasure driving. Returning from a lovely ride one morning, a sheet of wrapping-paper was blown across the street in front of our spirited horses. They began to back and paw the air at a frantic rate; they struck out with their front feet, and threatened destruction to anything in reach, and for a few seconds things looked serious, but in less time than I can write it there were two men at the head of each horse, three to drop the carriage top, four to hold the lines, five to help me out, and twenty-five to watch the performance in the ring, free of charge.

Nearly all the men of Helena who were not in commercial pursuits were interested in cattle, mining, or engaged in freighting.   There was no need for any man to be idle for a single day

There 's no place like home

in tne Northwest, if he wanted to work; neither was there need for people to leave Montana disappointed if they entered it with the spirit to work.   It required as steady, genuine application in that country as elsewhere to accumulate a fortune, but it required a shorter time, because wages were higher and work plenty, and opportunities for advancement everywhere.

Butte changed past recognition in two years.   Its growth and mining record was without an equal.   Its business men proved their confidence in her permanency for years to come by putting their profits into new business blocks and in business enterprises, though Butte has never to this day become a home city.

We left Butte on this trip, in 1880, to go south to Blackfoot, Idaho.   The stage was filled to the limit.   Pard had taken his seat on the outside, but it was so cold that the inside was more inviting to me, and as soon as the cry of "All aboard" was given, the crack of the jehu's whip sent the unruly bronchos spinning all over the road.

Among the passengers was a woman with two little girls, and the sudden starting of the coach set them to coughing so suspiciously that I at once asked the mother if the little girls had the whooping cough, and she promptly denied any such trouble, but one of the little girls turned her great surprised eyes up to her and said: "Why, yes, we have, Mamma."

I don't know where that chum of mine was raised that he had escaped all those plagues of childhood, and that he should reach maturity without measles, mumps, whooping cough or chicken pox, and I had to keep a net of watchfulness around him at all times. He never was more anxious to ride inside than after we were well out of Butte, and I finally had to pass him a note saying that whooping cough might be worse than mumps, and he better remain outside.

The Utah and Northern terminal had by this time been forwarded to Dillon and every trip into Montana meant a few less miles of stage travel and a few more miles of comfort. Dillon was bustling in its first trousers like a little hoodlum of the Bowery. Sounds of hammer and saw were ringing everywhere, and no one could believe it was the Sabbath day. Every mercantile place and saloon was wide open, and every corner of the settlement was bristling with life. It was a luxury indescribable to bolster one's self with plenty of pillows in a Pullman palace car and move smoothly over the rails and hear them sing the song of our destination—"Going to Blackfoot, going to Blackfoot, going to Blackfoot" until we dozed in happy forgetfulness of the tortuous roads we were soon to cross.

A little rest at Blackfoot made us eager to get on in our journey, and after a second trip to Challis and Bonanza we turned off to the Wood River country and thence to Boise City. The ride from Challis to Lost River Junction was a rocky one of a hundred and twenty miles, and on our arrival, about 11 P.M., learning that the Boise stage would not leave until seven o'clock the next morning, we called for a bed, and we were rather gruffly informed as we had been once before that there was not a bed within twenty miles. It was a question of again rolling up in our blankets on the little store floor or sitting up out in the stage-coach and we chose the former. We chose our corner and settled ourselves as well as we could, and it was not long before there was a chorus of snores such as Sancho Panza never heard when he said, "God bless the man who first invented sleep." The whole scale of sounds was there—one man ran the whole octave and then let go like the escape valve of a steam engine; another gave the squawk of the guinea hen, and a third struck a note on a high key and gave a chromatic descendo of four or five notes, as if his body might be crushed by a wedge. Still another gave a yep-hoo; one more gave a squeal like a pig under a gate, and ten or twelve good healthy snores made a chorus not soon forgotten or forgiven.

A doleful incident of the Overland Trail

Sleep seemed a long way from my corner, and then a strange odor began filling the room, and as it increased there came a rescue to reason, and I knew something was on fire. Just then a little glimmer of light shot up in a far corner, and I quickly roused Pard and gave the alarm. The man who was afire was soon rescued with little loss except a part of his blanket. He had carried a bunch of matches in his pocket, the old-fashioned California matches, where about fifty would stick together in a bunch less than an inch square. They were sulphur tipped and easily ignited, and in turning himself on his hard bed he had rubbed the whole cluster into a blaze. Had I too been asleep it might have been the last sleep for all of us. There was a bit of satisfaction for me in the morning when I discovered that he was the man who the night before had said women had no business travelling in such a country, and he had expressed himself in no gentle terms. But when he knew it was the woman who saved him from burning, he was most effusively apologetic.

It was along through a part of that section of the country which was still marked on the school maps as unexplored territory that the road led to Bellevue in Idaho, and there, too, was where the great lava beds of Idaho are most prominent.

Bunches of greasewood and sage-brush are the only products that vie with the black masses of basalt in that vast domain of volcanic origin, unless snakes, jack rabbits, and coyotes might be termed products of that part of the world. The lava assumes most grotesque shapes at times, and again it rises in tall minarets that stand as watchful sentinels. With a little imagination added one can see almost any shape chiselled in the black hard substance. It is just the kind of a country that the Indian loves to fight in, because of the dark and devious places to hide and to entrap the unsuspecting victim of his vicious nature. Indians will never come out boldly in the open to fight unless they know they have every advantage on their side.

The only bit of brightness was the few richly colored lichens that grew on the rocks and gave all the charm that the panorama possessed. The roads were rough, but fairly free from dust, making the ride as agreeable as could be expected through such desolation and the lack of all that makes our world so beautiful.

A night was spent at Fish Creek, in a cabin of two rooms, with a dirt floor. One bed was in the kitchen and two in the living-room, with some calico curtains around them. Sixteen people had to stay there that night. We arrived in the second coach, but ladies were few, so we got one of the beds. From Fish Creek to Bellevue the next day the scene changed to beautiful meadows, ribboned with crystal streams, and flanked to the north by the Wood River Mountains, which were carpeted to their summits with a thick turf of bunchgrass, cured to the golden hue of the ripest wheat field.

Bellevue had a population of about four hundred people, and the hotel was a log cabin of four rooms. The office and bar occupied one room; the dining-room, kitchen, and living-room were a trinity in one; a small bedroom, without a window, opened only from the bar, and the upper half story was a corral, where a score of beds were known by numbers.

From Wood River Junction to Bellevue there was among the passengers a young girl who came from Salt Lake City to meet her lover and be married. An uncle had come with her to see that the service was properly performed, because he did not like the would-be husband, and had been unable to persuade the girl

to give up the man of her choice.   The bridegroom did not show
up when the stage arrived, nor for several hours afterward, but
the uncle rounded him up and had the marriage take place at once.
After the evening meal some of the village rounders kidnapped
the benedict because he would not treat them, and he was kept
locked up for three days until he would open his purse in the
proper way.   Word was sent to the bride that her husband

The way they make the desert drink

was all right, though too stingy to deserve a wife, and he would
return in due time.

We were given the one single room off the office and bar.   It
had no outer door or window, and the office was full of men smoking all kinds of tobacco and drinking all kinds of liquor.   The
room was black with smoke most unendurable, and it was a
relief when the last man had gone to his bunk, and one thing I
must say in their favor is that they were kind enough to go early.

Bellevue was the *entrepôt* of the then brand new Wood River
mining country, and a boom for the town seemed near at hand.
Mines were being developed and sold, and good news of that kind
came in every day.   There were many branches of business not
yet represented, and not a bank in all the Salmon River country,
or on Wood River.

The tonsorial artist of the town was working in an enclosure of logs, with no roof over it, and when Pard went in to enjoy the luxury of a shave it was snowing so hard that he was soon covered with sleet and snow.

Ketchum was eighteen miles up the valley and the town of Hailey later located between Ketchum and Bellevue was not yet incubated. Hailey ultimately quite absorbed Bellevue, and when that time came houses dotted the entire seven miles of roadway between the two towns that were being taken bodily to the more fortunate location up-river and to the nearly total abandonment of the old.

There was a funny little chap came into the hotel and recognized Pard as an old travelling companion in Montana and an acquaintance of the Black Hills. He was a little, short Canadian, with black hair, eyes, and mustache. With a weird toss of his head he called Pard to him and said he had the finest saddle horse in the country, and if Pard wanted it for me he could have it while we remained on the river, but he would never lend it to a man.

The public stage had been taken off the route to Boise, which was 150 miles to the west, because of the limited business and the coming on of winter, and we seemed stranded on a desert, sure enough, with but little prospect of anything but a winter where we were. It made us feel pretty frosty at once to think that we had been so trapped in the outset of our trip to the western sea. But there happened to be a Mr. Riddle in town with a covered wagon, in which he had brought a load of fruit from Boise, and we engaged him to return at once and take us as passengers. The morning was clear and frosty, with mercury down to zero. He had a fine large bay team to drive and an extra horse tied behind the wagon as a sort of emergency animal.

Twenty miles from Bellevue the vast open valley of Camas Prairie, which contains 600,000 acres of choice grazing and farm lands is where the Indians have fought almost inch by inch to retain the land for their own ponies and for the camas root which grows there so abundantly. The camas is a bulbous plant, much like an onion, and is greatly prized by the redman for food.

There were no houses in sight at noon, and we camped by the wayside and built a fire. There was meat to broil, potatoes to fry, and coffee to make, but it was soon done, as our cook was most expeditious. The horses munched their oats from a box at the end of the wagon with a monotonous content, and the dog went through all sorts of canine antics while waiting for his share of the noonday meal.

We reached a log cabin for the night, which had a door but no windows, but it was large enough to make us quite comfortable.

One of the horses was taken sick, and caused Mr. Riddle to put the emergency horse in the harness next morning, and tie the sick bay as he had tied the other one, behind the wagon, but the sick horse had no inclination to submit to any such indignity. He would brace himself and pull back with all his might, giving the vehicle a jerk that

Where the Indians fought for the Camas Root

nearly pulled it apart. When the driver tried to reach the beast with the whip, it would jump sideways and balance the wagon on one side until it seemed that he would surely be the death of us. The streams were frozen over and we could only tell by trying them whether the ice would hold up. Just as we were fairly in the middle of one stream, the horses broke through, with one side of our wagon. At that stage of discomfort one of the horses balked and we were in a distressing, as well as dangerous plight that required patience and skill to be safely extricated from. When the balky horse was finally ready to go, the one behind was not, and he took such a rigid stand that his halter broke and he went off at this own pace. Our trials were many, and there still dwells in my mind some unfriendly remarks about that old horse Billy.

Emerging from that episode and spending a precious hour or two in catching the animal Pard thought he would walk up a steep hill behind Billy and use a persuader to make him keep up with the procession. But if that horse was sick, it must have been with St. Vitas dance, for the persuader was fatal to Billy's good nature and he jumped from side to side, rocking the wagon on a wheel balance until I, too, was glad to escape from it. The next day he was put in the harness again, but the emergency horse refusing to be led any more was finally turned loose in the hope that he would follow, but he preferred to graze, and as far as we know he is grazing yet. Surely the animal was well named the emergency horse, for it kept us in a crisis from first to finish.

It was late in the afternoon of the fourth day out from Wood River when we reached Boise City. The weather had been

" The Ovelrand Hotel was a two-story ramble shack, but quite palatial after our hard experiences"

intensely cold at night time, even two degrees below zero, but the days warmed near noon and were clear and bright, and in spite of many discomforts we made a good deal of a picnic out of the trip.

A big lot of mail awaited us at the Overland Hotel, and kept my heart full of joy for a long time. We had a grand visit with friends on paper as we sat by our warm fire, in real rocking chairs, with good oil lamps to illuminate the pages. Home friends begged us to give up such rough travelling and come back East, not knowing that now it was only thirty miles more to Walla Walla than it would be to go to Kelton (260 miles), the nearest railroad point toward home. They could not realize what it would mean to give up the coveted trip down the Columbia to the sea. To miss the finest river scenery in the world would be too great a disappointment not to speak of the trip on the Pacific

Ocean, the sail into the Golden Gate, basking in the orange groves of Los Angeles, and generally enjoying the grandeur of the Pacific slope, all now within our grasp.   The hardships we had endured would only make our joy the greater.

Boise is on the north bank of the Boise River, where the land is quite level, but it is encircled by a ring of foothills rising to the more majestic snowy range.   It is at the head of the extensive and fertile valley of the same name, which is one of the greatest fruit-producing districts in the West.   It had a population of about 2500 people and boasted two good newspapers, the *Semi-weekly Democrat* and *Tri-weekly Statesman*.   They later became dailies and are still the leaders in the State distribution of news.

The buildings were mostly one-story structures, but many of them were of brick.   The hotel was a two-story ramble shack, but quite palatial after our hard experiences since leaving Salt Lake, and we were glad for its comforts and conveniences, meagre as they were.   There was a public school having three hundred and seventy-five pupils and also an Episcopal school under the charge of Prof. C. H. Moore and of Bishop Tuttle.

A distillery, U. S. mint, packing house, and flouring mill were doing a fine business.   I name the distillery first, because it coined more money than the mint, though in a way peculiar to the business.   Boise then as now was the capital, and the social, political, and business centre of the territory.   There were many charming people and much enterprise and thrift, with the breezy far-west hospitable atmosphere we had so much remarked at Helena.

A half dozen stage lines centred there.   The one to Kelton, on the Central Pacific Railway, 260 miles, was the nearest rail connection, and had it not been for the little fruit wagon and the courtesy of Mr. Riddle, we would have had to go back from Bellevue to Blackfoot and Ogden, and around to Kelton, to reach Boise.

One other important stage line was west through Baker City to Walla Walla and Umatilla, to connect with the narrow gauge rail and portages down the Columbia River, and the one over which we must soon go.

Idaho at that time was bringing in some 6,000,000 pounds of freight annually, and its shipments of gold and silver through Boise even then were ranking it as a very important mining territory.

East of town there was an extinct volcano crater whose mountain is 1500 feet above the valley and the crater is perfect except for a section of the rim on the northwest side. It is at least a hundred feet across the top, and one can see many feet down into the orifice. On the imperfect side there is a vast deposit of lava.

Immense stone quarries lie along the foot of the nearby mountains, some of which had already been used for the penitentiary, and other pretentious buildings.

More hot medical springs were within two miles of Boise,

Idaho ox teams were bringing in some 6,000,000 pounds of freight annually

which bade fair to make Boise as famous as a certain liquid, which was not all foam, had made Milwaukee. That prophecy has been fulfilled; the water has not only been piped into the town for family use, but for heating purposes generally, and a veritable palace of a natatorium is the chief pleasure attraction of the present city of 20,000 people.

Idaho means "gem on the mountains," a name given by the Indians. When the morning sun first rests upon a certain mountain it produces the dazzling brilliancy of a great gem on the mountain top, and hence the name was applied to all that territory. The name was first published according to correct translation by Joaquin Miller.

CHAPTER XXV

BOISE TO WALLA WALLA VIA BAKER CITY AND PENDLETON

UR coach was severely crowded from Boise City, and nearly every passenger felt inclined to be a little c r o s s. There was one, however, who s a i d s h e never was ill-natured in her life, but was always jolly and making fun. The first "fun" that she made for the company was to call for a little bag of apples which was somewhere in the coach. Everybody had to move and assist in the search, and when it was found the coach had to be stopped and baggage stowed away again to the accompaniment of words known only to a stage driver. She was a gay young widow, with a male encumbrance about three years old. While in the full enjoyment of her apple she began to sing in a loud, coarse voice a song that Pard declared must have been entirely original. One verse ran:

> "There's Billy and Sammy and Duncan
> And Johnny and William and Joe.
> They can't make love worth a button,
> Or else they're eternally slow."

Then came the chorus:

> "I'm sighin', I'm dyin', mere friendship I ever shall spurn;
> I'm sighin', I'm dyin', to love and be loved in return."

This chorus was sung before and after each verse, then repeated with a voice full of longing, and there were about eight or ten verses all about wanting "to be loved in dead earnest" and the half dozen boys that "could n't make love worth a button," something about oysters, dinners, etc. The monotony of the song was varied by an occasional slap on the baby's face for some mischievous freak, which made her sing the louder while the baby cried. There were one or two other songs, and the peculiar drawl of her words made them quite ludicrous. One of them was on the Chicago fire, and ran:

"O Mary, sisture Mary, cling firmer to my arum
And I will guide you safely through all the fire allarum-ah.
O Mary, where is mother, and little baby too-oh?
They 're numbered with the dead, doh, whatever shall we do-ah?"

Chorus:

"'Fier, ah! fier, ah!' hear the dreadful sound-ah!
Chicago is on fier-ah and burning to the ground-ah."

The men had a chance to change about as we reached the various stations along the way, to climb up on the outside and smother their wrath in a drink or a smoke, and otherwise express their feelings, but poor me! I had to sit in the seat with her and her boy and when my patience reached the limit in her abuse of the poor child, I took the dear little fellow up on my lap and soon had him fast asleep. I never saw a more beautiful child or more senseless widow. It was like sunshine after a storm when at early dawn we stopped at the breakfast station and had her desire to be loved drowned in a cup of poor coffee. When we were well rid of her at Baker City we devoutly prayed to be delivered from any more such "joyous" dispositions.

Seventy-five miles northwest of Boise City we reached the Snake River again. For many miles it forms the dividing line between Idaho and Oregon, and after following its crooked ways some distance to the north we were again ferried over the river to the Oregon side, and continued our way through sage-brush and bunchgrass, and very little timber, westward to Baker City, 140 miles from Boise.

Baker may well be called the pride of eastern Oregon, as it nestles among its shade trees on the banks of Powder River. The enterprise of its educational leaders should be made a chapter of history. There was a boy's college, the Notre Dame Academy,

an Academy built by the State, and a fine public school.   They
were all in use, with students from far and near.   Baker boasted
of these attractions, for she claimed but 1500 inhabitants.   Mr.
Virtue's bank block was of cut stone and there were several other
store buildings of cut stone and several of brick.   The merchants
carried heavy stocks of goods and enjoyed large patronage.

The nearest gulch mining to the city was eight miles, but for

" We were again ferried over Snake River to the Oregon side "

twenty years there had been an average of $600,000 worth of
gold dust shipped annually from the county through Baker
banks.

The first gold discovery on the Pacific Coast was made in
1845, about one hundred and fifty miles from Baker, and at the
time no one knew what it was.   They used to flatten the gold out
with hammers and use it for ornamental purposes.   They knew
it to be some kind of metal, and said they found it by the pocket-
ful.   Those people were driven from the spot by Indians, as
many people have been since then in making attempts to find that
gold deposit again, but all efforts have been in vain.   One aged
mountaineer, and one of the original discoverers, still worked and
toiled in the vicinity, and declared he would die in the search

if he did not find it again. Frequent expulsions by Indians seemed but to renew his courage.

We spent our Thanksgiving in Baker in 1880, and there was indeed much to be thankful for.   There were but few bounties on the table, and we well remember how difficult it was to dismember the poor chicken that was served as we thought of the luscious brown turkey in the old home oven.   But we had come through many experiences with whole bodies and good health.   There

Copyright, Gifford, Portland, Or.

Sheep range among the pines of Oregon

had been no serious casualties with us or at home, and our hearts were indeed full of thanksgiving.

The ever charming feature of all our travels on our great frontier was the hospitality of the people wherever we dropped our hats for even a day.   It is of course true that the business which sent Pard into all these wilds was the building of new hopes and ambitions for the people already there, and every man was glad to tell of his acres, his sheep and cattle, and their increase, or to tell of the output of mines, the export and import of merchandise, or explain any interests they had that Pard might make reports and prove quickly how well it would pay to build railroads into the vast territory. His business known, it was an "open sesame" to the best homes and the best of all the towns afforded. It was like the swaying of a magic wand and we numbered many lifelong friends from those pioneer days. Senator Teller and Gov. Adams of Colorado; Senator Warren and Judge Carey of Wyoming; Hon. Tom Carter, Col. W. F. Sanders, and the Fisk brothers, Col. Broadwater and others of Montana; Gov. Steunenberg, Congressman John Hailey and Senator Shoup, of Idaho; Chas. H. Gleed, director and attorney for the Atchison, Topeka and Santa Fé Railway, who was Pard's assistant at the Union Pacific headquarters at Omaha, with many more we fondly recall, were then men in modest walks of life, but with loyalty of spirit and ambition, and an energy of purpose that has carried them to the leadership of the great States which they served.

Powder River valley is very productive of fruits, vegetables, and farm products. North of this valley, across a low divide, is the famous Grande Ronde valley, which is not only rich for agricultural purposes, but where many thousands of cattle and sheep have been raised. Eastern Oregon and Washington had exported upwards of 180,000 head of cattle and many thousand sheep the past season. Union, La Grande, and Pendleton valleys, through which we passed, were all thriving farming localities.

It had been but two years since the battle of Willow Springs against the Piute and Bannock Indians. All the Indians on the Oregon frontier from the Blue Mountains to the Cascades were in a bad temper, and they resolved to drive the whites out of the country. The battle of Willow Springs was the first check to their depredations and it aroused a decided defence. The Piute and Bannock Indians had hoped to join the Umatillas and the Yakimas and have a complete victory.

Here, as in other portions of the West, the story of its early settlement is a romance in which the hardy ranchers are the heroes, though they claim no such distinction. To make their story interesting requires no coloring, for the simple picture of the bunchgrass plains and rimrocked hills, with the men who rode over them under burning suns or through winter's blizzards, is a convincing proof not to be gainsaid.

Pendleton was the centre of a large farming country then as now, with far less population, and every man, woman, and child was taught the lesson of self-defence. In 1880 it was a modest village, with few trees and a few sheltered lawns, but the start had been well made toward the beautiful town of to-day. We put up for the night at the Foley House and, in fact, stopped over in Pendleton for twenty-four hours. The luncheon menu we had that day was unique for its orthography if nothing more. We had "stued beef, countery stile," "German fride potatos," "stued cabbage," "Appricot pie," and "Plum sause."

Copyright Lee Moorehouse, Pendleton, Oregon

Fish Hawk, war chief of the Cayuses

Leaving Pendleton at seven in the morning, our route was directly north, and for twenty miles we rode over the rich, uncultivated lands of the Umatilla reservation. Just across Wild Horse Creek, the dividing line between the red man and the white, fine farmhouses and well-filled granaries and storehouses proved plainly the value of the soil. For miles and miles the stubble of grain fields spread away on every side, even away up over the tops of the foothills, and held out in bold relief the golden land against the setting of the dark Blue mountain range.

Soon after dinner the tall church spires and flagstaffs of Walla Walla rose in view and by three o'clock we were comfortably located in the Exchange Hotel, after the pleasantest and quickest stage ride of our whole experience, 290 miles from Boise City and over 600 miles from Ogden, Utah.

I know of no place prettier than Walla Walla in the midsummer months. Its six thousand people moved like so many bees around a hive, and the four-story cut stone business blocks were marvels of beauty. The neat and elegant homes were embowered in shade trees and creeping vines that had not yet lost their summer leaves or colorings.

Walla Walla River was six miles from town, but pure, bright, sparkling Mill Creek ran through the town, and, divided into a hundred tiny rivulets, it danced in and out of everybody's garden, carrying coolness and fertility to every home. The avenues were broad, well improved, and shaded, and there were over five miles of well-graded streets.

Six thousand miles of staging had ended at Walla Walla, Washington, and we awoke next morning with glad hearts. For a time at least there would be no more "rough and tumble" of jostling, rocking stage-coaches, no more rising at ghostly hours to take the rough wheeled vehicles for a jog along through weary days and nights, no more fear of a sudden lurch sending a fist into a neighbor's eye or butting a head against a crossrod or a sidebrace of the lumbering, clumsy old dirt-laden transportation wagon. No more fear of a pitch down a steep mountainside or of being stuck in a mudhole.

How much it meant all over the West to hear that cry "Stage!" The sonorous voice of the stage driver, the clatter of hoofs, the creak of heavy brakes, and the grinding wheels as they bumped into the sidewalk, gave notice of the arrival of the daily mail and passengers. All over the western country it was the same great event of the day. Hotel lobbies and sidewalks were full of loiterers waiting for some kind of news to spread through the town, and the idle curious to see who was aboard.

The blankets and robes were tumbled out upon the sidewalk with a vigorous shove and perchance a little kick of joy to help them along. It had been a hard and toilsome journey, mingled with manifold joys and pleasures, the troubles to be for gotten and the pleasures to live always in our memories. Our ways were generally those of peace but we had at times the gay red men on our trail.

Over mountains and through the vales, through dense forests and broad open plains, through rivers untold and forest fires, through sunshine and storm, through mud and dust, with companions of all nationalities, and experiences unrivalled by any of my sex, we had reached a point of rest. We bade a long farewell to the "six-in-hand" and the characteristic stage driver, whose oddities and peculiarities had ever been an amusing study, and whose eccentricities would fill a volume, and put him in a class as distinct as a race itself.

For a time at least we would be far enough from warring Indians to rest in peace and tranquillity, without the fear that every red man we saw was on the warpath, and whose image was distorted by the eye of fear.

Yet all at once the thought came with a rush that sent me reeling with homesickness, of the long distance between us and home, and either that arduous, toilsome stage ride or the long

A Umatilla ranger

slow trip by water loomed up like an unscalable wall. But Pard never gave opportunities for such feelings to get rooted. He was quick to dissipate troubles, ever looking on the bright side, and it was always his pleasure, as soon as he found a comfortable place for me to rest, to skirmish out for reading matter and writing materials, and have my wants supplied before he started in on his rounds. This done, it was always his greatest delight to work; he was an indefatigable worker and never stopped for an hour's rest if the time was propitious for doing things. If ever a man earned laurels, he certainly did during our days of pioneering, when Jay Gould, Sidney Dillon, and Thomas L. Kimball were the leading spirits of the Union Pacific, and they were as proud of him and his work as I was.

Speaking of Sidney Dillon reminds me of an amusing incident that happened on a train coming west from Omaha.

President Dillon's private car was attached to the train, and at a junction point where the train was delayed he strolled up and down the station platform and attracted much attention by his New York air of simple elegance.   He was a fine-looking man, always faultlessly dressed and groomed, his white "Burnsides" seemed to make his face look younger, and his smile was good to see.   There was a little weazen-faced woman sitting opposite to me, a typical New England old maid, who looked as if she had been saying "prunes and prisms" all her life, and had enjoyed but meagre pleasure.   I turned and told her who the fine-looking man was attracting so much notice but instead of looking out of the window she deliberately turned her back to it, puckered up her prim little mouth, gave her head a little toss, crossed her hands, and said "I don't know him."

With time to catch my breath at Walla Walla, I began to figure out what we had been doing.   The year 1880 was nearing a close, and with it numbered three thousand miles more of stage travel for us, or six thousand miles in all since we started out on such adventurous experiences only three years before.   We had run about the whole gamut of exploration—the great stock ranges, the profoundest forests, the broad grain lands, and the varied attractions for the pleasure or health seeker, with everything else that could have any possible bearing on future transportation interests.   These things were gone into with a "fine tooth comb," as Pard sometimes put it.   Mines of the base or precious metals were everywhere, and down in the heart of mother-earth we had explored hundreds of them.   By winze and ropes and tunnels we had followed the gold, copper, and lead hidden in rocky rifts or sandy bed, or yet again from its black soft blanket of porphyry, out into the sunlight and through arastra, crusher, amalgamator, or smelter to the bright coins of commerce.   The advantage of future rail routes, or even of more stage lines, was nowhere overlooked.

We had come through it all with life, health, and experience worth more than tongue can tell; yet, as it turned out, we were only well started, so no wonder the few days' rest in the quiet little town of Walla Walla was a boon to be craved—to rest, to think, to write of what we had seen.

It was a great surprise to find all classes of goods lower in price than anywhere farther inland, but it was because of its nearness to tidewater. The people were bright, intelligent, and pleasant to meet, but not with the ambitious and progressive natures of

Copyright Lee Moorehouse, Pendleton, Oregon

**"White Bull spent his allotment of seven thousand dollars
in six weeks, then went to sleep on the railroad
and ended his career"**

other places we had visited. The feeling of self satisfaction, possessing the thought that Walla Walla was the hub of the universe, was like the old feeling of the Bostonian for his beloved Boston.

As we continued down the coast then and afterward we learned that it was a disease from which the whole population of our Pacific lands was suffering to such an extent that they would sniff and snuff at the bare suggestion of another coast of equal magnitude on the east side of our continent. The Pacific Coast people think there is no other country worth mentioning in the whole world. Loyalty to one's home and country is one of the most commendable virtues when it does not carry one into bigotry and perverse ignorance, but most Pacific Coasters in those days did go to the limit.

I was revelling in the thought of hardships over for a time when Pard came in with the news that we must nerve ourselves for one more hard trip, and do it quickly, for the season was getting late. We must make a hurried trip to Lewiston and Spokane Falls before going on down to Portland.

Travelling in the mountains by stage is ever a joy. Every mile reveals some new scenic wonder that repays the hardships, but when dragging along through long stretches of sand and alkali flats the time and the distance is endless to the weary traveller. The very horizon seems ever to be an eminence from which one should see the end of the journey, but that eminence is as far away as the mirage of Death Valley, for it is always just ahead and never reached. All of southern Idaho had that delusive expanse, without a tree or green field worthy of the name. Along that great highway, with its dust clouds and ashes and black lava beds, a story of sorrow and suffering is often told by a pile of stones or a cross by the wayside. I felt as if the end of the tether had been reached when we were rolled out of the coach at Walla Walla, and to make the trip to Spokane Falls required a renewal of courage and endurance that was hard to summon; but a few days' rest kindled life anew and hastened us on our way, to cover this unexpected five hundred mile round trip by stage and horseback.

CHAPTER XXVI

SPOKANE FALLS, MEDICAL LAKE, AND BEAUTIFUL LAKE CŒUR D'ALENE

THE Northern Pacific began laying rails northeast from Wallula to Spokane in the fall of 1879 but the work was very slowly pushed that year and even in 1880 the quickest way to make the trip from Walla Walla to Spokane was by stage via Pomeroy and Colfax. Another way was by Pomeroy on to Lewiston and down Snake River to Almota and then by stage again to Colfax and Spokane Falls.

The season was getting late and though time was precious we took the longer route by Lewiston. It was an interesting town because it was the first capital of Idaho and because of its location at the junction of the Snake and Clearwater rivers with towering bluffs rising more than two thousand feet above. The town was also at the head of navigation and that seemed to be its best excuse for existence at that time, although the vast mineral, forest, and agricultural resources that have since been developed prove that the founders builded better than they knew.

Its early settlers were the same restless pioneers who are the forerunners of civilization everywhere—the searchers for gold and lovers of adventure who are carried on wings of avarice, romance, adventure, and discovery and even fairy tales, to the remotest corners of the earth.

How glorious the experience of riding on the great river which we had watched from its birth in trickling rivulets to the

majesty of the seventh great artery of commerce! As romancers
we, too, sat on the steamer deck and revelled in the sweet air of

Our ferryboat at Lewiston which had been running ever since 1859

the uplands free from dust and grime and jolting chuck-holes
of the stage highway.

" Much of its course ran through magnificent canyons of its own carving "

Few had tried to follow the winding course of Snake River
through its wild and forbidding extents of lava and the lifeless
desert that bordered it. Much of its course ran through magnifi-

cent canyons of its own carving where upheavals of earth had added to the indescribable chaos of fantastic masses of melted rocks, of peaks and precipices.   Then, too, for nearly its entire length a treeless land completes the barren waste of the Snake River desert.   For three hundred and fifty miles there is not a stream that runs into it from the south.

When it reaches the Washington state line it loses much of its wildness and more gently rolling lands add a seductive inducement to settlers.   After its junction with the Clearwater for

Grain chute from the uplands down to the river

a time its basaltic walls are the most imposing and colossal of all its course; then the last hundred miles before its junction with the Columbia it runs on through what is now the greatest wheat belt in the world.

Even in 1880 wheat was raised along the river and one of the most interesting sights of the trip was the loading of wheat on the steamboats from the bluffs through flumes or chutes that were two and three thousand feet long.   In the experimental stage of thus handling wheat it was ground into unbolted flour by its own velocity and weight by the time it reached the boat, but that trouble was soon rectified by making checks in its downward course in such a way that the grain was made to clean itself in the race and flow into the boat bins in prime order.

From Almota to Colfax overland was but a short trip and there we considered the quickest way to accomplish the Spokane Falls trip to the best advantage. We had already used four days since leaving Walla Walla, and days were precious when winter was coming on.

Saddle horses and a couple of packs with a good guide were sent on ahead to make a camp near Spokane River, and we followed on the Kinnear Stage. In that way we lost no time in

City of Spokane Falls in the early eighties

getting into the saddles and riding among the beautiful hills and dales and lakes around Spokane Falls.

The weather was glorious in spite of the lateness of the season. Our greatest difficulty was in crossing some of the streams which owing to some unusually heavy rains were badly swollen. There were few bridges in those days, and it was a case of sink or swim at some crossings, and when we found a ferry, however primitive it was a luxury to be thankful for. Fording unknown streams were events to dread however confidently the road led down to them or marked the farther shore. Mountain streams with their delusive clearness were always deceptive in depth, and I generally curled up squaw fashion on the saddle in the hopes of keeping dry. I had my lesson in Colorado in going over the horse's head when he jerked the bridle from my hand as we went down a steep incline and he suddenly bent his head to drink. I went after the bridle into the stream, which fortunately was not deep, but it was awfully wet. The cunning horse did not even stop drinking, but he blinked his eyes at me as if he enjoyed the situation.

The virgin grandeur and beauty of the Spokane country appealed to us as no other place had done in all our travels. The little village of four hundred or five hundred people straggling over the parklike openings among the pines impressed us as one of the most pictur-

Old Hudson Bay post near Spokane

esque in America. As we stood on the banks of the beautiful river and saw its wonderful falls with the magnificent valley, its rich bunch-grass carpet then yellow as gold in its autumn garb and recalled the vast grain-land empire stretching to the southeast and southwest, the wonderful mines opening up nearby on the east, the ample forests, and the possibilities for power, the majesty of the situation made Pard declare that "Here will be the greatest inland city of the whole Northwest." How little he then knew his untiring energy and unflagging faith would make him one of the greatest promoters of the end he prophesied and that as President of an important railway company he would so materially add to the city's transportation facilities.

We took most of our meals at a small hotel near the river, called the California, but spent very little time in the town. We made the trip on horseback out to Medical Lake and bathed in the soft soapy water which was delightful; also northward to the entrancing Little Spokane with its frowning battlements and myriad of wondrous springs. It was impossible to tarry long anywhere though the banks of the rivers and the shores of the lakes were seductive with their enchanting beauty and the echoing anthem of the various waterfalls. The unfettered Spokane laughed in jubilant defiance of restraint as we built an imaginary city along its shores, little dreaming how soon the dream would come true.

The Northern Pacific Railroad was coming slowly toward this inland mecca of the Northwest but it did not reach the goal until June, 1881, and not until September, 1883, were the East and West made one with the connecting spike driven by Henry Villard at Deer Lodge, Montana.   There was a great deal of rivalry

The Lower Falls of Spokane River

between Spokane Falls and Cheney with the advantage in favor of Spokane because of the great waterpower and the splendid citizenship already making itself apparent. Such honored residents as J. J. Browne, Samuel Hyde, Judge L. B. Nash, and J. N. Glover were then, as now, most effective workers for Spokane, as was the lamented A. M. Cannon.   Mr. Glover had a saw mill on the south side of the river between the falls, and was also doing a thriving trade with the Indians.   Spokane Falls and forty acres of ground from Front Avenue to Broadway and from Post to Monroe, now the very heart of the city, were donated by Mr. Glover to one Frederick Post to insure the establishment of a flouring mill. Of all that land Mr. Glover reserved but one block, and that now contains the Spokane Auditorium Theatre building. One of our diversions at Spokane was an exciting Indian horserace on the racecourse then used, which extended from about the present location of the famous Davenport Restaurant to a point well out toward Browne's Addition.

The Indian, Curly Jim, was a character of the locality in those days the same as in this latter century. He was an intelligent young buck and at times induced prospectors to tie him and bring him into town as a bad Indian just for the fun of hearing what the people would say when they learned it was just "Curly Jim."

The most humane lot of Indians I have known are on reservations around North Yakima in the State of Washington. They are a happy-go-lucky lot, most of whom have acquired a wealth of ponies or of lands and on festival days they make Yakima the most picturesque city in the United States. If you nod to one of them as you pass he instantly shows his teeth in a broad smile. Their saddle trappings and bridles, their beaded gauntlets, their embroidered vests, their gaily colored blankets, tell of the love for bright sunny colorings, and happy dispositions are usually the counterpart of such gay trappings. They have their own homes, many own carriages, and all own horses. The squaw mother sits on a horse with her papoose fastened in front with a sort of diamond hitch that she gets on the blankets that are wound about her own body and limbs, and also holds the child secure. Often from a window in the hotel have I watched them come by the hundreds into the vacant lots close by and mount or dismount, tie their ponies, and primp themselves before going out on the street, and again pack themselves and their belongings on their ponies for the homeward trip. Some scoured the town for what they could beg, even though they were not destitute, and when they bought blankets they were most critical regarding quality and colors. They are not a menace to the town but a valuable attraction and a necessity in the field of labor. They excel in hop-picking, berry-picking, and in gathering fruits, but they have less regard for morals than most of the wilder tribes have.

The warriors of the middle States are being gradually pushed into the far West and the picturesqueness of all this Pacific Northwest is being narrowed down to a last dwelling place. It will not be many years before all their old time environments will be obliterated and the onward move of civilization will cover the ground with homes of white men. Indian legends will form but a mental picture no longer verified by living examples, but surrounded by a halo of mystery and a shadowy sense of the mythical that lies beyond the pale of our own lives.   There have been noted chiefs who have had many characteristics of royalty. Cleanly of mind and body, honorable, brave, and valiant, their presence imposed a personal magnetism and hypnotism not to be denied.   Such were Spotted Tail and Sitting Bull of the Sioux, Chief Moses of the Nez Perces, and many others.

"Fort Sherman was the most attractive spot for an army post that one could imagine."

Fort Sherman had been established about two years on Lake Cœur d'Alene and my remembrance is that a man named King owned the stage line running from Spokane Falls to Lake Cœur d'Alene and Fort Sherman, but we went out there on horseback, noting the store of M. M. Cowley at Spokane Bridge and a few houses at Post Falls as the only habitations where now the valley teems with its cozy homes, fruitful orchards, and a half dozen railway lines.   Fort Sherman was the most attractive spot for an army post that one could imagine and it was a great pity to have it abandoned in later years.

The Cœur d'Alene mines had begun to make history in as thrilling and interesting a way as Butte or Leadville. There was a Territorial tax of five dollars a month on alien miners for five months of the year, and it was a source of enormous revenue. It was devised at first to keep out the Chinamen but it was not a successful ruse.

It was not until after 1880 that marked development began in the Cœur d'Alene, but there is an old piano that is still in use in Mullen that was taken there in the seventies. It has been through half a dozen fires, packed over mountain trails, accidentally slid into many a gushing stream, and after being fished out was

The old Mission on Cœur d'Alene River.

"thumped" by some disciple of Mozart just as usual. Until recently it was the standby for balls and parties, Fourth of July and St. Patrick's day frivolities. Every once in a while "Mag," as the instrument is termed, is pressed into requisition and the cobwebs shaken from its chords. Its original cost, when purchased from J. B. Nugent of New York, is said to have been in the neighborhood of $2500.

The first boats on Lake Cœur d'Alene for traffic ran from Cœur d'Alene City, or rather Fort Sherman, to the old Mission, carrying supplies and prospectors and returning with hay for the Government. The freight rate on the first load of hay for the thirty-eight miles from what is now called Kingston to Farmington, on the lake, was $40 per ton.

A great deal of freight and many passengers were poled up the north fork of the Cœur d'Alene in dugouts and bateaux, at a cost of twenty-five cents per pound to Hummel's Landing. From there freight was hauled by dog trains into Eagle City, a distance of three miles, at the cost of five cents per pound, or a total cost of $100 per ton. The three mile haul on sleds drawn by dogs from Hummel's Landing to Eagle City cost the same price as freight from Chicago to Wallace, Idaho, a distance of 2000 miles, at the present time.

Some ten thousand people went in to Eagle City in a season;

Copyright Detroit Photo Co.

Jim Wardner's pack train of 1884

many were without either shack or blanket. Living was very high, flour was a dollar a pound, and bacon sixty to eighty cents.

In the spring of '84 pack trains began going in and greatly reduced all transportation rates. Jim Wardner was then in the mercantile business with the firm of Wardner and Blossom at Murray, and ultimately bought and operated the first pack train brought into the Cœur d'Alenes, but if there was anything from a pack train to gold bearing tradewinds that Jim Wardner did not attempt to handle after that it was because he never heard of it, or could not imagine it. He was a wild cat operator even to having a black cat ranch where it was said he raised the felines for their fur.

Mail was carried on a man's back from Cœur d'Alene City to Eagle by Fourth of July Canyon, or the old Mullen road to Evolution. The postage on a letter was twenty-five cents, and newspapers were too heavy and bulky to carry at any price. But that too was changed in the summer of '84.

Many of Spokane's wealthiest citizens have drawn their fortunes from Cœur d'Alene's famous mines. Among them are Patrick Clark, A. B. Campbell, John A. Finch, Charles Sweeny, Warren Hussey, and Greenough brothers, while hundreds of others have made more modest fortunes there since the first of 1880.

It is a country with more romance and tragedy than any other in American mining history. Those who went into that district in the early '80's after our first visit are full of reminiscences of thrilling experiences of humor and tragedy, from locating "prospects" by a borrowed mule and thereby making the owner of the mule a partner in the mine, to starvation in snowbound cabins and death by bullets on disputed claims or in labor riots.

Our Tillicùms on the shadowy St. Joe

Our return trip to Colfax was made entirely in the saddle, and it was one of the trips that will never be forgotten for it wove in a series of mishaps from start to finish. We stopped at Cannon and Warner's store to get a few supplies, then galloped out of town with all the zest of winter hunted travellers. Every cloud had been watched and pleaded with for a week, and now to make our down boat before a freeze-up was a great incentive to speed.

Spokane Falls was the crossroads for all Indian tribes of the surrounding country. The Indians were as plentiful as the dust, and as there had been some bad Indian scares recently we had watched for the truants among them all the way from Colfax as

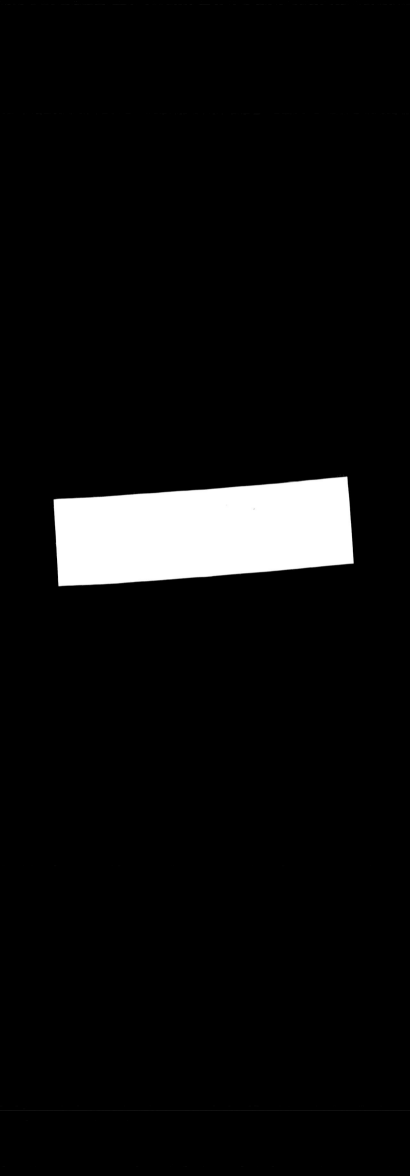

well as in our horseback riding around Spokane. Our guide had told us there was little to fear from them any more because white folks were coming in so fast. We became separated from him and our pack on the return in the hope of gaining some time but we got off the road somewhere near some springs north of Spangle and ran into a migratory band of the savages. Escape from them was impossible at the moment. The Indian wars were apparently over, but fearing peace had not yet full control of the red man's breast, we realized our situation might possibly be serious. We were urgently invited to dismount and reluctantly obeyed the signs. Our guide was to keep watch of our trail and we knew he would soon be after us and we tried to make the

"Spokane Falls was the crossroads for all the Indian tribes in the country"

Indians understand that other white men were coming. They looked longingly at our ponies and seemed much interested in some of their trappings. The camp was small in size and numbers but it was large in odors of fish and smoke and filth so inseparable from the Indians.

The young bucks stroked the ponies on their flanks and talked rapidly in their own tongue while making themselves familiar with the trappings about the saddles. One big buck was squeezing all the saddle bags and all of them made signs by pointing to the mouth and tipping the head back. We thought they were after whiskey and by signs and words kept repeating that we had none at all. But they were not satisfied and opened everything up until they got to the little medicine case, and the big fellow gave several grunts and pointed to a tepee and made us go over there. Inside his squaw was writhing in agony but I did not dare give her anything and shook my head again.   The old buck began to look pretty ugly, and his manner was so imperative that I finally took the case, doled out a large dose of bicarbonate of soda and with many flourishes of doing some wonderful thing I gave her the simple dope.   If I ever sent up an earnest prayer for help I did it then, for when medicine men fail among Indian tribes it is a serious matter and often means death to the doctor.   We had not long to wait for the medicine came up again in short order and brought relief to the favorite of the camp.   All we could understand as the Indians muttered among themselves was the one word "Skookum" and we heard that so often that we knew the spell had worked.   I then started to put up the case when the big buck came and took the bottle of soda, and he would not give it back to me.   I begged for it as if it were a precious parcel and the more I begged the more determined his "ugh! ugh!" and the shake of his head.

Just then we heard a far away call from our guide and his clear "hoo-hoo" rang out like an echo from the sky.   We hurriedly mounted our horses and were surprised that the Indians made not the slightest objection.   A lot of their own ponies were grazing close by and we wondered what mischief they were planning. Pard was just raising his whip to get a quick start when the big Indian grabbed the bridle and motioned with his hand to wait.

He turned about and said: "Spokane?" and we nodded yes. Then he pointed to the sun and made a circle under the earth and to the point overhead which meant the next day at noon, then he pointed to himself and said "Spokane" again.   He then pointed out five or six ponies in a line and two blankets, and continued "white squaw, me buy."   As near as we could make out he said he would be in Spokane at noon the next day to buy white squaw, meaning me, and would give so many ponies and blankets to Pard.   Then he gave Pard's horse such a blow on the flank that it needed no further coaxing to get under good headway, and we made the back trail as fast as we could go.

We still feared treachery for they were mounting their ponies and as soon as we were out of the camp Pard said: "Now, Dell, we must ride like the devil and get out of this."   We soon met the guide who was neither choice nor complimentary in his language used at our escapade and he threw a lash around the heels of the pack animals to give greater vent to his feelings as we ran on through the ravine.

That swerving from the main line did not take more than two or three hours' time but we found a bridle had been cut and

" If ever I sent up an earnest prayer for help I did it then "

other delays followed which made us late in reaching Colfax, and too late for the boat to Wallula. We had to ferry Snake River and go by stage via Pomeroy to Walla Walla again.

All that region is now as far removed from its virgin condition as its people are different from the wild race who once inhabited it. The most splendid inland city of the West fills the valley

and crowns the bluffs overlooking the falls.   Hills are no longer
covered with wild Indian ponies, and peppered with arrow heads,
but in their stead are miles upon miles of fruitful orchards and
willowy grain, with herds of cattle and sheep and the whole

The beautiful Falls of the Palouse

domain so covered with other thriving cities and villages, with
steam and electric communications, that distances are obliterated
and there is no more country.

It may seem strange that so little has been said in all these
adventures about the most important of Pard's missions.   His
confidential arrangement to carefully examine various routes
and regions with reference to railway extensions and possible

tonnage was a most laborious task. It was a matter of vast concern during the many years covered by this narrative. Most of the work was veiled under the popular guise of the hunt for statistics to induce immigration. Few knew with what zeal and care the railroad builders of our day have every possible factor examined, sifted, checked, and weighed often before even an engineer or right-of-way man is consulted. While Pard's

The awe-inspiring canyon of the Palouse on the Oregon-Washington Railroad and Navigation line

usual work never ceased other things were doing, and some of the best known and most profitable railway lines in the West were hatched during those long tedious trips across the frontier. It was a great secret then and the whole West has learned in later years that Pard can keep a secret so well that he has become popularly known as "the railroad sphinx."

It is no breach of confidence to tell of one bit of the work that meant so much to the Northwest. It was a matter of great study in the early '80's whether the Oregon Short Line en route to Portland should follow the water grade of Snake River around by Lewiston, go across central Oregon to the head of the Willamette Valley, and down that water grade, or take the short cut across the Blue Mountains through Baker City, La Grande, and Pendleton. Pard's report was wholly in favor of the Blue Mountain route which was finally adopted, and its justification has been that for thirty years no other route has had any serious consideration.

CHAPTER XXVII

DOWN THE COLUMBIA WITH ITS MANY PORTAGES

" Singing through the forests,
Rattling over ridges,
Shooting under arches,
Rumbling over bridges,
Whizzing through the mountains,
Buzzing o'er the vale;
Bless me! this is pleasant,
Riding on a rail! "

WINTER was indeed at hand and Jack Frost had already peeped in at the windows and left his congealed breath on the glass. It was no longer safe to tarry in Walla Walla; navigation might close and hold us there for the winter, or send us again eastward over the same tedious way that we had come with winter's hardships added to the ordeal.

The grain stubble in the vast wheat fields stretching away to the horizon told of the wealth of the valley lands, and in the many parts of eastern Washington and along the upper Columbia, where basaltic rocks had not been ground in time's crucible, there were many fissures where the rich and succulent grass grew abundantly for the great herds of cattle and sheep.

There had been a wheat transaction between Portland and Walla Walla amounting to $116,000, and it was considered a marvellous thing, but to-day it requires more than $3,000,000 to handle that rich valley product. The promise of the land was marvellous beyond conception, with its black, rich loam more than fifty feet deep.

327

How gloriously good it would seem to roll along on rails again and realize the cherished desire of a trip to the sea on the famous old Columbia River.

Pard's philosophy is, to want anything very much is the biggest half of getting it, for if the desire is strong enough, one will work with a will to gratify it.   So at last we moved on to that old historic railroad, which had been so long the connecting link between Walla Walla and its natural market on the west coast.   The company which built the road was incorporated in 1868, and with S. D. Baker as a leading spirit, the line was in operation between Wallula and Walla Walla in 1873.   The first

" The cowhide on the rails smelled good to the famished wolves "

ten miles of the road was built entirely of wood, fir stringers four by six being used for rails.   Later, a piece of strap iron was put on the face of the stringer and a few years after a twenty-six-pound rail was laid the entire distance.

Before strap iron was put on the stringers, Mr. Baker tried the experiment of putting down strips of cowhide.   The country was ransacked for hides, and for ten miles the leather was nailed on the stringers.   The experiment seemed to be working all right until the following winter, which was unusually severe. The cold weather and scarcity of food drove the coyotes out into the clearings along the railroad.   The cowhide on the rails smelled good to the famished wolves, and they proceeded to eat up Mr. Baker's railroad.

However, it was a money maker from the start.   A rate of

White River Falls near The Dalles, Oregon

$4.50 per ton was charged for carrying freight the distance of thirty-one miles. The little engine that hauled the half dozen cars over the line was capable of making only ten miles an hour. Part of the country between Walla Walla and Wallula was devoted to raising cattle. For fear some of the cattle should get on the tracks and be run over and cause damage suits, Mr. Baker bought half a dozen dogs, which were sent ahead of the "fast freight" to keep the cattle off the right-of-way.

The road was still the dinky little narrow gauge, but it was too great an improvement over the stage-coach to complain about. Mr. Baker's road was turned over to the Oregon Railroad and Navigation Company in 1882, and was then made standard gauge to grapple with the rapidly increasing traffic, and to harmonize with the rest of the road that was that year being built through from Portland to Huntington, where it would lock hands with the oncoming Oregon Short Line of the Union Pacific.

It was a cold December day for our coveted trip down the Columbia; it was a bitter disappointment to find the morning dimmed by a robe of heavy mist and fog; but how good it was to be on wheels that did not incessantly fall in a chuck-hole or make the brain reel with fear of upsetting over some precipitous declivity, to lean one's head on the casing for a little easement of mind and eyes without being hurled across the vehicle to bump one's cranium on whatever might come in the way!

The settlers also appreciated this railroad, rude as it was, for the wagon road to Wallula from Walla Walla was a volcanic ash mixed with alkali, like the roads are through southern Idaho, and the wagons would sink to the hubs in the soft road-bed. Freighting was expensive over such roads. It cost from ten to twenty dollars a ton to haul freight this thirty-one miles by teams and six dollars down the river, and still an additional charge for the two portages of Celilo Rapids and the Cascades. However, in these later days they are complaining at a charge of $2.75 per ton on their wheat from Walla Walla clear through to Portland!

The Columbia River rises in the Rocky Mountains of British Columbia and Montana, and flows northwest and then south through eastern Washington, and when it reaches the Oregon line it turns abruptly west and marks the boundaries of the two

States in its final northwesterly course to where all waters lose their identity in the western sea.

Steamboating on the upper Columbia and its tributaries is a revelation to those accustomed to the peaceful rivers of the East. The Columbia drains an empire 400,000 square miles in extent, from whose snow fields scores of rivers combine to quickly make it at times the equal of the Mississippi at its best. The variation between high and low water is almost incredible. A distinguished

Copyrighted by Geo. M. Weister, Portland, Ore.

Celilo Falls, the great barrier to navigation at The Dalles, Oregon

engineer estimates that for days at a time the increase in its volume each twenty-four hours is equal to the entire average flow of the Hudson. What a current to breast with ordinary craft and what ups and downs of its fickle bosom as it rapidly changes from highest to lowest stage! On no other inland water is a steamer's log so quickly filled with the romance of navigation. Near one of the rapids we found the *City of Ellensburgh* at anchor while her carpenters were giving her wheel a sprinkling of new paddles, the old ones having been knocked off the night before on a lava reef in mid-river. The powerful engines of this steamer were twenty-five years ago doing service in the famous old *Aunt Betsey* on Lake Michigan, which vessel later

came through Fox River and Beef Slough to the Mississippi and
sunk in collision on Lake Pepin.   The wreck was raised and her
engines transferred to the *City of Ellensburgh* with her chief
engineer, B. R. Rice, who has stuck by those engines ever since
and he said they would be in use after he is dead.

The Columbia was then navigable for more than two hundred
miles from its mouth for ocean vessels, and millions of dollars

The great Columbia waterway between Lewiston and Portland

have since been invested in improving the channel.   Many hundreds of miles of its tributaries are navigable beyond the borders
of Washington and Oregon.   Captain Gray, now mayor of Pasco,
navigated the first boat on the river in British Columbia.   For
forty-five years he operated steamers on the Columbia and many
times ran the gauntlet of hostile Indians on the banks.   Captain
White, who was another pioneer commander on the upper Columbia, repeatedly fought his way on *The Forty-Nine* through all
the rapids up to Revelstoke and beyond.

One cannot imagine the grandeur of a trip on the Columbia
River beginning a hundred miles from our own border line away
up in the Canadian Rockies whose summits are held in great
glaciers.   The slowly melting icebergs send down their powerful
arms that open vast fissures and make the great waterways of the
world.   The panoramic views of these great headlands of ice

and snow and the deep canyons and dense forestry of the lower watercourses on the Canadian side beggars description. From Revelstoke the river widens into the beautiful Arrow Lakes then it narrows as it flows to the southwest through the Chelan country in Washington, which is now famous the world over for its grand scenic effects. Lake Chelan's surroundings are but a shade less grand than those of the far North. It occupies a fissure unfathomed, but known to be 1000 ft. below sea-level. The vast summits and wooded slopes are reflected so perfectly in the smooth waters that an unpractised eye fears a collision with vast bulkheads mirrored so delusively. From canyons and rocky defiles the river runs into the more open country around Priest Rapids until reaching the great sand dunes of Snake River. After these waters unite the Columbia becomes more turbulent and treacherous with

A block house overlooking the Columbia River

falls and cascades, jutting lava rocks, and tide currents that tend to make navigation more difficult and they are obstacles that only locks and canals can obviate.

Umatilla was only a small village of two or three hundred people, but it was full of promise for a commercial centre in those early days. It has been a disappointment, and is almost as little known to-day as it was in the early '80's. The ground around the town was covered with small beautifully tinted shells, washed up by the high tides, and Indian arrow heads were found in large numbers. As this was the end of the historic railroad, the change from the cars to the steamer was soon made, and we

went sailing down the Columbia.   The scenery of this portion of
the river is not the most picturesque; basaltic rocks rise bold and
bare on either side, with scarcely a tree to break the monotonous
landscape.   Dinner was served on the steamer, and at 3 o'clock
P.M. we were again in the cars, and portaged to The Dalles, thus
avoiding another dangerous part of the river.

" Picturesque Indian camps of the Umatillas "

The whole country from Pendleton, Oregon, to Umatilla,
and on down the Columbia River, was dotted with picturesque
Indian camps of the Umatillas and many roving tribes.

The Dalles was an important business centre, with a population of about 5000 people.   The O. R. & N. Co. had extensive
machine shops there, and even manufactured its own cars.
At that point, too, the river channel was narrowed by projecting
basaltic banks into a space of a hundred yards, with depth unknown, for no line yet dropped had found a resting place.

When we arrived at The Dalles it was snowing furiously, with
a strong wind blowing; it seemed as if we had been floating backwards into the land of blizzards instead of approaching the soft

air of the Pacific. The train was late and everybody was ravenously hungry, but on board the steamer the supper hour was over, and coaxing for even a sandwich was without avail; finally, with judicious oiling, the steward was persuaded to give me a lunch on the pantry shelf, but Pard could not get a morsel for himself. He had to go out in that blinding storm to the hospitable old

Castle Rock on the Columbia

Umatilla House, which had apparently already fed more than its dinner quota. He was first seated at a table that had been used to the limit, and the linen was too much soiled for endurance. The head waiter responded courteously to the request for something better, and seated Pard again, on the opposite side of the room, where there were two ladies at the table. The linen was of spotless and inviting whiteness. But alas for his pride! when his supper was served, his sleeve caught the end of a table spoon in a tureen of stewed tomatoes, and splashed out a fiery spurt of the liquid that spread a roseate glow from the roots of his hair to the very plates of the ladies. He said he never knew that one tureen could hold so much trouble, and he was not long in making an exit to cool his humiliation in the wintry blasts

outside. The snow was so blinding he could scarcely see his
way to the steamer, and our long coveted trip seemed hovering
in clouds of disappointment.

The steamboat as the forerunner of the railroad is an important factor in the development of a country, but it has never
held its prestige after railroads were built; yet it was the profits

Copyrighted by Benj. A. Gifford
The rocky abutment of the Bridge of the Gods

made in the golden age of steamboating that furnished the first
money used in the railroad building contiguous to the Columbia.
It was the wonderfully rich traffic which appeared with the discovery of the Salmon River mines that enabled the steamboats
on the Lewiston–Celilo run to make records for money-making
that have never been equalled. The steamer *Tenino* on a single
trip from Celilo to Lewiston in May, 1862, collected $18,000 for
freight, fares, meals, and berths.

With completion of the rail lines to Wallula it was found
impossible for the steamboats to compete with the railroads in
the carrying trade. Although the fleet then in service between
Celilo and Lewiston included much finer and larger steamers
than any that have since appeared on that route, and represented an investment of several hundred thousand dollars, they
were practically abandoned, and most of them were taken down to
the lower river.

Whatever regret there may be in substituting the steam trains, the commercial fact stands out in bold relief that the difference in cost is too great. A single engine with sixty cars and a train crew of five men can make the round trip from Portland to Lewiston and return with 1800 tons of wheat in less than two days. To move a similar amount by the largest size carriers that could be operated on the water route would require a boat carrying a crew of twenty men more than two weeks.

It is unfortunate and although we may say that freight-boats and stage-coaches are things of the past, let us hope for the day when tourist travel will demand the restoration of steamers in Oriental splendor on the great waterways of the Columbia and Snake rivers.

Copyrighted by Benj. A. Gifford, Portland, Ore.

Gigantic balustrades of lava along the Columbia

There is an old Indian legend that the Columbia River once flowed through a hole in the mountains at The Dalles, with a great natural bridge of wooded land above called the Bridge of the Gods. An old Indian tells the legend of his grandfather passing through there in a canoe, and that the way was very, very long and dark. Then there came a battle of the mountains and fire and water, which is believed to have been an earthquake, and broke asunder the natural bridge, leaving the water full of massive rocks and forming an impassable barrier to navigation.

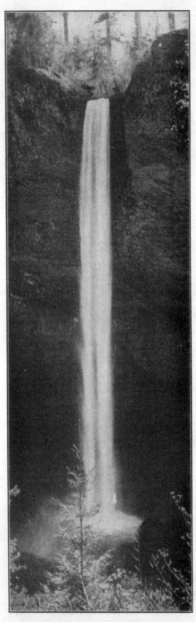

" La Tourelle Falls leap four hundred
feet in a graceful curve "

The broken mountain range on either side of the river carries convincing proof that such a condition must have existed. The precipitous banks and detached rocks on both sides carry out the theory, but how many hundreds or thousands of years ago that was no one can tell. Vast quantities of molten lava were poured out over the lands, destroying the forests of the mountains and leaving the great black masses piled in hideous array on both sides of the river.

The bridge with its forest of trees was destroyed and the banks of the river caved in, which accounts for the many dead tree trunks strewing the river bed from the little town of Mosier, Oregon, to the Cascade Locks, which, although submerged, still stand like gravestones telling the tale of a dead and forgotten past.

Mt. Hood and Mt. Adams, both of volcanic origin, and the pride and joy of Oregon, may at one time have been more closely interlocked than they are now and such a union is indicated by the deep canyons and high waterlines far above those of the present day.

From The Dalles we had only dim views of the grandeur

that we knew was on either bank, for the storm continued without cessation. However, the rocky pinnacles were clothed in the living green of the stately pines, and diversions of Nature's foliage, and the emerald islands and graceful curves of the river held us in a worshipful admiration. At 10 o'clock we made a third portage of a few miles around the roaring, wild cascades, and boarded the princely steamer *Wild West.*

It is two hundred and fifty miles from Walla Walla to Portland and sixty miles from the Cascades. The river forces its way through the Cascade range, leaving walls of 3500 feet in proof of its erosive power. Two miles below the Cascades "Castle Rock" rears its beautiful head which can be seen for fifty

Rounding Cape Horn

miles down the river. It stands alone at the water's edge and rises abruptly to a height of a thousand feet. It covers an area at its base of fifteen acres, while the apex is a level circle of several acres.

There were numberless waterfalls leaping down among the rocks, but "Multnomah" and the "La Tourelle" are those of greatest fame. The Multnomah Falls are seven hundred feet high and are divided into two leaps. The first one falls into a receptacle of its own carving and in this rocky basin, twenty feet in diameter, are myriads of mountain trout; from this granite enclosure Multnomah makes her second leap, with beauty and grandeur so appalling that one is frightened at the echo of his own voice as it rebounds from cliff to cliff.

La Tourelle Falls are possessed of a very novel feature. They are four hundred feet high and the ledge or shelf from which the water leaps projects out from the main wall some seventy feet; the water falls with a graceful curve that is almost half a circle, leaving ample room for a driveway behind the grand colossal water column.

Away to the left a rift in the storm clouds revealed the white head of Mt. Hood, the landmark of ages. Its altitude is about 11,000 feet, rising almost alone from the sea-level. Its pyramidal beauty and magnificence is that of which Oregonians are justly proud. No picture of Oregon, of pen or brush, seems complete without Mt. Hood's hoary head as it stands in untiring, faithful guardianship.

Farther down the river the tall concrete minarets proved the nearness of Cape Horn, but increasing storm gradually hid it from view; at last even the shores were lost in the fog, and the constant shriek of the whistles gave warning of a dangerous way.

We stopped for a few moments at Vancouver, Washington Territory (as it was then known), which was and still is a government reservation. It is one of the spots earliest inhabited by white men on the North Pacific coast. It was largely of military population, and so far as we could see from the liner it was one of the prettiest towns in the West. Its population was then about 2000.

CHAPTER XXVIII

PORTLAND AND PUGET SOUND

WE were two hours or more sailing up the Willamette River after turning from the Columbia, before we landed at the Portland wharf. I smiled at my own ignorance in having believed that Portland was on the Columbia River and near the ocean instead of being on a crossroad a hundred and twenty miles from the drunken liquid of the Columbia Bar.

When the gangplank was flung out and the passengers began wending their way to carriage and omnibus, it was gratefully amusing to hear the hotel runners singing their calls in musical rhythm, instead of shouting in the usual harsh, stentorian way and it deprived the heraldry of its unpleasant features and gave one a happy impression of Portland at the very start. All the omnibuses were free to the hotel, but when one left town he was surprised to find a collector at the door as he landed at the depot to collect a dollar fare.

Providence was indeed kind to guide us down the river in the very nick of time, for the freezing storm had closed in behind us, blocking navigation for the winter, severing all communication with the upriver country until spring, save as an occasional mail bearer could flounder through the snow-locked passes on horseback or snowshoes.

Sleighbells jingled merrily in a way to surprise the natives of that choleric clime, for snow enough for sleighing was an unheard-of occurrence.   It was amusing and, in a way, pitiful to see the helplessness of the people under the burden of snow. The walks were not cleaned anywhere and merchants let people get into their stores as best they could.   There were all kinds of improvised sleds, from a drygoods box to a rocking-chair, and all kinds of bells, from sleighbells, cowbells, and teabells to Portland belles, making a conglomerate of tones hard to describe;

Portland, Oregon, of to-day

but it was withal a very merry time for the usually rain-laden Coasters.

The St. Charles was a pretty fine place in '80 and we folded our weatherbeaten, stage-worn selves away there in dreams of luxury not enjoyed for many a day.   The luxury, however, was all in the rooms, for the table, as described in my notes and letters home in a way more forcible than elegant, was not far from detestable, and we had to search elsewhere for viands palatable.

I rang the bell in our room for some service without getting any response, so again and again I pushed the button and heard the tinkle way off somewhere, so it was surely in working order.

Nearly an hour passed before a great, fat, 250-pound darky came shuffling, flapperty-flap, down the hall to our number and knocked. I opened the door with a measure of impatience, to find him standing there with a broad grin on his big, black face that revealed every tooth in his head. With eyeballs bulging he wiped the moisture from his brow with his much soiled sleeve and said: "I guess you thinks I'se awfully slow, Missus, but when you all's been heah six months yous' 'll be just as lazy ez anybody." The impertinence was inexcusable, but slowness of movement and thought was in reality a strong characteristic of that semi-tropical climate, and he was but a fair sample of his colaborers.

Courtesy of Lee Moorehouse, Pendleton, Ore.

A native belle of Oregon

There were three railroads, seven steamboat lines on the rivers, and three ocean steamship lines for passenger and freight traffic that centred in Portland, and it was an open question whether these companies were to make this the strong commercial centre of the Northwest, or whether it would be changed to some more accessible seaport. Its business blocks, although not of huge dimensions, were models of architectural beauty; in fact, it was the best built town of 20,000 people anywhere west of the Mississippi River. The old residents were wealthy and had a good degree of enterprise, which promised to hold Portland's supremacy.

The *Oregonian*, the pioneer paper, had reached the mature age of thirty years, and was a sheet of thirty-two columns, issued daily.   This makes the *Oregonian* now a stately matron of more than sixty years, and we hope that she may keep the bloom of youth for aye, but wish she would please tell us where to find the fountain of that elixir that we may keep apace.

The entire products of the State and largely of Washington were first turned into the storehouses of Portland by rail or river boats before being loaded upon the ocean steamers that sailed at stated intervals to California, the far East or across the big pond.

The bright sunny days in which we had taken so much pride and pleasure in our frontier travels were now of the past, and encased in rubber coats and boots we wandered up and down the country quite disconsolate.   Morning, noon, and night the patter or steady pour of rain constituted the chief music of the outside, while comments on the unending shower filled the atmosphere within doors.   Residents, however, were quite delighted; they were happier wading around in the mud and water than when they received God's smile through a bright radiant sun, for the long summers were so dust laden that life was one constant wrestle against a sandy covering.

In a driving rain and several inches of melting snow, we were carried through the streets of Portland at seven o'clock one morning to the ferry which crossed the Willamette River, then waded ankle deep in the slush a couple of blocks to the train of the Oregon and California Railway Company, which was to take us through the Willamette valley to Roseburg.   For eight years Roseburg had been the terminus of the Oregon and California road, and there also the stages started for California to cover a gap of 250 miles to California rails.   Roseburg is two hundred miles from Portland, in a southwesterly direction, and only seventy-five miles inland from the coast.

The Willamette valley, fifty miles wide, was as charming a landscape as ever eye dwelt upon.   It was justly called the garden of Oregon, and contained at least half the population of the State.   Little villages and sprightly towns dotted the way from four to eight miles apart.   The clouds broke away for a little while and revealed deep forests, rich meadows, and groves of moss-covered drooping oaks; pleasant homes embowered in living green, and the sparkling rivers bordered with slender birch and more stately trees. Orchards had been so full of fruit that the market was depressed, and bushels, yes, carloads, of apples still clung to the mother limbs or clustered on the ground without value enough to be gathered.

Nearly all the farm homes were well improved and betokened

In the shadow of the pines in Central Oregon

a good degree of prosperity. Some of the best farming land in the valley was cleared timber land, which in the virgin state was sometimes so dense that the eye could not penetrate it; then again there was the gently rolling uplands, and near the middle of the valley it was as level as a marble slab.

At Oregon City the famous woollen mills were doing business just as they are now, making some of the best woollen goods in the United States, and just above the town were the picturesque winding falls of the Willamette River, which have made the country famous.

At Salem we caught a glimpse of the State House, university, and many fine homes. The State university was still further south at Eugene, the prettiest town in the valley. The day had become so mild and pleasant that students were out playing ball without hats or coats.

The Cascade Range of mountains form the eastern and the Coast Range the western boundary line of the Willamette valley, and where these unite at the southern end of the valley they are called the Callapoia mountains. Between the Willamette river and the summit of the Callapoia mountains, where the road crossed into Umpqua valley, was the only untenanted tract of land. It was very rich, but land speculators had taken possession of it and held it then at fifty dollars an acre in its rough and unimproved state. The Umpqua valley contained about 2,500,000 acres. Thunderstorms were almost unknown, and hailstorms and hurricanes were phenomena of which the people were ignorant.

The combination of mountain and valley, woodland and prairie, and river and sea, is beautiful indeed in this locality. Stretching at the foot of snowy mountain ranges were broad expanses of green swards and running waters, while the spruce, cedar, oak, pine, fir, different kinds of ash, maple, balm, larch, and laurel, with many other trees of the forest, dotted the valleys and hillsides until the picture was complete.

It was interesting and amusing to see the dense growth of moss on the housetops. No matter whether the roof was new or old, unless it was painted, a warm rain would bring out an astonishing growth of rich green moss. Should such a thing occur in the East, it would be ascribed either to the age of the town, or to the slow, lazy laggard, who took no pride in his home; but here every board and shingle, wherever it might be, had to be scraped every few years to keep it from decay, because of this moss growth.

Roseburg had a population of about two thousand people, and had the trade of the rich farming country for over a hundred miles inland and far to the south. It had been our intention to take the stage here for Redding, the terminal point of the Central Pacific road, which came from Sacramento River, but hearing the mud was bottomless, and being tired of that sort of thing, we preferred to feed the fishes all the way from Portland to the Golden Gate to so soon renewing the hardships of stage travel, and so went back to Portland. Our time had been well spent in getting that double view of Willamette valley in its glory, for from 1882 to 1897 that valley sent out more people than came in, because of the high price of lands as held by speculators, and people went to the country contiguous to the Palouse and Yakima, where the wilderness of Government lands was made fruitful in a year's time.

We had some personal experiences in Portland that were

On the top of the world

quite new and interesting, if they were not pleasant. In fact, it was our first acquaintance with the Pacific Coast flea, and we were not at all pleased with its familiarity. Life became almost unendurable in the indescribable misery of that association. It was far worse than all the bumps in the stage-coach, or sleeping on rocks under the open canopy of heaven. We could not liberate ourselves from them and, furthermore, soon learned that they were not confined to Portland but that the Puget Sound country, the steamships, and all California would hold out the same health-giving exponent to every arrival. I say "health-giving" because with all my later experiences in California I was led to believe that the activity required to rid oneself of the vicious marauders was what produced such a new and active circulation of the blood as would expurge from the system the most virulent disease and, therefore, through its fleas

California has become a wonderful cure-all.   Disbelievers should try it.   The California flea is an electrical vibrator that should be given its full commercial value.

There was much cause for alarm at the great prevalence of smallpox which was raging up and down the coast.   Every one had to pass under the rod of the law and be vaccinated.   It did

Copyrighted by Geo. M. Weister

A crevasse in the glacier of Mount Hood

no good to be angry; one might as well smile and put up his arm at two dollars per.   The surgeon amused himself jabbing the needle deep in the flesh and telling about the real bovine virus which he used, and which was so hard to get.   But the virus was good enough not to work out its mission with us, although it made showing enough to let us get through the lines when we tried to pass quarantine.

Pard was very proud of his dainty "Burnsides" in our early pioneer days, although they were but little tufts to relieve the slenderness of his classical features.   He went into a barber shop in Portland where the tonsorial artist had such a bad eye that he shaved off one side and not the other, and it was not noticed until he came back to the hotel. When "the man with the hoe" was assailed for his carelessness, he declared that they were so small he had not seen them, and that the mistake was in not taking them off on both sides, which he proceeded to do. Pard wanted to hibernate and nurse them back again, but instead it was a final farewell to whiskers. Tonsorial experiences were manifold on the frontier, and Montana was not without its episodes in that line. In Virginia City it cost two dollars for a hair cut and a shave.

That Oregon is a progressive State is due to a number of its enterprising men, who resorted to a little scheme of enticing fair maidens to come West, in the days when women were scarce. They sent a young man of large acquaintance back to his New England home, with instructions to select and escort back to Oregon one hundred young women, guaranteeing every one of them a year's employment. The active agent was a fine-looking young man, quite capable of executing such a mission, and he did accomplish it in about two months' time. On the way West he himself courted one of the girls, and by the time they had landed in Portland she had promised to be his wife. Of course the other men in the scheme thought he had not played quite square with them by taking the first pick, but there was a fine lot of marriageable material left, and in less than three years they were all married, some of them being to-day leading society ladies of the State.

The young man who did so much for Oregon in his youth was later sent for two terms to the U. S. Senate, and his wife has ever been one of the honored ones of his home town.

Oregon is a great State of plenty now, and beautiful women are considered one of its strongest attractions. They have grown more beautiful as generations pass, because of the luxurious and healthful foods that the State produces, and the influence of the soft, balmy atmosphere. Providence has been generous to all who will lend a willing hand to gather the substance of Oregon.

I think it was about the spring of 1885 that a stage-coach was overturned in a creek in southern Oregon by a rush of salmon. The salmon crowded the river from bank to bank in a school over a mile long. Hundreds of them jumped out on the bank and wriggled around until they died. Farmers fed their hogs on fish, small boys gathered them in their arms, and their elders speared

the larger ones for the sport of it.   Since those days the canneries
have been established and the fish are no longer abused and
wasted when they seek the spawning grounds, as they were on
that memorable occasion.

In later years it has been discovered that large areas of desert
land in Oregon were taken up under the Swamp Land Act, land-

At the ferry crossing of the Columbia

grabbers swearing they had ridden all over the lands in boats.
Their statements were true in the sense that they were carried
in a boat, but they neglected to state that the boat was loaded on
a wagon and pulled about by horses over the coveted area, and
thus they secured their holdings.

Twenty-five miles by boat was the only way to reach the
little narrow gauge road of the Northern Pacific on the Washington
shore of the Columbia, where the route lay to Puget Sound.   It
was not yet six o'clock in the morning when the *Emma Haywood*
pulled her nose out of the Portland dock and turned it down
stream to the mouth of the Willamette, then across the Columbia
River to the little junction point of Kalama on the Washington
Territory side.   There was a drizzling rain when the little boat

started and it enveloped everybody in clouds of irritability as well as water; everything was water soaked and promised a dismal day, but, happily, it was not long before the storm abated and sank quietly away; the stars twinkled down, gladdening all hearts with a new hope for clear skies, and soon the winter morning sun merged from the mist, lighted the horizon with its rays of red and gold, and brought Mt. Hood out in bold relief against a roseate sky. The quiet beauty of the morning seemed to make all nature glad, and even the mighty river sang to the ebb and flow of the

The rock of ages

sea. Ten o'clock came only too soon, and the clang, clang of the bell in the engine room was the signal to turn off the steam, and anchor at Kalama, an important point only as a landing for the southern terminus of the railroad.

Northern Pacific Railway cars were ready to start out for the Sound soon after we arrived. The passengers did the usual scrambling for the best seats, but there was little choice. There was not sufficient business to warrant anything but mixed trains of passenger and freight cars. The cars were peculiar to the section of the country; the frames of the seats were of light-colored wood, covered with black leather and gilt tacks. They were very narrow, and every jerk of the engine afforded amusement for the passengers, as they were hurled from the little slippery seats repeatedly, then hastily glanced around to see how their neighbors fared. The backs of the seats were not more than half high enough, and the natural inclination was to slide down until the shoulder blades hooked over the top of the slippery slabs behind, while one's feet searched in vain for a brace below.

The windows were so arranged that they suited any one else better than the ones for whom they were intended, and in consequence of this, to enjoy the scenery I found that I must recline my head on the shoulder in front of me, or thrust my hat in the face of the stranger behind me.

"The oldest bell tower in the world"

A moderately tall man would need to discard both hat and boots to walk erect through the car without scraping the ceiling, and nearly every one had to bend his head to get through the door; in fact, the car was so small that it only needed my little dishes and doll to believe myself in an old-time playhouse. But we made excellent time and were so handsomely treated by the officials and employes of the road that we soon forgot the quaint cars and little discomforts and thought only good things of the narrow gauge and the great power the corporation might some day sway in Washington.

The headquarters of the Northern Pacific Company were then at New Tacoma. The narrow iron arms were rapidly folding the Territory in their embrace as they reached on eastward to clasp the brotherly hand of the division coming westward from Bismarck.

Short feeders were being constructed to penetrate many desirable portions of the far Northwest, and with the $40,000,000, then subscribed for its use, it compelled the railroad world to admit it as a peer. The branch from Kalama spanned many a stream, penetrated deep forests, and crossed the great Chehalis farming lands.

New Tacoma residents thought the name of their little hamlet was on every Eastern tongue, so great were their hopes and strong their belief in future greatness. The population was a little over a thousand, as it had doubled in a year. Some very good residences had been finished, and the bluff just back of the town overlooking the sound was dotted with pleasant homes.

The principal sources of revenue aside from the railroad were, just as they are to-day, coal mines, lumber, hops, and fish. The coal mines were being rapidly developed, and hundreds of men were employed whose trade was thrown into the hands of New Tacoma merchants. The principal part of the lumber traffic was carried on at Old Tacoma, a mile distant, but virtually it was a part of the same place.

The bell tower of St. Peter's Church in Old Tacoma was then as now one of the interesting features for sightseers, for it is one of the oldest bell towers in the world—it is the remains of a giant cedar, many centuries old, and overgrown with ivy. The tones of the ringing bell float from its hidden top, where fancy makes music for the soul and imagination thrills the mind.

It did not, however, interest me as much as the Baptist Church that stands in the city of Santa Rosa, Cal., which enjoys the distinction of having been constructed entirely from a single tree. The tree from which the timbers, lumber, and shingles were cut was a giant California redwood, and a considerable quantity of the timber was left over after the church building was completed. It has a spire seventy feet high, an auditorium seating five hundred, a parlor seating eighty, a pastor's study, and a large vestibule. There are not many buildings in the world in which all the timbers, including its finishings, have been obtained from a single tree.

The hop culture in the Puyallup valley near New Tacoma was a subject of great interest and value. Great difficulty had been experienced in years gone to secure the requisite help in the hop-picking season, and that, with want of proper knowledge of the culture, had been a source of loss, but the year 1880 had been one of great success.

At least 2000 Indians were attracted thither in that year from beyond the Cascade Mountains, from around the sound, and even as far north as Sitka, for the sole purpose of picking hops and fishing. For the first few days of the season Tacoma Bay was covered with canoes of all sizes, laden with Indians, their camping outfits and dogs, the dogs and children faring alike and together. Besides the Indians there were many whites in the fields, but at least half of both classes were of a kind to make the city tremble with their wickedness when the day's work was done.

Hop vines grew to great size, and the fields were like shaded arbors, the merry pickers dodged among the trellised vines, while nimble fingers gathered the harvest, each trying to outdo the other in the day's work.

The *Geo. E. Starr*, on which we journeyed around the sound, was considered a veritable floating palace, and it was the little steamer that President Hayes chartered for his trip around Puget Sound. Human mind can scarcely conceive a body of water more beautiful than this inland sea, with its 2500 miles of shore line bending in and out to make its myriads of bays and trysting places for the ships of commerce and the joys of seafaring.

The straits of San Juan de Fuca is the ninety-five mile neck of water connecting the sound and the sea, and although its thirteen miles in average width narrows down to only eight miles at its mouth, there is no treacherous bar of sand and rocks as there is at the mouth of the Columbia. Neither are there hidden rocks or shoals where danger lurks unseen. The rise and fall of the tide is about eighteen feet, and the water of the sound is deep to the very shore line, making it possible for deep sea vessels to go to shore at will. Evergreen islands lift their emerald heads at frequent intervals in contrast to the distant setting of the snowy Olympics and the stately Mt. Rainier, Mt. Baker, and other silver peaks that crown the wooded shore line.

It seemed incredulous that any one could be hopelessly lost in a thicket within ten feet of the water, but it would be true if one had not the knowledge that the water must be *down* the slope. So dense is the growth of vines and shrubs, so luxuriant and yet so tall that one must mark his way by cutting a passage or blazing the trees if he would return again to the same starting-point.

Wild berries grew in profusion—blackberries as large as our eastern wild plum, and hazelnuts actually grew on trees. There were a lot of hazel burrs on the ground, and looking for their source we discovered ourselves standing under a hazelnut tree not less than fifty feet high, and myriads of the burrs were clinging to the branches way beyond the hope of getting them.

The first steam sawmill built on the sound was in Seattle, in 1853, by H. L. Yesler, and had a capacity of 15,000 feet per day, a marked contrast to a mill's capac- ity for 1911, but there was small demand for lum- ber in Mr. Yesler's earlier years of pioneering. The greatest manufac- tory that Seattle had in 1880 was for the making of barrels, and the tall cottonwood trees were sliced, moulded, and bent into two thousand barrels a day.

The county jail had its quota of inmates but they were dry shod, while people on the outside waded about ankle deep

Growing hops and hop-pickers

in mud, climbed slippery hills and absorbed climate until man and the native elements of soil and water were so mingled in person- ality that it was hard to distinguish one from the other, to say nothing of separating them. It was a place for an optimist to dream of maritime power, to peer into the future and build great commercial docks, and hold the key of the great Northwest for both Orient and Occident. To dream—yes, then, but now to realize—to see the miles of paved streets, miles of warehouses, miles of docks, miles of ships, and miles of steam cars, and miles of electric motors, is a dream come true beyond the hope of man in 1880.

Chief Seattle for whom the city of Seattle was named

The city of Seattle was named after the Indian Chief Seattle, who with his daughter, Princess Angeline, were noted characters for many years and were known by all the residents of the upper Sound country.

The sound cities did not have the thrill of energetic forces brought in by the ox teams or mule teams, with their covered wagons and loads of merchandise and bedraggled appendages, but they watched the sea craft throw out their *mal de mer* humanity to lose itself in the forests, to come out again loyal devotees of the place of their adoption. Perchance one might stand veiled in his own wrath and be stuck in the mud until the blue air about his head and the clinging mass about his feet fairly won his affection by their very tenacity and kept him there even when the streets were paved under him.

Many a man of the interior who has led civilization will take up his belongings and move on to a new wilderness when the iron horse invades his solitude and brings its commercial and social changes and responsibilities. He loves the wild free life of the Bohemian and follows in its quest. The man by the sea is differently constituted; there is an odor of the sea that holds him enthralled; he loves the swish and roar of the water; he loves the mist, the rain, and the mud. The ceaseless motion of the ocean waves quiets his own overcharged, restless body and mind, and he finds a content that commerce and civilization cannot change.

The first shipment of lumber from the sound consisted of a cargo of piles in 1851, by one Lafayette Balch, for which he paid eight cents per running foot, delivered to the vessel, and which brought him cne dollar per running foot. The first sawed lumber was shipped by James McAllister and sold in San Francisco for fifty dollars per thousand feet. In 1880 there were 125,000,000 feet of lumber shipped from the sound.

The trees grew so tall, so straight, and stately that it was a sacrilege to nature to hew them with an ax or saw; it seemed like striking down our own great people in the very hour of perfection. There is no other place in the world where so many trees are transported for shipmasts, unless it may be far away Norway. And now steamers, barks, schooners, great warships, and many other kinds of water craft are made and completed here of such strength and texture as has long since proved the value of the woods of the great Northwest.

Across the sound from Seattle, Port Townsend reminded one of Mackinaw, away off in northern Michigan. The sleepy villagers, the occasional squaw and papoose, the military fort perched on a cliff, and the long stairway leading to the best residential portion were novel features of the home beside the sea. From the heights one could look down upon the commercial part of the town and across to the opposite bluff, where the "boys in blue" stood at duty's call, and then the gaze floated across to the British lands.

The incoming Victoria steamer had such a furious wind to battle against the day we were in Port Townsend that she called to our boat to come out to sea for her cargo, and together they went about eight miles into a sheltered cove to exchange their mails and freight.

A few hours later, when the wind had somewhat abated, we boarded the old *Eliza Ann* and started across the straits to Victoria, but when about a third of the way over the captain would not take the risk of getting the old boat safely through the storm, and he turned back to anchor again at Townsend. To La-conner and Whatcom there was a mail boat once in two weeks, but in the few years intervening Whatcom has lost its identity in the rhythmic melody of Bellingham, and has its scores of daily steamers tooting in the harbor oblivious of the ages of silence that were broken only by the booming waves upon the shore.

Princess Angeline, a daughter of Chief Seattle

Oysters and clams are plentiful on the sound, but the native oysters, though very good, would make a Baltimorian turn his head to smile, for they are not the fat, plump bivalves of our eastern shores, as they are no larger than a silver dime, and even that size would be a big one. However, in these later days the eastern oyster transplanted to these western inlets results in the most tender and delicious morsel in all oysterdom.

Port Townsend is so situated that it feels the first throb of the commercial life as it comes through the straits of Fuca and it was there where all sea craft must clear and enter. It was the great *entrepôt* of all the Northwest, yet why the town has never risen above its station of those days seems hard to understand.   Perhaps it will some day awaken from its Rip Van Winkle sleep and wield the power that is its own by location, but lacks the energy and persistent effort to sustain.

Tucked away down at the southwest end of the sound the territorial capital, Olympia, nestled cosily on the sea-kissed shore. Why the capital of so great a territory should be there I do not

The largest tide-land spruce in the world, nearly 33 feet in circumference

think any one could tell then or now.   It had some attractive scenic features and was famous for its oysters.   The De Chutes river emptied into Budd's inlet, about a mile and a half from town, with a fall of eighty feet in the last half mile of its course, furnishing a thousand horse-power for the mill burrs.   These falls were in a picturesque location, embodied now in a glorious city park, the natural beauties of which are unexcelled.

The town had a fine water supply, wooded shores, and pleasant drives, and such few advantages as a capital city offers, but the query still stands: "Why is the capitol of so great a State hidden away in an oyster bed, where ships of sea draft can anchor only at high tide?" But for all its little tuckaway retreat, it was a pretty little town of two thousand people, with aspirations, some of which have since been realized.

The sound fisheries were then as much of an interesting study as they are to-day, though of far less magnitude. The chief fishing was for salmon, but there were cod, herring, sturgeon,

Drying and mending fish-nets on Puget Sound

flounder, perch, sardines, and many other kinds of sea food. Now also halibut are caught in large numbers.

The shipments of canned salmon did not exceed six hundred thousand cases in a season, and now one firm alone puts up ten thousand cases daily. A trip on a steam yacht to the traps to see how the fish are caught and then follow them into the can is an educational achievement not to be ignored. At certain seasons there was fine sport trolling from the deck of a steam launch and pulling in the tom-cod, salmon, and other big fish that would weigh as much as the fisherman himself, or at least one seemed that heavy on the end of a line.

We were indebted to Mr. and Mrs. C. X. Larabee for such a treat in a later year. Everybody knows Mr. Larabee from his famous Montana horse ranch and great mining exploits in Montana to his townsite scheme on Bellingham Bay with his stately hotel, and his later exploits in Portland's financial field.

With half a dozen lines trailing behind our gently moving steamer there grew a great rivalry among the fishermen for first place, and the landing of the first fish. But the excitement of first place was all lost in the tension of landing the fish, and I was surprised to be obliged to hand my line to stronger arms to land my ten pound tom-cod and my eleven pound salmon. Pard declined such unsportsmanlike fishing and was the butt of a score of jests because he used only his light trout rod and line from a canoe, and took two hours to land his three ten and twelve pound salmon, which he ultimately did without breaking rod or line.

When our party gathered for the evening to talk over the events of the day's fishing and compare them with other experiences, every one was surprised at the silence of one member of the party, who was generally in the foremost rank of story tellers, and when he was summoned to do his share of the entertaining he told a story entitling him to the champion prevaricator's belt.

The old rounder cast a glance around the room to see that he was given the proper attention then said: "Well, friends, I had a little experience of my own once that just knocks the color off these salmon of to-day. I went up Hood's Canal to visit an old friend. He had often told me of the splendid fishing there, and I was anxious to try it. It was late in the evening when I got there, and I retired early, so as to be ready for the fun next day. I asked how far it was to the creek, and they told me it was only a few hundred yards, just beyond the fence. Before light next morning I was up, and, securing a good tackle and a little bait, started off toward the creek. The fog was heavy, for it was woods burning time and I could not see any distance ahead of me, so groped my way as best I could across the little clearing. Reaching the fence I climbed over, and picked my way carefully, for I did not want to fall in the creek. I proceeded slowly down the slope until I thought I must be near the water's edge. Baiting my hook I threw it forward, and just about time enough for it to strike the water I felt a pull, and with a jerk I brought in a fine fellow. For ten minutes I stood there and pulled them in, and then, fearing that I would spoil the day's sport, I regretfully returned and by accident reached the house through the fog. After breakfast the fog lifted and we got ready for a day's enjoyment.   You may imagine my surprise when, on going to the place where I had caught so many fish early in the morning, I found that it was a full hundred yards from the bank of the creek. The truth is, I had not touched the water but just stood there and caught them out of the fog."

For an instant or two there was a dead silence, then as the

Mt. Rainier as seen from the waters of the Sound

rumble and roar of life began to manifest itself again, our friend slipped out of the door and did not show up again until the next day, when he could feel reasonably safe from lynching.

It was said there were only two seasons on the sound, the wet and the dry, and we surely struck the wet season; yet the days were not full of rain, for there were many rifts in the clouds where the sun came through to gladden our hearts and to encourage us to renewed action.

Washington Territory, with its 60,000 people, was a bud of promise that needed no grafting.   It was the best timbered and watered land between the two great seas.   Its snowy peaks fed perpetual springs and hid treasures untold; its sunny slopes afforded the finest grazing lands; and its broad valley acres

waving in the golden grain nodded joyously to distant lands to
hush the cry for bread.

Seattle was a veritable mudhole with its cowpath streets
meandering over the hills, and giving but little sign of the commercial metropolis it is to-day.   Our feet came out of the mud
with a sock-sock-sock that was as ludicrous as it was annoying,
and as we steamed out southward again, I sang out to our new-
found friends:

> "You may sing your songs of the shells and the sea,
> But the hills and the vales ring their bells for me."

CHAPTER XXIX

A NON-STRIKABLE UNION

THERE were many inducements offered to have us visit Klamath Falls in southwestern Oregon. The beauty and grandeur of the trip were painted in most glowing terms and the temptation seemed almost too great to resist. We could not see, however, that Pard's company interests would be advanced at that time, as there could not be any railroad in that direction for many years, and in spite of the wonderful resources in the locality we decided not to use our time that way. Besides the season was too late.

It was no sooner decided in the negative than our friends began telling some different stories about the country. First and foremost it was the breeding land of snakes. The shiny, crawling reptiles were so numerous they could be taken up by the shovel full, and their little heads would glisten from every crevice. A photograph taken at Klamath in recent years shows a good, steady increase from that time up to the present day, and if the new summer home of the late Mr. Harriman at Pelican Lodge, on Klamath Lake, shares the fate of more humble habitations in that locality its occupant will doubtless some day find snakes wound around the mirrors, adorning the walls, hanging from the chandeliers, and creeping into his own warm bed, to say nothing about clogging the chimneys, raising their families in unused stoves, and vieing with the pet cat for the cushioned chairs.

They may haunt the dreams and clothespress of Mr. Harriman's successor but they have the one great virtue of being harmless for if they are plentiful, they are non-poisonous and playful. He may really become quite attached to the slippery fellows and go back East with his pockets full of them. It may be that the railroad magnates have heard of the great profits in snakes and

A happy family near Klamath on a sunny day

go into their domain to work up a snake trust. The greatest inducement any one could have in organizing this particular snake trust is that in spite of the great unions among them they never strike.

This possible solicitude upon the part of captains of industry not to let a good deal even in such livestock as snakes get away was probably suggested by the experience of a local dealer at Klamath who started in, not very long ago, to build up a permanent traffic in this line.

Some firm in St. Paul, hearing of the great abundance of these reptiles at Klamath, and having some special use for snakes by the wholesale, wrote to the local merchant offering to take all the live snakes he could ship, at a price which was very attractive. The Klamath man lost no time in raking up a *ton* of snakes, large, small, and indifferent, and shipping them by express as directed to his correspondent.   The snakes were shipped in boxes of convenient size for handling, and seemed to be fairly well content with the rough usage of the wagon haul to the railroad, but, after being disposed of among the many other packages in the warm express car on the Southern Pacific, they limbered up, grew uneasy, and by the time the train had gotten half way across the Continent the smaller ones especially had wriggled themselves out

The Harriman Lodge on Klamath Lake

of the boxes all over the car floor, and many of them had crawled into other express packages, so that by the time the miscellaneous consignments were delivered to their respective owners every package which was not air tight and under seal contained anywhere from one to half a dozen good, lively snakes, while the snake shipment itself reached St. Paul minus a goodly portion of the original number.

It is easy to imagine the consternation of the recipients of those express packages and the stream of abuse and complaint which was showered upon the railway and express officials, as well as the dissatisfaction of the St. Paul people at receiving such short measure.

The upshot of this snake deal was that no temptation in the way of high express rates, and not even a compulsory order upon the part of the Interstate Commerce Commission could induce the railways to accept any more snakes for shipment.

On Klamath Lake's wooded shores Mr. E. H. Harriman bought a summer home, and he was enchanted with the grandeur of the environment.

Doubtless Mr. Harriman, if he had lived, with his long experience in circumventing business situations even far more refractory, would have been enabled to turn this superfluous

A party of pelicans

supply of reptiles to a good purpose. It might not have been a ten per cent. investment but something that would grow. But as there never can be a successor to that gentleman in business acumen, so it is unlikely that Klamath will realize adequately upon this unique resource for many years to come.

Another local resource which will doubtless be brought to the attention of those looking for business openings may call for somewhat greater ingenuity to utilize, but will work in with the snake business. This is the great showers of toads which sometimes descend upon Klamath, and which are swallowed up almost on sight by the snakes.

Of course any financier of acute perception who might wish

to combine the snake and toad business would naturally ship his snakes just after the arrival and disposal of the toads by these voracious Klamath enemies of theirs.

Pelicans just dote on snakes and frogs, and from the moment the birds are out of the incubators they could be trained as personal attendants for Klamath visitors who are foolishly sensitive about snake companionship.   They could also be trained as house pets to keep snakes out of the bookcases and from under the sofa pillows.   They could also patrol the Klamath streets and see to it that the cracks in the board walks are no

Copyrighted by Miller Photo Co.
An   hour of inspiration at Crater Lake

longer ornamented by protruding heads of the many bodies wriggling underneath as in days of yore.

But in all seriousness too much cannot be said of the natural wealth and beauty of the Klamath country or the glories of Crater Lake.   With its better railway facilities recently afforded by the completion of the Southern Pacific road through Klamath Falls, the great government projects in the way of irrigation and drainage of vast areas will soon make Klamath one of the most important agricultural regions in the whole West and with development of local water-power, Klamath Falls bids fair to be the Spokane of Oregon.   The railway extension referred to and the co-operation of Uncle Sam in rendering the wonders of Crater

Lake National Park more accessible will quickly conspire to send thousands of tourists to enjoy that unique wonderland of southern Oregon.

And, gentle reader, don't let what I have written about snakes deter you from considering a trip or a permanent location in any part of the West. Civilization and snakes don't go together. The rattlers move on or disappear as they have always done and Klamath snakes are harmless and unsociable.

It is in southeastern Oregon where Crater Lake lends inimitable charm to the State's attractions. Its mirrored reflections,

Crater Lake's phantom ship rises two hundred feet from the surface

its phantom ship rising two hundred feet above its midwater surface, its caves in the shore line, and its grand abutments are a combination that holds the eye entranced. But it has a rival for mysterious depths and chemical actions in the great ice cave of a central Oregon mountain. When it was discovered men were let down into the cavernous depths with ropes and found a large body of ice. In the course of time means were provided to get the ice out for use as it was far from any running streams and where the climate was too mild the year around to make ice. It is a better investment than a gold mine, for now the ice is exhausted in the cave every day, but it renews itself every twenty-four hours, much to the consternation of the chemists and other wise men who have studied the peculiar phenomenon.

It is a most fortunate dispensation of Providence that the snakes in south Oregon are so harmless, for it is not the case in most parts of Oregon.   On Snake and Columbia rivers the snakes

Ice Cave near Bend, Oregon.   Ice is cut every day.   It freezes over night and next day there is the same amount of ice left

are rattlers, and one has small desire to be caught out on a warm night with a rock for a bed, without a hair rope, else that peculiar buz-z-z-z might warn him against turning over or stretching himself too suddenly.

Rattlers have great fear of one another, and a small one will always run from a large one, but when they get into mortal combat their fighting is terrific; they wind around one another until they can wind no more, and squeeze one another to the limit of their strength.

The snakes of Arizona and most of the southern countries are poisonous, and the rattler is the most prevalent, as in parts of Montana and along the great rivers. In the rattler's country one's ear is always attuned to catch the warning "buzz" for they never strike without giving notice of their intent if given any opportunity to do so. They love the expansive wastes and deserts and the desolate rocky fastnesses. Along the coulées of the Mississippi and the upper Missouri, across the Mojave and the Colorado deserts, across the bad lands of Montana, and through the great wheat fields of Washington and Oregon, and along the Snake and Columbia river lava cliffs, they live and multiply and fight for freedom from the on-moving civilization. Rattlesnake dens are all over the great stretches of lava beds, and one man declared that he saw one coil of rattlers as large as a ten gallon keg. We did not learn his Kentucky brand.

In going through a section of Montana between Helena and old Fort Benton I heard so many snake stories that I expected every revolution of the old stage wheels to throw snakes in upon us, and I was glad when I was offered a chance to ride on the top boot and be out of range. Bunches of them would coil in the warm sand in the middle of the road, causing the untamed bronchos to buck and jump clear off the road in one wild plunge. The driver was one who had pulled the ribbons for forty years, and he was an adept in telling impossible things. He thought the time propitious for telling of the time when he tried to drive over a bunch of snakes and after he had been past them a spell his wagon tongue began to swell; he had to stop and get another and leave "that there one" behind and it just kept on a swelling until it was sent to a sawmill where it was sawed up into lumber which made over one thousand feet of fine hickory.

Many pioneers are obliged to get their living off the country through which they pass, as well as the place wherein they drive their home stakes. First and foremost comes the sturdy little sagebrush that kindles into a hot, quick fire. It burns rapidly and completely but it engenders a fierce hot flame that gives much warmth and hurries the wayside meal. The streams have multitudes of the finny tribe, the foothills are filled with antelope and deer, and the lakes are covered with feathered game in the great unfrequented trails; but on the open stretch of arid land the buffalo and the rattlesnake have been the saviours of many lives. It would seem to one unaccustomed to hardships that to eat snakes would be the ditch of last resort, but through necessity it became a custom that has prevailed down to the present day.

The hunter for the rattlers for food must catch them unawares, which is usually done with a forked stick fastened down quickly

Ready for business

over the head, for when a rattler is cornered and has to fight for its life it will quickly commit suicide by piercing its own body with its poisonous fangs, and will soon die. There is no poison in the snake flesh unless the reptile is allowed to bite itself and then it is destroyed for food purposes. For roasting they are skinned and cut into small pieces and held over the campfire until they are crispy brown, then seasoned with salt and pepper. If there are more conveniences for preparing them they can be baked with butter, pepper, and salt, or fried in a skillet.

The snake meat is white and tender and Mrs. Frederick Burbidge now of Spokane, when entertaining a party from New York in her Montana home, served them a rattlesnake salad. She had the kindness to tell her guests what it was that they might refuse it if they desired. It certainly was a novelty that they will never forget.

Indians will eat snakes, coyotes, grasshoppers, dogs, crickets, and lice, all of which I have seen them do.

First post-office west of the Rockies, built at Astoria in 1847